By exploring new assemblages of youth, technology, and governance, these wide-ranging essays offer fresh and theorized insights into contemporary young people and the politics of youth. For example, the chapters on sexting provide a review of current perspectives from sexual citizenship to pleasure to criminality. This is a smart, critical, and engaging collection.

Nancy Lesko, Maxine Greene Professor,
Teachers College, Columbia University

Youth, Technology, Governance, Experience

How do adults understand youth? How do their conceptions inform interventions into young lives or involve young people's experiences?

This volume tackles these questions by exploring adults' ideas about youth. Specifically, *Youth, Technology, Governance, Experience* examines the four titular concepts and their implications for a range of relationships between youth and adults. Utilising interdisciplinary methods, the contributing authors deliver a broad range of analyses of young people differentiated by gender, class, race, and geography across an array of contexts, including within the home, in media representations, through government bureaucracies, and in everyday life.

Youth, Technology, Governance, Experience also interrogates the meaning of technology and governance for youth studies, considering a range of ways they interact, including through social media, technologies of regulation, and educational tools. It will appeal to students and academic researchers interested in fields such as youth studies, cultural studies, sociology, and education.

Liam Grealy is a postdoctoral research fellow of gender and cultural studies at the University of Sydney, Australia.

Catherine Driscoll is a professor of gender and cultural studies at the University of Sydney, Australia.

Anna Hickey-Moody is a professor of media and communications at RMIT University, Australia.

Youth, Young Adulthood and Society

Series editor: Andy Furlong, University of Glasgow, UK

The **Youth, Young Adulthood and Society** series brings together social scientists from many disciplines to present research monographs and collections, seeking to further research into youth in our changing societies around the world today. The books in this series advance the field of youth studies by presenting original, exciting research, with strongly theoretically- and empirically-grounded analysis.

For a full list of titles in this series, please visit: https://www.routledge.com/Youth-Young-Adulthood-and-Society/book-series/YYAS

Published:

Youth Homelessness and Survival Sex
Intimate Relationships and Gendered Subjectivities
Juliet Watson

Spaces of Youth
Work, Citizenship and Culture in a Global Context
David Farrugia

Transitions to Adulthood through Recession
Youth and Inequality in a European Comparative Perspective
Edited by Sarah Irwin and Ann Nilsen

Youth, Technology, Governance, Experience
Adults Understanding Young Lives
Edited by Liam Grealy, Catherine Driscoll, Anna Hickey-Moody

Forthcoming:

Rethinking Young People's Marginalisation
Beyond Neo-Liberal Futures?
Perri Campbell, Lyn Harrison, Chris Hickey and Peter Kelly

Youth, Technology, Governance, Experience
Adults Understanding Young People

Edited by
Liam Grealy, Catherine Driscoll and
Anna Hickey-Moody

LONDON AND NEW YORK

First published 2018
by Routledge
2 Park Square, Milton Park, Abingdon, Oxon OX14 4RN

and by Routledge
711 Third Avenue, New York, NY 10017

Routledge is an imprint of the Taylor & Francis Group, an Informa business

© 2018 selection and editorial matter, Liam Grealy, Catherine Driscoll, Anna Hickey-Moody; individual chapters, the contributors

The right of Liam Grealy, Catherine Driscoll, Anna Hickey-Moody to be identified as the authors of the editorial material, and of the authors for their individual chapters, has been asserted in accordance with sections 77 and 78 of the Copyright, Designs and Patents Act 1988.

All rights reserved. No part of this book may be reprinted or reproduced or utilised in any form or by any electronic, mechanical, or other means, now known or hereafter invented, including photocopying and recording, or in any information storage or retrieval system, without permission in writing from the publishers.

Trademark notice: Product or corporate names may be trademarks or registered trademarks, and are used only for identification and explanation without intent to infringe.

British Library Cataloguing in Publication Data
A catalogue record for this book is available from the British Library

Library of Congress Cataloging in Publication Data
Names: Grealy, Liam, editor. | Driscoll, Catherine, editor. | Hickey-Moody, Anna, 1977- editor.
Title: Youth, technology, governance, experience /
edited by Liam Grealy, Catherine Driscoll, Anna Hickey-Moody.
Description: Abingdon, Oxon ; New York, NY : Routledge, 2018. | Series: Youth, young adulthood and society | Includes bibliographical references and index.
Identifiers: LCCN 2017060369 | ISBN 9780815362319 (hardback)
Subjects: LCSH: Youth. | Information technology. |
Intergenerational relations.
Classification: LCC HQ796 .Y6255 2018 | DDC 305.2–dc23
LC record available at https://lccn.loc.gov/2017060369

ISBN: 978-0-8153-6231-9 (hbk)
ISBN: 978-1-351-11267-3 (ebk)

Typeset in Times New Roman
by Taylor & Francis Books

This book is dedicated to students of youth and youth culture.

Contents

List of tables	xi
Preface	xii
Acknowledgements	xiii

1 Youth, technology, governance, experience: keywords for youth studies   1
   LIAM GREALY, ANNA HICKEY-MOODY AND CATHERINE DRISCOLL

PART I
Governing minority: surveillance and media classification   27

2 Common sense in the government of youth and sex   29
   LIAM GREALY

3 Regulation beyond government: Weber, Foucault, and the liberal governance of media content   46
   TERRY FLEW

4 Classifying adulthood: A history of governing minority in media classification   65
   RACHEL COLE, CATHERINE DRISCOLL AND LIAM GREALY

PART 2
Young people and technologies: ethical research and sexting   85

5 Ethical issues in qualitative research addressing sensitive issues with children and young people   87
   CATHARINE LUMBY, KATH ALBURY, ALAN MCKEE AND SKY HUGMAN

6 Sexting pleasures: Young people, fun, flirtation, and child pornography   103
   THOMAS CROFTS, MURRAY LEE, ALYCE MCGOVERN AND SANJA MILIVOJEVIC

7 Representations of sexting and sexual violence on legal dramas. Implications for teenagers' sexual citizenship. 123
EMILY LOCKHART

PART III
Ethnographies of young people's education   **139**

8 MOOCs and widening participation in higher education: From competency to capability in the evaluation of educational technologies 141
REMY YI SIANG LOW

9 Technologies of orientation: Pathways, futures 158
ANNA HICKEY-MOODY AND VALERIE HARWOOD

10 The use of mobile and new media technologies in a health intervention about HPV and HPV vaccination in schools 175
CRISTYN DAVIES, S. RACHEL SKINNER, HARRISON L. ODGERS, GEORGE P. KHUT AND ANGIE MORROW

Index   196

Tables

4.1	Changes to the BBFC's ratings categories	67
4.2	Changes to Australian ratings categories	74
8.1	Capabilities derived from participation in MOOCs	152

Preface

This collection is largely based on papers presented at the symposium 'Youth and Technology: Pleasure and Governance' in the Department of Gender and Cultural Studies at the University of Sydney in December 2013. That symposium sought to bring together researchers from a range of fields, including cultural studies, media studies, education, policy studies, and public health. The key themes – governance, technology, and pleasure – provided a broad framework for discussions about interventions into young people's lives and their responses, which is continued in this collection, with pleasure incorporated within wider examinations of experience. The editors would like to thank all the authors for their thoughtful contributions and for their patience throughout the publication process.

Acknowledgements

The symposium at which most of the chapters in this book were first presented was supported by funding from the School of Philosophical and Historical Inquiry at the University of Sydney. The production of this book was supported by Australian Research Council funding for the Discovery Project *Media Classification Systems: An International Comparative Study* (DP150101226).

1 Youth, technology, governance, experience: keywords for youth studies

Liam Grealy, Anna Hickey-Moody and Catherine Driscoll

This introductory chapter provides an overview of the collection's keywords and the ways these concepts inform the essays drawn together in this book. Our approach is inspired by Raymond Williams's *Keywords: A vocabulary of culture and society* (1983) – a landmark text for cultural studies – and by the subsequent *New Keywords: A revised vocabulary of culture and society* (Bennett et al. 2005). In *Keywords*, Williams offers short essays on the 'general usage' of his collected keywords (1983, p. 12), attuned not only to historical changes in meaning, but to how such changes articulate with political and social circumstances. *Keywords* is Williams's 'record of an inquiry into a *vocabulary*: a shared body of words and meanings in our most general discussion, in English, of the practices and institutions which we group as *culture* and *society*' (1983, p. 13). His inquiry aimed 'to provide a useful, intellectually and historically grounded guide to *public* questions' (Bennett et al. 2005, p. xviii), where conflicts over terms indicate 'historical and contemporary substance' (Williams 1983, p. 21) rather than semantic disagreements of definition.

This introduction is written in the spirit of *Keywords*, framing our collection's aim to be broadly useful to students and scholars working on youth, youth culture, and young people. The enormous field of research that can be collected as 'youth studies' contains myriad investigations of relations between youth, technology, governance, and experience. All the chapters collected here are centrally interested in youth, although they bring to this subject different disciplinary approaches and field orientations, including cultural studies, media studies, the sociology of education, and criminology. The collection's keywords are used variously across the book, signalling differences in authorial preference and disciplinary location, but also the wide social and cultural uses of these terms, from which youth studies scholars directly draw. This introduction provides historical background and examines the use of the keywords youth, technology, governance, and experience, as the broad parameters organising the chapters that follow. We begin, in greatest detail, with the contemporary critical conception of youth as simultaneously a life stage and a category of disciplinary knowledge.

Youth

Possibility. The future. Investment. Care. Youth is a concept widely associated with positive aspects of life in that it represents all that might come to be. Youth is also understood as a time of vulnerability. Being young consolidates the related needs for care, protection, and education. Beyond individual experiences, youth simultaneously symbolises potential and futurity, but also vulnerability and immaturity. However recognisable this apparent ambivalence, it raises questions about how youth continues to be constituted as such.

In discussing 'youth' and 'young people' we need to move beyond such general categories, and not just because we must acknowledge the historical and cultural contexts in which these terms hold different meanings. A typical ontology of youth begins with age and associated developmental categorisations of age. The Australian Bureau of Statistics (ABS 2016), for example, circumscribes the 'youth unemployment' rate to include unemployed individuals between the ages of 15 and 24. The same age range underpins the UN's definition of youth, which overlaps with the definition of the child under the United Nations Convention on the Rights of the Child (individuals below 18 years of age). Such crossover is inevitable for a category that is simultaneously cultural, social, and biological.

The mutability of meanings associated with age is exemplified in adaptations of Shakespeare's *Romeo and Juliet*. In the 1597 play, Juliet is explicitly 13 years old and, past menarche, is considered to be of marriageable age. Though Romeo's age is not specified, he too is called a youth, and both his actions (his identity drama) and how others treat him are compatible with the period's ideas about youth, with his judgement and temperament deemed immature and rash. By the time the play began to be adapted for the cinema, Juliet's age was no longer considered appropriately marriageable and the practice of using adult actors to play these youths on stage was exported to film until Franco Zeffirelli's 1968 adaptation (Brauborn et al. 1968), which courted controversy by casting lead actors who were respectively 17 and 15 years old. Concern over the representation of diegetic sex between minors in Zeffirelli's film was fuelled by contemporaneous concerns over new forms of youth culture and of discourse on sexual freedom. By 1996, Baz Luhrmann's *Romeo + Juliet* indicated further care to cast actors over the age of sexual consent, now 22 and 17 years old (Brook et al. 1998). The shifting meaning of age in these adaptations reflects changing adult anxieties around youth sexuality as well as historical changes in conceptions of minority and gendered ages of sexual consent (Grealy 2013). The adaptations exemplify the mobility of youth as a concept opposed to childhood and adulthood and framed as an orientation to culture, or judgement, rather than straightforwardly reflecting an individual's years since birth.

For both scholarly and popular approaches to youth, there are characteristics and tendencies associated with youth that can overlap with and even override definitions of adulthood. Lawrence Grossberg (1994, p. 34), for example, argues that youth is defined by an 'affective extremism' and by 'lines of flight that attempt to escape the dominant organization of everyday life'. Such lines of flight centrally include the pursuit of pleasure over productivity, and investment in ephemeral activities rather than future-oriented thinking as well as, contradictorily, an orientation towards remaking the future as different from the present. The characterisation of an older person as having a 'young spirit' and the condescending imperative to 'grow up!' each signal the mobility of 'youthful' actions and beliefs across age-based demographics. Such conceptions of youth as an orientation, often tightly associated with identity-making and with resistance to social convention, are not necessarily circumscribed by age.

The ambiguous relationship between youth and age is often exemplified by the figure of 'the teenager': nominally an individual aged between 13 and 20 years but in practice an assemblage of orientations, associations, and practices. The meaning of the teenager has also changed over time and points to the importance of historically contextualising any discussion of youth. In *Teenage: the prehistory of youth culture 1875–1945*, Jon Savage (2007) locates the emergence of the teenager at the end of the Second World War and especially links it to the effects of the military draft in the United States, which had removed young adult men from public life. The 'Teen Canteen' movement, for example, burgeoned from 1944 in response to the new visibility of youth during wartime and related concerns about young people frequenting saloons and drinking alcohol. Coca-Cola distributed pamphlets detailing how to start neighbourhood centres like the Teen Canteens, which frequently included a vending machine alongside a jukebox, dance floor, and ping-pong table (Savage 2007, p. 447).

In addition to new social spaces, Savage conveys this relationship between youth and post-war consumer culture as a generational identity informed by magazines like *Seventeen*. Featuring celebrity biographies, fashion articles, photomontage, Hollywood gossip columns, popular culture reviews, and dating and etiquette columns, *Seventeen* openly connected the formation of girls' identities to consumer culture (Savage 2007, p. 448). Such conflation of girlhood and consumption-as-identity-formation was not new, as we can see in Eliza Lyn Linton's notorious 1868 diatribe against 'the modern girl', in the girl's recurring presence across cultural theory as the exemplary passive dupe of popular culture, and in earlier girls' magazines (Driscoll 2008, p. 18). However, the interpellative modes of address characterising girls' magazines, as well as the audiences these might attract, clearly expanded across the early- to mid-twentieth century as part of a burgeoning consumer culture through which the teenager might construct a set of preferences, affiliations, and personal style.

At least by the 1920s, in contexts as diverse as Japan, Germany, Australia, and the US, youth had come to be equated with processes of identity formation tied to broadly gendered forms of consumption (Weinbaum et al. 2008; Driscoll 2010). But the teenager as a demographic category produced by market researchers and the popular cultural industries is only one of many concepts whose intersecting meanings and histories come to bear on any common-sense notion of youth. The seemingly new centrality of youth across the twentieth century is not only a product of the expansion of youth-oriented commodity culture. Rather, the increasing weight placed on youth in modern theories of identity formation meant that associating youthful identity formation with cultural commodities helped undermine the centrality of productive and domestic relations to social identity in general.

The concept of youth has always attempted to capture the process and experience of development. Puberty is one aspect of this, as a metamorphosis of physiological events that historically emphasised growing a beard or breasts, but now more commonly denotes a person developing the capacity for sexual reproduction. The relationship between puberty and age has varied, across time and between cultures. Across the nineteenth and twentieth centuries, however, the discursive significance of puberty was subsumed by adolescence, a broader concept denoting changes in behaviour and social status. The contemporary sociological meaning for adolescence continues to suggest liminality, as 'the transition period from dependent childhood to self-sufficient adulthood' (Muuss 1974, p. 4), and as examined by anthropology in seminal studies of rites of passage (Turner 1967). But contemporary conceptions of adolescence far more explicitly emphasise the management of expected difficulties and also conscious adjustments to one's behaviour shaped by an increasing awareness of and training for a future unfolding towards adult civic, sexual, and work freedoms and responsibilities.

This expanded definition of adolescence derives its popular use from psychologist and educator G. Stanley Hall who in 1904 published the two-volume *Adolescence: its psychology and its relations to physiology, anthropology, sociology, sex, crime, religion and education*. From Charles Darwin's theory of evolution, Hall developed his 'law of recapitulation' under which he argued the human organism must mature through stages from savagery to citizenly civility. As a vitalistic period of 'storm and stress', Hall's adolescence is the definitive stage in this trajectory, 'before the decline of the highest powers of the soul in maturity and age' (Hall, in Lesko 2001, p. 55). In accounting for Hall's historical significance, however, it seems as important to notice the way his theory modelled the contemporary focus on youth as the site for resolving the broadest possible social problems, and detecting signs of future problems. For Hall (1904 II, p. 448):

> Youth, when properly understood, will seem to be not only the revealer of the past but of the future, for it is dimly prophetic of the best part of history which is not yet written because it has not yet transpired, of the best literature the only criterion of which is that it helps to an ever more complete maturity, and of better social organisations, which, like everything else, are those that best serve youth.

Hall's work also draws attention to the fact that adolescence is both a set of cultural norms and a biosocial fact organising an array of institutional approaches to young people (Lesko 2001). Hall drew heavily on current debates in the still emerging field of developmental psychology, notably sponsoring Sigmund Freud's lecture tour of the United States. In an open letter to a Dr M. Fürst on the sexual enlightenment of children, Freud (1986, p. 138) described adults' investment in the idea of childhood innocence and its protection, and argued that a young person's sexual education should take account of 'each stage of [their] learning'. The famous model of sexual stages in childhood development that Freud developed from this principle may have long been contested in the discipline of psychology itself, but the core concepts of his broader developmental model continue to be important, often more directly through the work of those he influenced, including ego psychologist Erik Erikson.

Erikson's own model of life stages gave special weight to adolescence as the temporal site of subject formation. For Erikson, each age involves the development of a specific vital strength or basic virtue, and youth is understood as a period in which the prepubescent development of 'competence' is displaced during adolescence proper by the centrality of 'fidelity', devotion, or strong attachment. During this 'psychosocial moratorium' (Erikson 1968, p. 242), the individual becomes focused solely on the activity of identity formation. For Erikson, the adolescent desire for attachment drives a potentially bewildering search as 'the sense of identity becomes necessary (and increasingly problematic) wherever a wide range of possible identities is envisaged' (p. 245). The necessity of identity development, and the adolescent's growing freedom to encounter a range of identity possibilities gives rise to a basic conflict between identity and diversity, and Erikson's (p. 244) contention that 'In no other stage of the life cycle ... are the promise of finding oneself and the threat of losing oneself so closely allied' has continued to influence ideas about the blend of risk and possibility in the experience of youth. In Grossberg's (1994, pp. 32–33) terms, youth for Erikson 'does not so much involve an ideological search for identity as an affective search for appropriate maps of daily life, for appropriate sites of involvement, investment and absorption'. And consumer culture, Grossberg notes, is one important terrain on which this search takes place.

Published in the same year that Zeffirelli's *Romeo and Juliet* was released – 1968 – Erikson's writing also reflects the emergence of 1960s counterculture and the spirit of the May '68 riots in Europe, both of which tended to resist the commitments of previous generations (Williams 1970). We should not miss the echo of Hall in Erikson's (1968, p. 258) claim that

> no longer is it merely for the old to teach the young the meaning of life. It is the young who, by their responses and actions, tell the old whether life as represented to them has some vital promise, and it is the young who

carry in them the power to confirm those who confirm them, to renew and regenerate, to disavow what is rotten, to reform and rebel.

Nevertheless, since the 1960s it has become increasingly common to frame youth as a time and place of potential social critique and to discuss young people as political agents (Grossberg 1994, p. 28) who may resist sexual and domestic but also social and governmental norms (Frith 2005). Those particularly influenced by Erikson's model of youth often frame this potential for resistance in generational terms. They stress that those experiencing Erikson's adolescent life stage simultaneously inhabit some shared historical experience (Mannheim 1952). However, generation is also a troublesomely homogenising concept, effacing difference within an age-stratified population. It also underpins the dismissive assumption that the concerns of 'youth today' are passing and thus trivial. Any such generational claim thus requires some care in its application.

The Chicago School of Sociology had paid particular attention to urban American youth in the 1920s and 1930s, taking young people as exemplary sites on which to see the formation of social identities and groups in relation to a social environment (or 'ecology') (Shaw and McKay 1942). But as the new cultural visibility of youth in the 1950s and 1960s demanded new attention from psychology it also fuelled new directions in studies of youth. For Pierre Bourdieu (1993) at this time, generation seemed a useful concept for characterising broadly changing cultural aspirations – for example, the normalised expectation that a family would own a car – as well as broad social shifts in relation to an education system – such as the universalisation of high-schooling or the expansion of access to bachelor-degree programmes. However, Bourdieu's (1984) interest was primarily with class difference, including within generations, and socioeconomic inequality continues to be widely explored in contemporary sociological literature on youth in transition. From a sociological point of view, the end of adolescence might be observed through phenomena such as financial independence, full-time employment, or marriage. But such achievements do not necessarily indicate psychological independence and maturity, and their significance and likelihood are highly variable across time, place, and population demographics.

The conception of youth mapped across these ideas underpins the emergence of a visible field of 'youth studies', which took different forms under various disciplinary and institutional influences across the twentieth century. For cultural studies, the work emerging around the Centre for Contemporary Cultural Studies at Birmingham in the 1960s and 1970s has remained influential because of its interdisciplinary approach, its use of both structuralist and post-structuralist theory, and its framing commitment to political analysis of contemporary culture and society, which is now often described as 'conjunctural' (after Stuart Hall), but was then often characterised as 'Marxist'. This work consistently focused on instances of (usually male and working-class) youth subcultures that appropriated popular cultural meanings to signify their double articulation with and against mainstream and parent cultures alongside attempts to win social space (Clarke et al. 1993; Hebdige 1979; Thornton 1997). These ideas remain central to the 'post-subcultural' work that has more recently prioritised the fluidity of young people's cultural identifications through lifestyle consumption and temporary experiences of togetherness (Bennett 1999; Malbon 1999; Huq 2006). CCCS scholars galvanised a sense that specific cultural objects and practices are particularly fundamental to defining youth and to the experience of youth, despite recent accounts of subcultural participation by adults that problematise any presumed relationships between subcultures and age-stratified populations (Hodkinson 2012; Brabazon 2013). *Youth culture*, like (the mobility of) youth itself, remains inevitably difficult to define: it is not only the culture sold to youth but also the diverse cultural meanings circulated among youth from an array of practices that may not be exclusive to them, and the culture made by young people themselves.

Gill Valentine, Tracey Skelton, and Deborah Chambers (1998) identify two dominant discourses that organise adult thinking about youth and youth culture: youth as trouble and youth as fun. In governmental terms, this opposition appears in policies designed to manage risks particularly associated with youth – including the risk of being improperly or inadequately trained – and those designed to nurture or celebrate youth. The many figures representing this opposition have been historically produced by institutions charged with managing young people, but these figures are also sites of pleasurable investment by adults and young people alike. In popular cultural forms we can identify this opposition in the ubiquitous figures of the 'juvenile delinquent' and the 'clean teen'. In teen film, for example, consider James Dean in *Rebel without a Cause* and Sandra Dee in *Gidget* (Doherty 2002; Driscoll 2011). Both the juvenile delinquent and the clean teen represent cultural fantasies of youth in relation to normative trajectories of progression towards stable, self-sufficient adulthood. Moreover, like all such figures they represent the nexus of youth/adulthood as concretely gendered, raced, classed, abled, and otherwise distinguished by forms of social access and restriction that are powerfully invested with lived meanings during youth. Elizabeth Freeman (2010) characterises this trajectory as underpinned by a 'heteronormative chronobiopolitics', in which developmental time is structured as a linear progression across supposedly key events. Such progression is organised by strategies including the accumulation of wealth, education, marriage, reproduction, and child-rearing. It is the cultural force of presumed movement along this trajectory that defines the liminality of youth as inherently risky, given that at any point the normative progression may falter or divert with presumably extensive consequences. Where culture positions youth and young people as the hope for the future, the risk of a stunted or misdirected trajectory is a collective as well as individual problem. Youth as an image of becoming and potential crisis thus exist together, centrally providing justification for adult intervention, not only at the level of individual management of minors but institutionally.

We have been drawing connections between discourses and images of youth that span a long historical period, and, at the same time, acknowledging historically specific spikes in the visibility of youth and shifts in the way youth is discussed. Youth cannot now be credibly understood as cross-culturally homogeneous, despite the evident internationalising impact of ideas about child and adolescent development, about education and training, and about youthful tastes and leisure practices. Nor has 'youth' in any culturally specific context remained static. In Australia, the UK, and North America, the contexts on which most of the chapters in this collection focus, recent decades have seen high rates of youth unemployment (albeit lower than in continental Europe), combined with the requirements of prolonged education and increasingly exclusionary property markets. Such circumstances require young people to remain ambiguously dependent for longer, in need of state and parental financial support even while they engage in other 'adult' activities, such as paid labour, unpaid care work, sexual relationships, and drug consumption (Grealy 2017). Of course, this process of extending youth itself has a now long history, tied to the emergence and ongoing transformation of interlocking social norms and governmental agendas for training youth and licensing adulthood (which we turn to below). As Joanna Wyn and Rob White (1996, p. 96) point out

> the concept of *transition* offers a deceptively simple notion of a linear and uni-dimensional process of growing up, contradicted by the actual experiences of young people. These transitions into maturity – such as leaving home, or finding full-time work – are often transitory, reversible, and impermanent.

As a normative category, youth expresses a set of expectations both drawn from and yet not continuous with the diverse empirical experiences of those who identify with youth as a particular social identity. When we talk about youth, whether in popular or academic discourse, we variously invoke meanings associated with concepts as diverse as the teenager, minority, adolescence, and generation, including their disciplinary foundations. Like any form of common sense, youth remains knowable to us – as 'youth today' or via an array of other important clichés – precisely because it can incorporate these competing meanings. These ways of knowing youth may be cultural constructions which form the basis for conflicts over how we should engage with young people, but they also constitute the social context in which anyone experiences their own youth and the competencies and identities it is expected to produce.

Technology

Our stress on the multiple and often contingent meanings of 'youth' in the previous section is not simplified by the fact that this collection discusses youth through varied and particular relations to technology. Technology itself is a concept with diverse meanings employed to various analytical ends. As Jennifer Daryl Slack (2016, p. 1) puts this point, 'technology' is a promiscuously broad concept that reveals 'more about the cultural circumstances within which it is used than about real, consistent, and fixed meanings of the term'. Slack identifies four features linking the varied, sometimes conflicting, accounts of technology: 'that technology discloses and transforms the natural order; that technology is a transformational process; that technology embodies knowledge; and that technology is a certain kind of object' (2016, p. 1). It is salient here that we could replace each use of the term 'technology' in this list of features with the term 'youth' and have described principles in relation to which all accounts of youth take some kind of position. As the previous section outlined, the sense in which youth represents a natural developmental order, although still crucial to the importance placed on youth and to its experience, is now clearly overlaid with ideas about youth as a transformational process, as an orientation in or perspective on the world, and as a category of not just people but objects and practices.

The possibility of rephrasing an account of technology into an account of youth indicates some of the reasons why youth has come to have a special relation to conceptualising technology. Youth has been increasingly associated with *new* technology in particular, reinforcing the association of both with images of social transformation. These associations are presently most visible in the popular oppositions between old and new media audiences, centred on now familiar narratives about a digital or online generation that has succeeded narratives about the TV and then the MTV generations, which themselves succeeded the rock-and-roll and jazz age generations (Buckingham and Willett 2006). The generationalisation of youth culture thus remains closely tied to technological change in the field of popular or leisure culture, but the extent to which these stories feed back into stories about how young people should be educated (Marofsky 1990), and for what set of future skills, points to a more broadly generationalised image of technology – the progression of what Slack (2016, p. 6) calls 'technological-cultural' eras or communicative modes. Overall:

> Youth as a trope for accounts of media change allows a positive spin (by implication it is vibrant and full of potential), an inevitable spin (because generations can be neatly assumed to have different presumed knowledge of changing technology), and a threatening spin (insofar as it invokes some inevitable redundancy for what is now and has been).
> (Driscoll and Gregg 2008, pp. 79–80)

In each respect youth and technology are invoked to tell stories about one another.

There is, however, a tendency to think of the relationship between youth and technology predominantly in these terms – that is, in terms of how young people use technology, and what this means. One of the key features of this collection is that it stretches the understanding of technology in relation to youth. The chapters included in Part II of this book engage with specific innovations in communications technology that have impacted heavily on the popular imagination of youth as well as on young people's lives. These chapters, by Catharine Lumby et al. (Chapter 5), Thomas Crofts et al. (Chapter 6), and Emily Lockhart (Chapter 7), are to various degrees interested in 'sexting', which became a key site for new anxieties about youthful experiences of gender and sexuality in the first decade of the twenty-first century. Together, however, they indicate that popular concerns about how young people use digital communications technology to develop and represent sexual selves and relationships may nevertheless understand the relation between youth and technology in very different ways. Sexting provokes concerns about young people's sexual innocence or vulnerability, gendered coercion, and sexual rights or autonomy, which encourage conflicting responses that variously appeal to criminal sanctions, technological restrictions, reformed sex education, the protection of young people's sexual citizenship, and new principles for ethical research. In each instance the relationship between youth and technology is mediated by the age of sexual consent, which is itself a proxy for a set of assumptions about age, vulnerability, capacity, and the risks associated with young people's sexualised participation in social worlds.

The choice of sexting as a case study nevertheless points to the historical context of this book, and to the way technologies can inflect dominant understandings of youth. If other chapters in this collection are not focused on technology as 'a particular kind of object: a machine, a structure, or a medium of communication' (Slack 2016, p. 8), all remain invested in 'technology as integral to the culture within which it emerges' (p. 6). The communicative horizon of the digital is itself a factor in this collection, underpinning forms of concern about and communication with and between youth that are important not only to the uses of technology in Part II but to the assumptions about a present digital era underpinning the chapters in Part I and the purposes and means of contemporary education as discussed in Part III.

Notwithstanding this important context, this volume also includes chapters that approach forms of knowledges and even institutional apparatuses as technologies. Such approaches often take as a starting point Michel Foucault's (1988a, p. 18) famous proposition that 'there are four major types' of 'technologies' by which human beings 'understand themselves':

> each a matrix of practical reason: (1) technologies of production, which permit us to produce, transform, or manipulate things; (2) technologies of sign systems, which permit us to use signs, meanings, symbols, or signification; (3) technologies of power, which determine the conduct of individuals and submit them to certain ends or domination, an objectivizing of the subject; (4) technologies of the self, which permit individuals

to effect by their own means or with the help of others a certain number of operations on their own bodies and souls, thoughts, conduct, and way of being.

Counter to the received classical distinction between knowledge (episteme) and craft (techne), Foucault approaches knowledge as itself transformative, in the form of discursive apparatuses like 'the sexual sciences' (Foucault 1978) as much as in concrete practices like the diary or the confessional (Foucault 1988a). In this context, the chapters in Part I, by Liam Grealy, Terry Flew, and Rachel Cole et al. (Chapters 2–4), are primarily concerned with 'technologies of domination and power' (p. 19) deployed by the state and other institutional authorities. The work of such technologies of power is frequently concerned with both the application of machine technologies such as surveillance tools or film, and with the ways that age should stratify access to various sign systems, as exemplified by media classification systems.

However influential, Foucault's is not the only critical lens that elucidates how forms of knowledge work to shape and define both selves and social relations. For example, Megan Watkins's (2012) study of how the skill of writing is taught and learned in contemporary classrooms draws on Foucault among a range of philosophies of knowledge and embodiment, but most centrally Bourdieu's concept of 'habitus', to show how learning the disciplined techniques of writing – mastering the technology of writing – involves learning an entire mode of comportment as a student. Foucault's specific version of expanding the definition of technology to encompass knowledge also points us to Martin Heidegger's philosophical engagement with technology. The modern elevation of science over metaphysics questioned the classical denigration of technology as a second order kind of knowledge only concerned with the practical or material world. Although technology continued to imply particular specialist knowledge, specialisation itself came to be more highly valued. As knowledge became increasingly specialised – divided by disciplines and hierarchised by specific expertise – technology itself became increasingly associated with concrete uses, such as machine technology, that might not only serve human purposes but direct human understanding (Heidegger 1977, pp. 115–154). Heidegger (p. 5) rejects the modern reduction of technology to what he calls its 'instrumental and anthropological' definition, focused on human mediation of the natural world, and seeks what he views as a return to thinking technology as 'techne', as a *revealing*. Technology is thus 'nothing technological, nothing on the order of a machine. It is the way in which the real reveals itself' (p. 23).

Within these broad parameters each chapter in this collection considers particular relations between technology and youth, or young lives, or what it means to be a young person today. While families, communities, and institutions remain central sites of young people's subject formation, an expanding array of machine technologies also influence the development of individuals' identities and their education in social expectations, at the same time as these offer youth diverse sites of experience and sources of pleasure. To return to the example of sexting, the advancement and proliferation of smartphone technology has facilitated new means and forums for sexual expression which are nonetheless understood through precedent cultural norms regarding youth, pleasure, gender, responsibility, and risk. Technology shapes young people's understanding of their world, as well as their futures, in ever-changing ways, and while that is clearly true of people who are not 'young', the additional pressures placed on youth to orient themselves towards the future, and their more limited ability, as minors, to determine what they need to know, adds to the importance of examining carefully just how technologies affect young people, both positively and negatively, and equally how we should research such questions.

The chapters included in Part III all address the place of technology in the interface between young people and education. Digital technology is widely seen to open new communicative possibilities for young people, particularly opportunities to expand their social relations outside their immediate or traditional environments. Remy Yi Siang Low (Chapter 8) and Cristyn Davies et al. (Chapter 10) consider quite different technologies in terms of their capacity to influence young people's sense of agency: Low examining the potential of online education to increase access to the higher education sector for disadvantaged young people, and Davies et al. focusing on the use of new mobile apps to educate young people and to manage their anxiety in relation to school-based health interventions. Between these, Anna Hickey-Moody and Valerie Harwood (Chapter 9) examine the lack of access to appropriate technologies experienced by young people in lower socio-economic areas, highlighting the absence of information pathways about higher education available to adolescents whose dreams for the future frequently lack practical understandings about how they might get to where they dream of going.

Governance

Standardised testing. Road rules. Youth arts programmes. Media content warnings. Young people are governed in multiple ways in their everyday lives. Modern schooling is the governmental institution par excellence in which efforts to train individuals to become citizens are in effect. Schooling within liberal-democratic nation states is simultaneously a civilising, disciplinary, and educative project, in which battles over what sort of subjects should be produced are contested, most notably in curriculum design and delivery. While the common end of liberal education is the development of citizens capable of participating in civil society through the development of collective knowledge as well as social and intellectual skills, the means by which this is pursued can vary significantly.

In the philosophy of education of two seminal theorists on the state and social contract – Jean-Jacques Rousseau and Georg Wilhelm Friedrich Hegel – dramatically different conceptions of youth determine the appropriate techniques by which the individual's education should take effect. For Rousseau (1979), the (boy) child's natural freedom requires the invisible guidance of a tutor, and learning through direct experience in the context of a rural idyll, so that he will preserve the 'amour de soi' (love of self) that girds the future citizen against the competitive influences of modern societies. For Hegel (2007, p. 57), developing the capacity for an ethical adult life (in which the particular can be identified with the universal) requires a disciplinary education during which a young person first encounters universal moral values embodied in the teacher: 'What the boy has to learn must therefore be given to him on and with authority; he has the feeling that what is thus given to him is higher than himself'. This contrast between the forms that education might take signals how different values can be attributed to freedom and discipline in young people's education, as remains evident today in competing teaching methodologies and forms of schooling. Both Rousseau and Hegel's philosophies depend on developmental models that justify the governance of young people in terms of their future significance to democratic participation, as well as their gendered roles in nuclear households. As in justifications for education in general, the citizen-to-be requires both the protection and the expertise of the governing adult – whether this is the omnipresent tutor or the ideal of ethical life embodied in Hegel's teacher – in anticipation of individuals' consent to be governed as citizens. This model of consent under the social contract depends on a fundamental majority–minority distinction, in which majority citizens are responsible for the government of minors who require their protection, education, and control (Grealy 2013).

Compulsory schooling is the most significant form of modern education, but the governance of young people takes many other forms. The successful progress of adolescence is marked by an array of official borders and milestones, in which the achievement of various licences and graduations marks the negotiation or passing of age limits placed on political, economic, and leisure activities. Such limits – on having sex, drinking alcohol, driving, adopting children, and so on – often depend on their recognition by the state, but their enforcement requires governance by authorities that are not necessarily congruent in their aims or actions. In this sense it might be useful to understand the state as 'the mobile effect of a regime of governmentalities' that operate in conjunction, overlapping and struggling with one another (Foucault 2008, p. 77), and as 'a dynamic form and historic stabilisation of societal power relations' (Lemke 2000, p. 11), including the reproduction of majority–minority distinctions. As the chapters collected in Part I suggest, the implementation of policies for governmental interventions in young people's lives rely on a broad set of common-sense understandings about youth. Grealy (Chapter 2) is centrally focused on the role of common-sense notions of youth, maturity, sex, and public good in the governmental protection of minors, but the chapters by Flew (Chapter 3) and Cole et al. (Chapter 4) also examine how the role of the state in managing media consumption by minors is tied to such a common sense.

All of the chapters in Part I examine ways in which the state, within but also working across national boundaries, works with religious and other institutions with interests in public pedagogy or advocacy, with large corporations and small businesses, with local communities, families, and with many other social agents, to manage regulatory networks affecting youth. As we suggested above, Foucault's (1991) conception of 'governmentality' has often seemed helpful for discussing how the state nurtures self-governance in youth, but it is especially useful for emphasising this dispersal of regulation (Tait 1993). Governmentality refers, for Foucault (1991, pp. 102–103), to the emergence of the administrative state through an 'ensemble' of institutions, social practices, and apparatuses of knowledge by which population is managed. This positions the liberal-democratic nation state not as an institution of domination but as a set of public claims to care for the population and to nurture citizens' regulation of the self and others. Knowledge production in academic fields ranging from psychology to social work, criminology, demography, education, and also youth studies, have established expertise on and conceptions of youth which orient practices and interpretive frameworks within institutions focused on youth, such as schools, juvenile justice facilities, movie theatres, and clinics (Kelly 2000). As Nancy Lesko (2001, p. 50) describes it:

> adolescence was a social fact produced through a set of practices, including emphasis on and control of sexuality, segregation of girls' and boys' curricular areas, increasing years of compulsory schooling, separate justice facilities for juvenile delinquents, and unrelenting emphasis on youths' futures. In this light, adolescence can be glimpsed as a *technology* to produce certain kinds of persons within particular social arrangements.

In Foucault's narrative about the emergence of the governmental state, the family assumes a central role in the assemblage of rationalities, authorities, and techniques governing youth. The family becomes 'an instrument rather than a model: the privileged instrument for the government of the population and not the chimerical model of good government' (Foucault 1991, p. 100). Regarding the administration of young people's sexuality in particular, modern forms of knowledge such as nineteenth-century masturbation phobia, the science of sexology, Freudian psychoanalysis, and the social purity movement all depended on parental surveillance of and intervention into young people's sexual lives such that these might be normalised with regard to moral and scientific standards (Egan and Hawkes 2010). These help to constitute what Foucault (1978, p. 104) calls the 'pedagogization of children's sex', producing demands on various parties associated with young people, in particular mothers' responsibility for their children's health (pp. 146–147), along with educators, doctors, and psy professionals. Foucault (1996, p. 166) suggests that 'Watching over this childhood sexuality, observing it, diagnosing it, discovering it when it is hidden has now become a fundamental obligation of the parents.' Thus liberal governmentality is not defined by the actions of the state alone, but by 'the totality of practices, by which one can constitute, define, organize, instrumentalize the strategies which individuals in their liberty can have in regard to each other' (Foucault 1988b, pp. 19–20).

Recognising that the governance of youth operates across interconnected official and unofficial operations of power has far-reaching implications for youth studies. Let us take up the example of sex education, which is particularly relevant to the chapters on sexting collected in Part II. Youth studies, criminology, and the sociology of education have each noted the disjuncture between youth sexual practices and sex education curriculum, a gap that signals the power of those anxieties about youth often discussed in terms of 'moral panic' (Cohen 2002). In the Australian state of New South Wales, the Department of Education incorporated sex education into the health syllabus for high school students in 1967, focused on 'family life' and including 'social, emotional, and sexual development' (Weaver et al. 2005, p. 176). As in other countries, social changes ranging from 'the medical "invention" of homosexuality, the gays rights movement, feminism's redefinition of femininity, [and] pandemics of venereal disease' (Nelson and Martin 2004, p. 10) have since impacted on the content of school-based sex education, as a secular scientific discourse of risk has overtaken explicitly moral discourse for understanding sex and sexuality.

Progressive critics of secular sex education frequently note that the centrality of topics such as reproductive sex and the biology of reproduction, the risks of sexually transmitted diseases and unwanted pregnancy, and contraception and safer sex, together preclude appropriate attention to issues of sexual consent, violence, pleasure, and ethical erotics, as well as the inclusive normalisation of sex, gender, and sexual diversity (Fine 1988; Allen 2012). In this context, while institutional models of sex education often presume heterosexuality and emphasise health risks, underage sex takes a range of forms in which health is only one of many considerations, if it is considered at all. Research with young people who have themselves identified the limited utility of contemporary school-based sex education (Hillier and Mitchell 2008, p. 220), indicates the insufficient consideration given to young people's dominant motivations for having sex – because it feels good and/or because they want to be socially approved – and to the relationship between such desires and what is recognised as sex itself.

This simple example illustrates the significant gap between systems designed to govern youth and the forces that shape young lives. The formal disciplinary training and regulatory ideals offered by such institutions as school or family are clearly not exclusive influences on young people's sexual identities and activities. Social identification and pleasure also inspire forms of peer and self-regulation; as, more generally, both belonging and resisting offer complimentary motivations for self-government. However, an opposition between formal institutions of governance and social influence is also clearly untenable. Foucault (1988a, p. 19) himself defined governmentality as the point of 'contact between the technologies of domination of others and those of the self'. Government and subjection have the potential to be identical processes when understood in this way, although their relationship is rarely so straightforward. The modern self is certainly expected to relate to the self, and for young people normative models of selfhood encourage particular sorts of investments, desires, and action alongside a range of prohibitions to orient their development. Through this Foucauldian lens, the identity work of adolescence translates 'coming of age' as the process of becoming, in various ways, a resistant, or a governable, subject.

Governmentality has become a key concern for youth studies scholars interested in the effects of peers, adults, and institutions in how young people become 'who they are'. The acute investment of adolescence in identity work both serves and is supported by the commodified forms of youth culture we discussed above; indeed, the active consumer identity that youth culture frequently involves is part of the training in citizenship that governmentality demands. Youth culture is thus both the target and the means of governmental interventions into young people's lives (Bennett 1998), for example in arts programmes such as legal graffiti walls and music production workshops (Cahill 2008). The key aspects of modern youth outlined in the first section of this introduction can all be understood as conducive to, if not produced by, modern governance – through the institution of normative if not compulsory mature (post-pubescent) education, through the governmental manipulation of labour and training markets, through the legal delimitation of appropriate forms of sexuality, and so on. The promise and difficulty of 'fitting in' that dominates popular cultural narratives about adolescence is in this sense continuous with explicit forms of governance, and most directly those that depend on models of at-risk youth based in statistical age-based norms. As young people become accustomed to school, for example, they may also be encouraged to start part-time work and to anticipate a career, or further study. They will often be simultaneously subject to peer pressure around youth cultural norms, and however awkwardly they sit alongside parental norms these forms of pressure constitute ways in which young people attempt to govern each other and thus reinforce the importance of 'fitting in'. This imperative to belong can relate to personal style, sexual lives, or subcultural or scenic practices of consumption and production, among other things, and the desire for peer recognition and approval further models a viable adult life because it requires the negotiation of contradictory social demands. Youth cultural belonging may need to be balanced, for example, with the public performance requirements of university entry exams or paid employment.

The chapters collected here suggest that governance is intimately entwined with the use of technology in the constitution of youth experience. While such relations can never be determined in advance, youth practices are nevertheless a cultural barometer by which we might develop future forms of governance and more productive uses of associated technologies. The chapters in Parts II and III of this book demonstrate that where the impact of technology on young people's lives is negative, as it can be in sexting, governmental interventions are always more effective and ethical when they include young people's opinions and experiences in their design. For example, Lumby et al. (Chapter 5) suggest that conceptualising young people as active co-participants in academic research can reduce the reliance on protectionist strategies in governing young people's relationships to sexuality, bullying, and drug use, which can further disempower them. And Crofts et al. (Chapter 6) explore the complexities of the intersections between pornography and sexual exploration, and freedom and harassment, to conclude that whole new categories of response need to be developed to constructively govern these situations. In Part III, the chapters by Low (Chapter 8), Hickey-Moody and Harwood (Chapter 9), and Davies et al. (Chapter 10) on the use of technology to improve access to education demonstrate opportunities for using young people's interest in and familiarity with particular technologies to ameliorate expectations of social disadvantage and increase participation in sexual health education. Across the collection as a whole, the authors reiterate the importance of governmental interventions acknowledging the particular experiences of young people themselves.

Experience

In *New Keywords*, Michael Berubé (1995, p. 121) writes that 'experience' is 'one of the most compelling and elusive words in the language', echoing Williams's opening to his own *Keywords* entry on 'culture'. As Williams (1983, pp. 87–8, 127) explains, there are historical and conceptual overlaps the changing meanings of culture and experience, as both came to e͏ tensions between the general and the particular or subjective. Williams the modern conception of experience as divided into two types: 'k͏ based on past events', and 'a particular kind of consciousness' (p͏ He goes on to summarise these as 'experience past' – situated in͏ of 'trial and observation' – and 'experience present' – a 'f͏ "awareness"' of 'an "experience"'. This is not, of course, the ͏ popularly understood when young people are discussed as l͏ In fact, Williams refers to just this 'troubled contrast' bet͏ experience, already familiar in the eighteenth century, ͏ usage that confuses political judgement with experience͏ seems significant that this simplistic opposition con͏ important in public and popular discourse on youth͏

The opposition between youth and maturity ͏ Williams calls 'experience past', in that this ve͏ taught, or learned by even the most avid stud͏ and thus privileges age. On the other hand, ͏ youthful experiences requires the model of ͏ as 'the moment of experience as a way ͏ p. 28). In thinking about experience bey͏ omy we thus might turn back to its co͏ pp. 128–9) notes the ongoing relevance of a 'fundamental' philosophical 'controversy' over whether experience names 'the ground for all (subsequent) reasoning' or 'the product of social conditioning'. Experience is central to phenomenology, for example, in which even apparently ordinary modes of experiences cannot be brought together as the mere accumulation of data, and sensory experience has complex relations to its subjective processing. In *Being and Time* (2010), Martin Heidegger distinguishes between two types of experience, one that names isolated events (our 'experiences') and one involving the subject's attempt to know the world through testing. These forms of experience would have very different relations to a distinction between youth and maturity. For pragmatism, too, experience is not a measure of knowledge, but its form. For William James (2013), who directly influenced important theorists of education and citizenship, including John Dewey, impressionability to experience is a key characteristic of the human mind, and while the young mind is more impressionable it is not innocent in the sense that its experiences are less valid or significant.

As adults we might suggest that our youth was only knowable after the fact. The cliché that 'youth is the time of your life' requires a retrospective temporal point of comparison from which former experiences can be cited and evaluated against the present. This aspect of the way adulthood co-constitutes youth reconstructs sporadic, differentiated events into an idea of youth that teleologically explains an adult present – how did I get here? It frames youth as a novel time of affectively intense and singular experiences that cannot be repeated, or whose repetition reduces their significance, and which are important to determining who one becomes and how that happens. We could just as easily characterise youth as 'the *worst* time of your life' for the same reasons. Regret sits alongside nostalgia in recollections of youth that frame adult responses to young people. Adult coming of age stories are variously inspiring, blaming, angst-ridden, hilarious, embarrassing, and traumatic: an assemblage of the opportunities, limits, lacks, and pleasures that the experience of youth opens.

Of course, these same ideas also inform the experience of youth *as it happens*. Even before we arrive at adolescence, and during adolescence, we are aware/expect that youth entails this kind of significance. An increased awareness of one's experience and one's role in directing that experience, however, is prescribed by some of the forms of governance discussed above, is central to distinguishing youth from childhood. The nostalgic claim that 'youth is at one's your life' is liable to prompt both feelings of excitement – subsumes itive freedom – and inadequacy – where apprehension time of on An individual's experience may well not live up to the posed oppo he gap between the imperative to seize youth's supit gets better one's ability to do so can be palpable. 'Don't worry, This cliché retrospective adult discourse on youth experience. experienced ntensity and importance of youth as apparently le, while simultaneously framing youth as a contingent immaturity, and attempts to provide consolation for its pressures. The 'it gets better' claim consolidates the sense that youth anticipates an adult future, but also defines the experience of youth as repeatedly and thus unavoidably difficult.

On the one hand the imperative to maximise the potential of life's 'best time' can incorporate an expectation of future adult nostalgia that heightens the significance of new experiences and incorporates an anticipatory melancholia that asks 'Is this it?' as youth unfolds. On the other hand, the anticipation of youth's completion looks towards adulthood as providing independence, and new opportunities, capacities, or solutions. Together, such affective experiences of youth and ageing provide two poles, suggesting simultaneous temporalities defining the experience of youth: a *suspension in the present* of singular or life-defining experiences, and the *anticipation of an adult future*. Framing youth through these conflicting temporalities is another way of explaining the academic claim that youth is a 'relational' concept designating a 'liminal' period. It also gestures towards the social roles played by ideas about youth outlined above, including in shaping adolescent experience.

As the previous section outlined, the chapters in this collection consider various governmental regimes that manage young people's experience of growing up. The innocence associated with childhood is often understood simply as the absence of experience and its disappearance is often figured as corruption, despite the fact that experience underpins learning and also effective participation in social life. The enlightenment philosopher John Locke famously argued that all knowledge is derived from experience and this perspective influenced Rousseau's model of ideal education described above. For Rousseau (1979, p. 390), 'Our first masters of philosophy are our feet, our hands, our eyes'. But while Rousseau claims that the independent experience of his fictional ideal student Emile should not be interfered with by others, Emile's inclinations should nonetheless be manipulated by his tutor for his own good (Bloom 1979, p. 11). This dynamic balancing of freedom and control is central to governmental systems aimed at regulating youth experience, which systematically defer to developmental models outlining the experiences appropriate to particular ages. In Part I, Flew (Chapter 3) and Cole et al. (Chapter 4) demonstrate how the hierarchised categories of media classification systems communicate assumptions about when young people should consume particular sorts of representational content – featuring sex, violence, drug use, and so on – and how such content might be appropriately experienced by young people – for example, by recommending parental guidance. But the fact that youth experience exceeds both developmental models and governmental norms is apparent in the fact that consuming content restricted in such ways is both a common experience for young people and a key site of youthful pleasure.

Pleasure as a mode of experience is both a defining characteristic of idealised youth experience and a focus of adult anxiety over the difficulty of governing youth. The exciting novelty of first events and feelings – of dates, graduations, love, sex, trust, responsibility, freedom, and so on – is integral to youth as an experience suspended in the present, even as the future makes its demands. Pleasure is simultaneously responsive, interactive, embodied, and social; at once intimate and collective. For young people, pleasure may lie in fitting into or resisting social positions and norms, such as those Judith Butler (1990, p. 194) describes as the heterosexual matrix: 'that grid of intelligibility through which bodies, gender, and desires are naturalized'. In this example, the identity work of gender and sexuality produce a range of pleasures, in conformity with and resistant to dominant subject positions through modes of self-representation, political affiliation, and embodiment. The desire for identity, familial or peer recognition, social visibility, and exciting sensuous experiences is central to a range of youth cultural practices ostensibly concerned with style, consumption, embodiment, and social transgression (Hickey-Moody 2012; Findlay 2017). Such practices driven by desire are world making, while simultaneously providing reasons for being in the world. The chapters in Part II of this collection by Crofts et al. and Lockhart (Chapters 6 and 7) illustrate how youth sexting is understood and responded to by concerned adults. Pleasure is not itself the problem, but it is conceptualised as a dangerous motivation for young people categorically understood to lack the experience which would properly inform knowledge of its consequences. The chapters in this book attempt to extend consideration of experience beyond the categorical opposition to innocence, and to recognise the complex exchanges by which immaturity and maturity are represented in individual as well as collective lives. They seek to critically analyse how relationships between adult anxiety, perceptions of risk, and material circumstances of disadvantage bear on young people's experience, but also to consider how technologies of the self provide opportunities for thinking through and pleasurably being a young person.

A number of the chapters collected here demand greater direct engagement with young people in youth studies and related disciplines. Lumby et al. (Chapter 5) argue for reframing youth as co-participants and co-researchers in academic research, as an important step towards recognising young people's agency in determining their own desires, decisions, and practices, including risky ones. Ethnographic research methods have been used by a number of authors here to convey young people's own accounts of their situations and fantasies, and to represent the diversity of material situations in which individual young lives are located. This reflects a commitment to characterising the situatedness of young people's particular perspectives on their capacities and potential in shared social worlds. Hickey-Moody and Harwood (Chapter 9) use interviews to collect young people's fantasies about their futures, focused on higher education, work, and travel, and to illustrate the importance of social location in determining the resources through which such aspirations might be achieved. Low uses narrative case studies of individual high school students completing Massive Open Online Courses

(MOOCs), both as a pathway to formal higher education and out of intellectual curiosity, to show how their educational experience sits alongside various familial, financial, and political obstacles. In these cases, the research methods as well as the arguments aim to effectively demonstrate the forms of stratification and difference amongst a population demographic too often and too easily objectified as 'youth'.

Attention paid to the experience of youth, as articulated by young people themselves, is an ethical obligation for youth studies. This is especially important, given the willingness of multiple academic disciplines, as well as public authorities and popular commentators, to speak on behalf of young people and to intervene in their lives in the name of a general social good that effectively excludes youth as immature. Youth studies must attempt to represent young people's agentic contribution to their own lives and to society broadly, while providing space for young people to articulate such contributions themselves. However, this now somewhat clichéd demand for youth voices, and for the recognition of youth agency through methods that allow or advocate participation, must remain aware of a number of considerations.

It will help to bear in mind Joan Wallach Scott's argument concerning the uses and disadvantages of experience for historians 'of difference' (Scott, 1992, p. 24; see also Berubé 2005, p. 123). For youth studies too, documenting the experiences of youth, and of the effects of discourse on youth, cannot reveal more than individual perspectives. What is opaque or alien to the young person concerned, or just not considered worth representing, will remain 'excluded' (Scott, 1992, p. 25). Three further points are worth making based on this recognition. First, we must recognise that the field itself objectifies and mediates representations of and by young people, which are selectively chosen and subject to scholarly interpretation. Acknowledging this inevitability of scholarly representation should curtail the seductive tendency to fetishise any individual voice as an 'authentic' youth position – as speaking truth about the experience of 'youth today' – instead remaining attuned to diversity and conflict among young people, as in any social demographic. Second, we should remember that providing space for young people to speak does not mean we will like what is said. Pleasure and social affiliation are not goods in themselves and as with all social groups (youth studies scholars included) we should approach such actions and commitments critically, not on behalf of establishing moral culpability, but to investigate their social bases and their effects. In this regard it is important that youth studies does not restrict itself to only studying young people it perceives as marginalised (and to whom it can 'provide a voice') and those whose resistance conforms to scholarly practitioners' own politics, but also engages with young people whose commitments and actions we find difficult to understand and support. Third, youth studies scholars must recognise that the language of increased youth participation has long been employed by government itself (Bessant 2000), and that the language of consultation can easily become a strategy for conservative containment. The representation of young people's experiences, in youth studies research or elsewhere, will have a marginal positive impact unless work is simultaneously undertaken to make the institutions that bear on young people's lives more just, equal, and open to incorporating their critique. These are difficult challenges for youth studies, but necessary to keep in mind to do justice to the experiences of young people, who exist as both research subjects and co-participants.

Structure of this book

This chapter has examined four keywords for youth studies – youth, technology, governance, and experience – which structure the collection of chapters that follows. Some of these chapters engage directly with debates over these terms, as they play out in everyday contexts, while others implicitly depend on various historical and semantic inheritances to analyse specific instances of youth representation or young people's experience. We hope this opening chapter attunes the reader to the multiple meanings of keywords as they appear across the book and youth studies in general, but also where such meanings are mobilised politically in attempts to regulate young people's participation in culture.

Following Chapter 1, the book is organised under three part titles: Part I Governing Minority: Surveillance and Media Classification; Part II Young People and Technologies: Ethical Research and Sexting; and Part III Ethnographies of Young People's Education. In Part I, Chapters 2–4 variously explore the regulation of young people's relationships with media, in particular through age-based media ratings systems. Employing discourse analysis of policy and archival materials, and drawing on Foucauldian approaches to government, the authors consider discourses on and approaches to young people's media consumption, and the conceptions of minority and capacity underpinning adult interventions into young lives. In Part II, Chapters 5–7 each examine the discourses of pleasure, harm, and sexuality associated with young people's use of new technologies. Chapter 5 provides a methodological framework for research involving young people and such sensitive issues, while Chapters 6 and 7 demonstrate how concerns over youth sexting are figured in law and television dramas, respectively. Chapters 8–10 in Part III each employ ethnographic methods in relation to schooling and various technologies. Respectively focused on MOOCs and tertiary education, imagined pathways into university, and apps in health delivery, these chapters offer examinations of young people's experience of the systems that govern them, analysed in the former sections.

References

ABS 2016, 'Paid work: youth unemployment', viewed 19 August 2017, www.abs.gov.au/AUSSTATS/abs@.nsf/2f762f95845417aeca25706c00834efa/2b67f865fdbbf38ca2570ec0073e383!OpenDocument.

Allen, L. 2012, 'Pleasure's perils? Critically reflecting on pleasure's inclusion in sexuality education', *Sexualities*, vol. 15, no. 3–4, pp. 455–471.

Bennett, A. 1999, 'Subcultures or neo-tribes? Rethinking the relationship between youth, style and musical taste', *Sociology*, vol. 33, no. 3, pp. 599–617.

Bennett, T. 1998, *Culture: a reformer's science*, Allen & Unwin, Sydney.

Bennett, T., Grossberg, L., and Morris, M. 2005, *New keywords: a revised vocabulary of culture and society*, Blackwell, Malden, MA.

Berubé, M. 2005, 'Experience', in T. Bennett, L. Grossberg, and M. Morris (eds), *New keywords: a revised vocabulary of culture and society*, Blackwell, Malden, MA, pp. 121–123.

Bessant, J. 2000, 'Youth participation: a new mode of government', *Policy Studies*, vol. 24, no. 2–3, pp. 87–100.

Bloom, A. 1979, 'Introduction', in A. Bloom (ed.), *Emile, or on education*, Basic Books, New York, pp. 3–29.

Bourdieu, P. 1984, *Distinction*, Routledge, London.

Bourdieu, P. 1993, *Sociology in question*, Sage, London.

Brabazon, T. 2013, 'Dancing through post-youth cultures' [book review], *Cultural Studies Review*, vol. 19, no. 2, pp. 314–323

Brauborn, J. and A. Havelock Allan [producers] and F. Zeffirelli [director] 1968, *Romeo and Juliet* [motion picture], BHE Films, United Kingdom and Italy.

Brook, P., Hall, P., Loncraine, R., Luhrmann, B., Nunn, T., Parker, O., Polanski, R. and F. Zeffirelli 1998, 'Shakespeare in the cinema: a film directors', symposium with Peter Brook, Sir Peter Hall, Richard Loncraine, Baz Luhrmann, Oliver Parker, Roman Polanski, and Franco Zeffirelli, *Cineaste*, vol. 24, no. 1, pp. 48–55.

Buckingham, D. and R. Willett 2006, *Digital generations: children, young people and the new media*, Lawrence Erlbaum, Mahwah.

Butler J. 1990, *Gender trouble*, Routledge, New York.

Cahill, H. 2008, 'Resisting risk and rescue as the raison d'etre for arts intervention', in A. O'Brien and K. Donelan (eds), *The arts and youth at risk: global and local challenges*, Cambridge Scholars, Newcastle.

Clarke, J., Hall, S., Jefferson, T. and B. Roberts [1975] 1993, 'Subcultures, cultures and class a theoretical overview', in S. Hall and T. Jefferson (eds), *Resistance through rituals: youth subcultures in post-war Britain*, Routledge, New York, pp. 3–59.

Cohen, S. 2002, *Folk devils and moral panics: the creation of the mods and rockers*, Routledge, Oxon.

Doherty, T. 2002, *Teenagers and teenpics: the juvenilization of American movies in the 1950s*, Temple University Press, Philadelphia.

Driscoll, C. 2008, 'Girls today – girls, girl culture and girl studies', *Girlhood Studies*, vol. 1, no. 1, pp. 13–32.

Driscoll, C. 2010, *Modernist cultural studies*, University of Florida Press, Gainesville.

Driscoll, C. 2011, *Teen film: a critical introduction*, Bloomsbury, Oxford and New York.

Driscoll, C. and M. Gregg 2008, 'Broadcast yourself: moral panic, youth culture and Internet studies', in U. M. Rodrigues and B. Smaill (eds), *Youth, media and culture in the Asia Pacific region*, Cambridge Scholars, Newcastle, pp. 71–86.

Egan, R. D. and G. Hawkes 2010, *Theorizing the sexual child in modernity*, Palgrave Macmillan, New York.

Erikson, E. 1968, *Identity, youth and crisis*, Norton, New York.

Findlay, R. 2017, *Personal style blogs: appearances that fascinate*, Intellect, Bristol.

Fine, M. 1988, 'Sexuality, schooling, and adolescent females: the missing discourse of desire', *Harvard Educational Review*, vol. 58, no. 1, pp. 29–54.

Foucault, M. 1978, *The history of sexuality: the will to knowledge*, Penguin, Harmondsworth.

Foucault, M. 1988a, 'Technologies of the self', in L. H. Martin, H. Gutman, and P. H. Hutton (eds), *Technologies of the self*, University of Massachusetts Press, Amherst, MA, pp. 16–49.

Foucault, M. 1988b, 'The ethic of the care of the self as a practice of freedom' [an interview], in J. Bernauer and D. Rasmussen (eds), *The final Foucault*, MIT Press, Cambridge, MA, pp. 1–20.

Foucault, M. 1991, 'Governmentality', in G. Burchell, C. Gordon, and P. Miller (eds), *The Foucault effect: studies in governmentality, with two lectures by and an interview with Michel Foucault*, University of Chicago Press, Chicago, IL, pp. 87–104.

Foucault, M. 1996, 'Schizo-culture: infantile sexuality', in S. Lotringer (ed.), *Foucault live: interviews, 1961–1984*, Semiotext(e), New York, pp. 154–167.

Foucault, M. 2008, *The birth of biopolitics: lectures at the Collège de France 1978–1979*, trans. G. Burchell, Picador, New York.

Freeman, E. 2010, *Time binds: queer temporalities, queer histories*, Duke University Press, Durham, NC.

Freud, S. 1907, 'The sexual enlightenment of children: an open letter to Dr M. Fürst', in J. Strachey (ed.), *The standard edition of the complete psychological works of Sigmund Freud*, Hogarth Press, London.

Freud, S. 1986, 'Three essays on the theory of sexuality', trans. J. Strachey, *The essentials of psychoanalysis*, Hogarth Press, London, pp. 277–375.

Frith, S. 2005, 'Youth', in T. Bennett, L. Grossberg, and M. Morris (eds), *New keywords: a revised vocabulary of culture and society*, Blackwell, Malden, MA, pp. 380–382.

Grealy, L. 2013, 'Reorienting the Henson debate: child pornography, consent, and the masturbating adolescent', *Continuum*, vol. 27, no. 1, pp. 67–79.

Grealy, L. 2017, 'Philosophy for youth', *Cultural Studies Review*, vol. 23, no. 2, pp. 174–178.

Grossberg, L. 1994, 'The political status of youth and youth culture', in J. Epstein (ed.), *Adolescents and their music: if it's too loud, you're too old*, Garland, New York, pp. 25–46.

Grossberg, L. 2010, 'Raymond Williams and the absent modernity', in M. Seidl, R. Horak, and L. Grossberg (eds), *About Raymond Williams*, Routledge, Abingdon, pp. 18–33.

Hall, G. S. 1904, *Adolescence: its psychology and its relations to physiology, anthropology, sociology, sex, crime, religion and education*, Appleton, New York.

Hebdige, D. 1979. *Subculture: the meaning of style*. Routledge, New York.

Hegel, G. W. F. 2007, *Philosophy of mind*, trans. W. Wallace and A. V. Miller, Clarendon Press, Oxford.

Heidegger, M. 1977, *The question concerning technology and other essays*, Garland, New York.

Heidegger, M. 2010, *Being and time*, trans. J. Stambaugh, State University of New York Press, Albany.

Hickey-Moody, A. 2012, *Youth, arts and education: reassembling subjectivity through affect*, Routledge, Abingdon.

Hillier, L. and A. Mitchell 2008, '"It was as useful as a chocolate kettle": sex education in the lives of same-sex attracted young people in Australia', *Sex Education*, vol. 8, no. 2, pp. 211–224.
Hodkinson, P. 2012, 'The collective ageing of a goth festival', in A. Bennett and P. Hodkinson (eds), *Ageing and youth cultures: music, style and identity*, Bloomsbury, London and New York, pp. 133–145.
Huq, R. 2006, *Beyond subculture: pop, youth and identity in a postcolonial world*, Routledge, Abingdon and New York.
James, W. 2013, *Pragmatism – a new name for some old ways of thinking*, Read Books, London.
Kelly, P. 2000, 'The dangerousness of youth-at-risk: the possibilities of surveillance and intervention in uncertain times', *Journal of Adolescence*, vol. 23, no. 4, pp. 463–476.
Lemke, T. 2000, 'Foucault, governmentality, and critique', paper presented at conference Rethinking Marxism, University of Amherst, Massachusetts, 21–24 September.
Lesko, N. 2001, *Act your age! A cultural construction of adolescence*, Routledge, Abingdon and New York.
Linton, E. L. 1868, 'The girl of the period', *Saturday Review*, 14 March.
Luhrmann, B. and G. Martinelli [producers] and B. Luhrmann [director] 1996, *Romeo + Juliet* [motion picture], Bazmark Productions, USA.
Malbon, B. 1999, *Clubbing: dancing, ecstasy and vitality*, Routledge, London and New York.
Mannheim, K. 1952, 'The problem of generations', in P. Kecskemeti (ed.), *Essays on the sociology of knowledge*, Routledge, London, pp. 276–322.
Marofsky, M. 1990, 'Training the MTV generation', *Training and Development*, vol. 44, no. 6, pp. 9–11.
Muuss, R. E. 1974, *Theories of adolescence*, Random House, New York.
Nelson, C. and M. Martin 2004, *Sexual pedagogies: sex education in Britain, Australia, and America, 1879–2000*, Palgrave Macmillan, New York and Basingstoke.
Rousseau, J. J. 1979, *Emile, or on education*, trans. A. Bloom, Basic Books, New York.
Savage, J. 2007, *Teenage: the prehistory of youth culture 1875–1945*, Penguin, New York.
Scott, J. W. 1992, 'Experience', in J. Butler and J. W. Scott (eds), *Feminists theorize the political*, Routledge, New York.
Shaw, C. R. and H. D. McKay 1942, *Juvenile delinquency in urban areas*, University of Chicago Press, Chicago, IL.
Slack, J. D. 2016, 'Technology', in K. B. Jensen, R. T. Craig, J. D. Pooley, and E. W. Rothenbuhler (eds), *The international encyclopedia of communication theory and philosophy*, Wiley, New York, pp. 1–11.
Tait, G. 1993, 'Youth, personhood and "practices of the self"', *Journal of Sociology*, vol. 29, no. 1, pp. 40–54.
Thornton, S. 1997, 'General introduction', in K. Gelder and S. Thornton (eds) *The subcultures reader*, Routledge, London and New York, pp. 1–9.
Turner, V. 1967, *The forest of symbols: aspects of Ndembu ritual*, Cornell University Press, Ithaca, NY.
Valentine, G., Skelton, T. and D. Chambers 1998, 'Cool places: an introduction to youth and youth cultures', in T. Skelton and G. Valentine (eds), *Cool places: geographies of youth cultures*, Routledge, London and New York, pp. 1–34.

Watkins, M. 2012, *Discipline and learn: bodies, pedagogy and writing*, Springer, London.
Weaver, H., Smith, G., and S. Kippax 2005, 'School-based sex education policies and indicators of sexual health among young people: a comparison of the Netherlands, France, Australia, and the United States', *Sex Education: Sexuality, Society and Learning*, vol. 5, no. 2, pp. 171–188
Weinbaum, A. E., Thomas, L. M., Ramamurthy, P., Poiger, U. G., and M. Yue Dong 2008, *The modern girl around the world: consumption, modernity and globalization*, Duke University Press, Durham, NC.
Williams, R. 1970, 'A hundred years of culture and anarchy', *The Spokesman*, 8 December.
Williams, R. 1983, *Keywords: a vocabulary of culture and society*, Fontana, London.
Wyn, J. and R. White 1996, *Rethinking youth*, Sage, London.

Part I
Governing minority: surveillance and media classification

2 Common sense in the government of youth and sex

Liam Grealy

Talking about young people, sex, and harm

I want to begin with three statements that I take as exemplary of different common-sense discourses on young people, sex, and government. First, from the former New South Wales Housing Minister David Borger, in relation to the removal of sex offender Dennis Ferguson from a Ryde neighbourhood: 'He does have to live somewhere (but) I don't think that [his current housing complex] is the right or appropriate location' (SMH 2009). Second, from the organisation Common Sense Media (2014), comes the claim that: 'We steer you away from things that are developmentally inappropriate, and help you to find the hidden gems that are right for your family and your kids'. And, third, from eBay (2014, p. 1), in an article entitled 'Ways to use surveillance equipment to protect your children', comes the assertion that 'The level of a person's security drops immediately when they leave the confines of a home. This is especially true for kids.'

Each of these statements reflects significant recent changes in Australian law, policy, and culture. In the first, Borger's concern over Ferguson's accommodation followed local community protest, facilitated legislation allowing for his removal, and occurred because laws inspired by Ferguson's actions did not apply to him. That is, Ferguson's release from prison in 2003 led to Australian state laws and institutions allowing for post-sentence detention of sex offenders on the grounds of community protection (see Grealy 2011; 2014). For many people, trusting Ferguson to live in the community without reoffending seemed to no longer make sense.

In the second statement, Common Sense Media's assurance aims to interpellate parents as responsible for their children's media consumption. This approach to responsibility is similarly articulated by the Australian Law Reform Commission's 2012 review of the Australian Classification System (see Driscoll and Grealy 2013). The key purposes of the ALRC review included 'providing advice to consumers to help inform their viewing choices' and 'protecting children from harmful or disturbing content' (ALRC 2011, p. 19; 2012, p. 24), and its key recommendations included platform-neutral regulation and an adult category for video games. Parental involvement in mediating children's media consumption is presumed common sense, and is increasingly important in relation to state and industry emphasis on education rather than direct intervention.

Finally, the assertion in the eBay article promotes 'responsibilisation' strategies to parents – strategies that encourage the purchase of new technologies (such as CCTV, device monitoring software, RFID chips, and GPS watches) to track and regulate children's behaviour and mobility. 'Installing a surveillance system is an important measure for parents to take to ensure their kids' safety', eBay (2014) claims. Despite significant debate about expanding state surveillance of citizens, comparatively little concern has been expressed over the surveillance creep of such technologies into parent–child relationships.[1] Common sense demands that parents are responsible for their children's public safety, and the consideration of new technologies to facilitate this is logical in the present context. This is so without framing any particular technology as good or bad, or presuming its use is characterised by a parent's desires to either care for or control a minor.

The post-sentence management of sex offenders, the regulation of media consumption, and the use of child surveillance technologies are complex areas worth consideration on their own terms. But they share an obvious overlapping interest in the protection of minors from various harms, primarily if not only sexual harms. These extend from sexual assault to all forms of 'premature' experience as designated by 'reasonable adults'. That is, in common-sense protections instituted by adults in relation to young people and sex, any consideration of the pleasure and intimacy provided by sex contends with powerful developmental discourses that prioritise caution and delay in terms of safety, harm, and linear models of youthful becoming. In their own ways, these quotations each provide entry points into considering common sense about young people, sex, and associated harms and pleasures. This chapter takes these examples as indicative of culturally dominant discourses and modes of reasoning about young people and sex. It aims to examine common sense itself, both in the particular instance of common-sense ideas and practices related to young people and sex, and in terms of the more general relevance of common sense as an object for youth and cultural studies.

Debate over the legitimacy of *particular* techniques or technologies employed to manage sex offenders post-sentence conceals the consensus that ongoing state surveillance *should* occur for community – specifically, child – protection. Argument over specific ratings categories and concerns about practical challenges for classification related to media convergence nonetheless indicates *ongoing* commitment to regulating media consumption in relation to consumers' age. And concerns over the ethics of new technologies applied to the surveillance of minors belies the fact that these are simply the most advanced techniques for fulfilling the modern family's role as an instrument of liberal government (see Foucault 1984, p. 100). Such disagreements nevertheless signal a *common* investment in the production of 'minoritised adolescence'. Elsewhere, Catherine Driscoll and I (Driscoll and Grealy 2015) define minoritised adolescence as the way governmental technologies like media classification systems locate conceptions of malleable, plastic adolescence on one side of the major-minor binary, consolidating adjacent notions of stable, reasonable adulthood. This is also a distinction between citizens and citizens-in-training. It is common sense for which adults are presumed competent and with which they should act on behalf of minors, driven by minors' best interests.

In this chapter, despite the primary focus of this collection on 'youth', I make no strict or consistent distinctions between childhood and youth. That is, I broadly accept Joanna Wyn and Rob White's (1996, p. 1) multiple conceptions of youth, 'as an age category, for institutional and policy purposes, [that] generally starts at age 13 and continues until age 25', as a 'social process' in which the meaning and experience of becoming adult is socially mediated (p. 4), and as 'a *relational* concept, which refers to the social processes whereby age is socially constructed, institutionalised, and controlled' (pp. 10–11). Modern youth combines the historical figure of the commodified teenager and the period of adolescence as one of 'storm and stress' to emphasise its liminal status between childhood and adulthood. Nonetheless, as David Archard (1993) notes, the boundaries, divisions, and dimensions that define competing conceptions of childhood (in his terminology), as distinct from adulthood, both distinguish themselves from and encompass the period elsewhere defined specifically as youth. Such definitions and distinctions are political, discursively local, and practical. And technologies such as media classification or home surveillance relate to and constitute both children and youth, in common and particular ways. Thus, my argument here is cognisant of Pierre Bourdieu's (1993, p. 95) claims that 'youth' always signifies a division of power, between adults and not, but that it also homogenises 'social universes that have practically nothing in common'. Common sense about youth is pragmatic, knowingly effacing differences about and between young people to make generalisations, and ever ready to acknowledge exceptions and complexities and the limitations of contemporary conceptions.

Publicising common sense

I began with three statements. To paraphrase: 'he has to live somewhere, but not here';[2] 'protecting children from harmful or disturbing content' (ALRC 2011, p. 19); and 'There are all manners of trouble that children can get themselves into when they are outside the home' (eBay 2014).[3] Located variously in media, policy, and marketing discourses, these are recognisable to us as clichés: shorthand representations of common sense. In public debate, the notion of common sense itself operates similarly to the figure of 'the public'. The politician acts in the name of the public and citing the common sense she shares with its citizens in order to legislate for the sex offender's removal. Common sense is the parent's explanation for not letting her 10-year-old watch *Eyes Wide Shut* or *The Texas Chainsaw Massacre*. Similarly, common sense facilitates the parental purchase of a mobile phone for an adolescent previously denied one, on behalf of safety as well as social and cultural capital. In what follows I provide an overview of common sense to set up an argument about its central role in the protection of minors from their own pleasure, sexual and otherwise.

Jean-Jacques Rousseau's (1987, p. 32) distinction between 'the general will' and 'the will of all' signals 'the public' as inevitably a rhetorical fiction mobilised to political ends. The 'reasonable adult' as a measure of 'community standards' in classification decisions is a similar representation or practical solution, at once representing and effacing differences within the population (Grealy and Driscoll 2015).[4] Contesting what 'the public' means, and thus the purported content of common-sense public standards, is at the heart of modern politics, and common sense in such contexts is a rhetorical device that effaces alternative positions, invoked explicitly during crises over consensus. Writing about 'law and order common sense', Russell Hogg and David Brown (1998, p. 43) suggest that this underpins public statements made by a range of social actors, including 'politicians, police, judges, lawyers, administrators, radio talk show hosts, newspaper executives and journalists'. Such figures often feature in public debates speaking in terms of common sense even if other forms of expertise or social capital grant them an audience. A politician is asked to comment 'as a parent' because it is understood that she represents the common demands of her constituency, but such speaking positions are also established for scientific, legal, and other experts. Where their views do not correspond to dominant norms about parenthood, for example, common sense consolidates ontological claims by appeals to its commonness, to common people, everyday life, and culture. In this way, common sense is not false knowledge but it is partial, and by disguising its modes of reasoning or appealing to experience – 'the world is its authority' (Geertz 1983, p. 75) – common sense is regularly drawn on, especially in political debate, to naturalise diverse claims.[5]

The most famous example fitting this account is perhaps Thomas Paine's ([1776] 2010) treatise, *Common sense*. His pamphlet sought both a style accessible to those with limited literacy and, despite its title, a dramatic break with dominant thinking in its advocacy for 'immediate American independence, a union of thirteen resisting states, and republican governments for the states in that union' (Taylor 2010, p. xi). As Sophia Rosenfeld (2011, p. 15) writes, 'common sense is typically evoked and held up as authoritative only at moments of crisis in other forms of legitimacy'. While I would suggest such crises can include banal disagreements over matters of little consequence, the appeal to common sense often signals the social application of some competing (i.e. silly, offensive, arcane) idea. Common-sense assumptions are usually left unstated while, 'The rest of the time, the speaker feels compelled to employ a preceding "of course" as a signal that he or she is stating the obvious and offering up a cliché rather than treating the interlocutor as childish or insane' (Rosenfeld 2011, p. 2). Of course, a parent sets limits on the media their child can consume, for example.

With a similar eye on how conflict is effaced through representation of common sense, Michael Warner (2002, p. 51) writes that '*A* public, in practice, appears as *the* public'. This is importantly a question of who gets to speak in and as the public. As Craig Calhoun (2005, p. 283) notes:

> Even when [public discourse] is about matters that affect the whole public, only a smaller public is active in it – and this is often a matter of active exclusion, not just apathy ... There is a distinction, thus, between the public capable of (or entitled to) political speech, and the public that is the object of such speech or its intended political effects.

Acknowledging the contested nature of claims concerning the public and purported common-sense standards is important. Elsewhere I have considered the relationship between minority, consent – in its sexual and political forms – and the public sphere (Grealy 2013). Consent is both an agreement to make oneself subject to external forces and a political capacity that signifies recognition of one's autonomy by external powers – a capacity not universally granted and one stratified by age. However, I am also interested here in whether we can think about common sense as *not only* a politician's tactic to efface specific interests, or as exemplary of supposed bad thinking. For cultural studies, common sense might have a more important place as that which fundamentally binds us to culture, and that which orients our everyday decision-making, including in matters involving minors and harm.

Common sense connotes the concepts or categories we use to make things sensible, but also our shared modes of reasoning relative to them. Raymond Williams's well-known concept 'structure of feeling' seems comparable: 'The general idea ... is that of a shared set of ways of thinking and feeling which, displaying a patterned regularity, form and are formed by the "whole way of life" which comprises the "lived culture" of a particular epoch, class or group' (Bennett, in Turner 2003, p. 47). However, the following consideration of common sense and young people is somewhat distinct from what both Williams ([1961] 1975) and Paul Willis (1990) describe as a 'common culture', the former as an argument against British class distinctions and the latter on behalf of celebrating everyday practices of appropriation and meaning-making. Ideology, too, can come close to glossing how common sense works, on Antonio Gramsci's condition 'that the word is used in its best sense of a conception of the world that is implicitly manifest in art, in law, in economic activity and in all manifestations of individual and collective life' (in Hall 1986, p. 20). Rosenfeld's (2011, p. 254) description of the relationship between the idea of common culture and the notion of common sense is useful: 'The idea of a common culture as either the basis or result of public discourse is starting to sound quaint. Yet as democracy has turned into the only acceptable global norm, common sense has become more valued than ever, both conceptually and rhetorically, in public life.'

In thinking about the government of young people in relation to sex, one central requirement here is to think through common-sense concepts and feelings as 'what [lie] so artlessly before our eyes [they are] almost impossible to see' (Geertz 1983, p. 92). This endeavour complies with John Hartley's (2003, p. 10) description of cultural studies as 'A critical enterprise devoted to displacing, decentring, demystifying and deconstructing the common sense of dominant discourses.' However, I am less concerned here with displacing common sense than with investigating its usefulness for understanding the government of young people. This does not forgo a commitment to cultural studies' 'critical' enterprise, but it does perhaps prioritise the banal, everyday contexts in which people act according to implicit ideas and habitual practices, including in 'expert' or 'professional' contexts. Thinking about common sense in this way can help us understand tricky decisions relating to young people and sex, made by parents and others, in terms of both the premises and processes of decision-making that are often implicit. I suggest this can also be useful for understanding the generic academic critique that highlights the harms of repression, control, and adult intervention in actions motivated by 'child protection'.

John Brewer, drawing on Errol Lawrence, offers us a useful description of how common sense is typically understood. Common sense is conceived as

> down to earth 'good sense', which is 'taken-for-granted', held to be 'legitimate', 'real' and 'proper', containing within it 'structures of knowledges', 'beliefs, ideas and practices', which are 'contextualised' or 'situated' in the 'experiences of people' and the 'social relations of everyday life'.
> (Brewer 1984, p. 67)

In Geertz's (1983, p. 84) terms, common sense is similarly 'what the mind filled with presuppositions ... concludes'. In other words, even if common sense – as both substantive knowledge and a mode of apperception – is historically determined it is not readily apparent as such, and it is thus the necessary grounds for social relations that are not characterised by overt conflict. Like culture itself, common sense transcends individuals who, constituted in relation to it, draw on its repository of knowledge, archetypes, and representations and combine these with experiences as a form of everyday reasoning for approaching particular, immediate problems. For John Dewey (1948, p. 202), common sense fuses the emotional, the intellectual, and the practical, and specific 'contexts of use' portray a particular emphasis rather than an absence in this 'indissoluble unity'. Common sense is thus 'embedded within actual material practices' (Brewer 1984, p. 68) and confirmed by individual experiences selectively chosen through reasoning that effaces its own processes (p. 69). Stuart Hall (1986, p. 20) describes common sense as 'disjointed and episodic, fragmentary and contradictory', and 'sedimented over time'. Thus, common sense is historical, even if it attempts to disguise its historicity through appeals to '"feeling", "personal experience" and immediate empirical perception' (Hall et al. 1977, p. 52). Existing somewhere between superstition and the arcane, common-sense appeals to experience typically set themselves 'in opposition to complexity, expertise, inside knowledge, urbanity, jargon, conflict, partisanship, and debate' (Rosenfeld 2011, pp. 14–15). For Hall (1986, p. 20), common sense is

> the terrain of conceptions and categories on which the practical consciousness of the masses of the people is actually formed. It is the already formed and 'taken for granted' terrain, on which more coherent ideologies and philosophies must contend for mastery ... if they are to shape the conceptions of the world of the masses and in that way become historically effective.

We should remember, as Williams (1958) noted, that 'To other people, we are also masses'; somewhat like the public, the concept of the mass is a political figure mobilised to represent others. Acknowledging its similarly performative capacity, I suggest that common sense is central to imagining and experiencing modern, pluralist communities, as well as modern conceptions of youth, even if its substantive content differs between groups and individuals (who are often surprised by this experiential diversity) (Ezrahi 2012, p. 87). In contemporary politics, where populism is a dominant style, common sense is the epistemology that 'expert' knowledges must contend with, including the epistemological assumptions of other expert knowledges that have become 'sedimented over time'.

That minority is naturalised as an object of governance is, of course, common sense. Ethel Mannin conceived her famous guide to parenting, *Commonsense and the Child*, 'as a protest against all the highfalutin theorizing about children, all the physical fussing, and the mention and emotional fingering' (1947, p. 25). Mannin defines common sense concerning children in opposition to their neglect (p. 277). While Mannin's preferred conception of common-sense parenting emphasises the child's freedom 'consistent with its own well-being, and the protection of one's own and other people's property and privacy' (p. 277), the appeal to common sense is important here, as well as the presumptions on which this is based. That adults must act in the best interests of young people, intervening in and managing their lives in relation to developmental markers and timelines, is basic to the majority–minority distinction foundational to liberal government.

None of this is to claim that common sense is deficient relative to some other mode of reasoning or some other discursive formation that classifies the world and organises responses to it. Rather, I am interested both in the provenance of common sense within particular youth-related governmental discourses and in how common sense constitutes communities, situating individuals in certain shared structures of feeling and judging. Minority provides us with a pre-eminent example of contemporary common sense; for example, the common sense that situates the child sex offender – alongside the terrorist – as one of contemporary culture's most significant threats. Nonetheless, any discussion of *common* sense stands on shaky ground in cultural studies, given the generalised scepticism of totalising anthropological conceptions of culture, and an emphasis on conceptions of culture that acknowledge its administrative dimension (see Bennett 1998), or which emphasise culture as imbricated with the social and characterised by ongoing negotiations and conflicts (see Frow and Morris 1996). Indeed, discussions of common sense in cultural studies are most prevalent in Hall's work, where it is inspired by Gramsci's (1992) writing on hegemony. Tony Bennett's shift from Gramscian understandings of hegemony and cultural consent to Foucauldian conceptions of dispersed relations of power/knowledge organised by multiple authorities is typical of cultural studies generally, as it shifted to investigate political and discursive conflicts that did not map easily onto class interests or assumptions about common culture.

Yet, I want to contend that common sense is a useful analytic for understanding ideas about young people and government. Our ideas, or our basic presuppositions in this field, highlight collective investments in fundamental cultural–legal categories: childhood and adulthood, minority and majority, citizenship, rights and consent, and community and government. Sex – in terms of both its potential pleasures and harms – is obviously significant in organising relationships between these concepts in terms of development and delay, and quotidian strategies both protect and exclude minors from sex, and some forms of sex more than others. As Lauren Berlant and Michael Warner (1998, p. 552) famously argue, sex, and in particular heterosexuality, is not a thing but a culture, which 'never has more than a provisional unity'.

Instead, what comes to count as sex depends on intersecting spatial, temporal, representational, and normative practices to regulate and stratify desire and intimacy in relation to bodies, practices, legal entities, and so on. Such strategies, embedded in apparatuses that manage adult–child relations, draw on expert and common-sense ideas about puberty, sexual latency, adolescence, and the modern family. And, as the first section of this chapter made clear, such strategies are legitimised in everyday speech through performative shorthand statements for deeply held ideas about young people, which often take the form of cliché.

Cliché, youthful harms, and common-sense responses

Taking potential harms to minors into account, common sense knows it is better to have a convicted sex offender live further away than next door – 'he has to live somewhere, but not here'. It says young people may not understand the 'significance' of graphic violence, 'adult themes' or sex on-screen – 'protecting children from harmful or disturbing content' (ALRC 2011, p. 19). And common sense assumes minors will be safer the more time and money parents dedicate to their surveillance – 'There are all manners of trouble that children can get themselves into when they are outside the home' (eBay 2014).

Cultural studies often responds to such clichés by exposing universal claims, outlining problematic assumptions, and mediating between them and expert knowledge gleaned from other fields: child sexual abuse is most often committed by a known adult in the home; media classification has tended to classify sex higher than violence, and non-heteronormative sex higher still; and surveillance technologies assuage parental anxiety rather than increase child safety, are easily subverted by young people, and could just as easily be exploited by the cliché man in the white van.

Such statements are important contributions to academic and public debates, but these clichés shouldn't be dismissed as signalling misunderstanding, and especially not as moral panic. In a consideration of post-Romantic literary reading, Ruth Amossy (1982, p. 34) describes clichés as 'reading effects' that 'emerge through an act of recognition'. Clichés are recognisable because repeated, and Amossy (1982, p. 35) suggests that in the cliché 'The reader recognizes ... speech that is both his own and radically foreign to him'. No cliché, of course, determines the reading processes by which it will be deciphered (Amossy 1982, pp. 36–38), however across different approaches to reading 'the cliché posits a relation with a pre-existing discourse – anonymous and blurred talk, the insistent buzz of social discourse' (p. 38). In an essay on Baz Luhrmann's film *Australia*, Meaghan Morris draws on Amossy's call to treat cliché in terms of 'the ways it is used within various programmings of reading', or watching (Amossy 1982, p. 38). As more than 'static markers of a legacy that always remains the same' (Morris 2013, p. 86), Morris considers clichés as providing openings for debate about shared cultural histories and values, thus central to blockbusters seeking international audiences (p. 88). For Morris (2013, p. 94), 'the power of cliché is to ask an unsettling question: *do you recognize me?*', a 'probe' that establishes potential for identification, agreement, disavowal, or refusal. The production and recognition of cliché are necessarily collective endeavours, constituted in *Australia*'s case through texts that circulated commentary on that film (Morris 2013, p. 99). While she says they will usually not do so, Morris (2013, p. 101) characterises clichés as 'materially open elliptical spaces and times of involvement in which it is possible for change to occur in habitual ways of thinking and feeling'.

The recognisable, repeatable features of cliché thus signal both a claim to consensus and an invitation to review such a claim. Cliché is historically grounded by the reiterative exchange of speech acts (including in the forms of gossip and anecdote; see Grealy 2016) that performatively constitute communities around shared values and practices. But cliché's shorthand nature underpins its capacity to efface difference. The common sense represented in the claim that minors should be protected from harmful content or experiences leaves ample room for disagreement over what that content is and how we should understand it (e.g. films featuring adult sex, the production of sexy selfies on Snapchat, participation in child pornography). Conflicts over how best to respond to commonly conceived risks to young people find clichés mobilised by parties with competing positions: 'he has to live somewhere, *but not here*' and 'he has to live somewhere; *why not here?*'. The fact that no cliché is enunciated alone, but is determined by collaborative, interactive social discourse, provides opportunity for recognition *or* disavowal of the common sense it represents.

Debates about the government of young people's relationships to sex draw on normative, progressive models of development in which harm, in particular the harm of thwarted or disordered development, is a perpetual spectre. The child-at-risk is a common and much critiqued figure in youth studies (Kelly 2001) and her emergence signals a wider shift towards risk in criminology, education, and sociology. Whereas dangers can be unknown to us, risks exist in our knowledge of them, as estimates of the likelihood of a particular event occurring. Risk thinking attempts to make the future calculable in the present: to tame chance (Hacking 1990). David Garland (2003, p. 71) claims that modern societies have become more adept at identifying and managing risks, which has increasingly become a responsibility of government and an expectation of citizens. Responding to Ulrich Beck's risk society thesis, Garland (2003, p. 71) writes that 'We are not a "risk society" in the sense of being exposed to more, or more serious dangers. If we are a risk society, it is because we have come to be more conscious of the risks that we run and more intensely engaged in attempts to measure and manage them.' In criminal justice and in education, the uncertainty of dangerousness has been supplanted by risk (e.g. of offender recidivism or failure to graduate), a trust in numbers that generates graduated assessments of future probabilities based on past outcomes in like circumstances (Simon 2005, p. 414).

While risk assessment is now standard practice in formalised educational and social work approaches to young people at the level of the population, the normative parent's approach to potential harms is importantly different. Parental government of children operates through a localised, domesticated perspective that invests the individual case with special value, while nonetheless informed by the norms associated with population distributions as public standards for common-sense parenting. For Clifford Geertz, common sense – totalising, dogmatic, and ambitious (1983, p. 84) – consistently reveals certain 'stylistic features', what he calls 'naturalness', 'practicalness', 'thinness', 'immethodicalness', and 'accessibleness' (p. 85). 'Naturalness' represents matters 'as inherent in the situation, intrinsic aspects of reality, the way things go', in the sense that children and adolescents are straightforwardly smaller, and more easily harmed, than adults. The 'practicalness' of common sense is not only the pursuit of utilitarian prerogatives but a sensible prudence, or level-headedness (p. 87), which is not simply responsive to issues demanding immediate responses, but which defines what it is 'practical' to know. This practicality is determined by a sense of contemporary necessity, and now includes, for parents adequately concerned with risk avoidance, young people's acquaintances and those acquaintances' parents, their criminal histories, their diets, their favourite TV shows, and online lives. 'Thinness' for Geertz is like 'simpleness' or 'literalness': 'the tendency for common-sense views of this matter or that to represent them as being precisely what they seem to be, neither more nor less' (p. 89) – such as, this offender harmed children, and that's that; you're too young for that, because I told you so. 'Immethodicalness' recalls Stuart Hall's characterisation of common sense as 'sedimented over time', but also connotes 'the pleasures of inconsistency' in wisdom that is 'shamelessly and unapologetically ad hoc' (Geertz 1983, p. 90). Experts on offender recidivism, media effects, or child development can be dismissed as promoting positions that are narrowly rational. Mediating multiple knowledge claims, the common sense directing parental governance is framed as most 'capable of grasping the multifariousness of life in the world' (p. 91), especially for one's own children. Finally, 'Accessibleness' is 'the assumption, in fact the insistence, that any person with faculties intact can grasp common-sense conclusions, and indeed, once they are unequivocally enough stated, will not only grasp but embrace them' (p. 91). Such an assumption is central to populism as a style of politics that supposes a legitimating notion of 'the people' defined collectively by common sense (Rosenfeld 2011, pp. 227–228), the dismissal of which becomes bad or unrepresentative government.

Common sense, where it is informed by threats of child sexual abuse, by images that might cause 'precocious' questioning, or by the undesirable influences of other children and the necessity of immediate, situational decision-making, frequently invokes a precautionary principle into parenting. 'Better to be safe than sorry', the parenting cliché goes. Bill Hebenton and Toby Seddon (2009, p. 345) suggest that in regulating risk the precautionary principle urges governmental authorities to 'avoid steps that will create a risk of harm until safety (security) is established, be cautious ... and do not require unambiguous evidence before acting', it implores. Kevin Haggerty (2003, p. 198) writes that 'Precautionary logic is non-calculative', as compared to risk assessment based on population data. For individuals and communities organising their behaviour as harm prevention, precautionary decisions are embedded in 'situational' rationalities that include 'non-calculative motivations, anxieties and desires' (Haggerty 2003, p. 197). While both actuarial risk assessment and precautionary politics are based on taming chance in the future, the latter evades scientific predictions with the position that one negative outcome is too many. The governance of young people is a pre-eminent example for understanding the future orientation of risk prevention, where the personal inflection of parenting adds urgency to the feeling that one negative outcome is too many. False positive predictions – the sex offender who was never going to reoffend; the child who was capable of maturely understanding the image or using the technology; the teenager who wasn't doing drugs anyway – are not simply tolerable but evidence of sound government, or responsible parenting. These are further justified regarding young people through the notion that these restrictions are temporary – 'one day, son'.

The precautionary principle is a dominant feature of common-sense reasoning in discourses of child protection. The conception of security at its heart is both an unachievable ideal and a means towards its fulfilment. There is of course no point at which a responsible authority is able to say the individual in her care is definitively safe or secure and she is thus left in the difficult position of determining the right types and levels of harm her young people should be exposed to. So too must a responsible authority determine the point at which a possible harm becomes an important learning experience, or is sufficiently counteracted by pleasure under a classical utilitarian calculation. We can characterise this, drawing on Lucia Zedner's (2007) notion of 'pre-crime societies', as *pre-harm parenting*: 'whereas risk threatens, security promises' (Zedner 2003, p. 176). Of course, there is no ontological given that directs us to favour the reduction of false negative over false positive outcomes. When and where a precautionary approach is taken depends upon how we understand the harm (and pleasure) involved, who is included in the 'we' that conceptualises the effects of action, and how this public (parents, community leaders, media industries, state officials) distributes responsibility for particular risks. Where young people are understood via a *tabula rasa* model or especially in terms of innocence, the disappearance of which is so easily mourned, the precautionary principle is especially alluring to common sense (see Kincaid 1998; Faulkner 2011). Contrasting innocence with experience rather than corruption, and thus in terms of pleasure, resilience, education, and citizenship is important for conceiving young people's sexual development in terms other than destruction or loss.

Conclusion: common sense, young people, and cultural studies

Teaching a unit called 'Youth and Youth Culture', I conduct an activity in which I distribute to students a worksheet on which they are asked to specify what they think the legal ages for consumption of alcohol, sexual consent, school leaving, and adopting children should be.[6] Students individually provide justifications, discuss these in pairs and then as a large group, subsequently comparing Australian legal and policy approaches with those from other national jurisdictions. In developing their justifications, students draw on and employ common sense, among other forms of expertise, to establish positions that generally resemble Australian legal standards.

Considering intersections between young people, processes of social maturation, potential harms that might affect them, and dominant ways of conceptualising and responding to those harms, I have found it pedagogically productive to investigate those proposals or programmes that offend or upset deeply held values and approaches to child protection and education: the ridiculous, the impractical, the arcane, and the irresponsible. For my Youth and Youth Culture students, for example, Rousseau's (1979) approach to the fictional student Emile's pastoral education seems not just impractical but potentially neglectful. Michel Foucault's (1988) historicisation of discourses on child sexual abuse and sexuality appears acceptable until he shifts into advocating the abolishment of the sexual age of consent. The human rights of sex offenders are acknowledged by students, but their resettlement 'in communities with kids' is deemed problematic, if not inappropriate. And unsupervised parental approaches to children's media consumption and social mobility are deemed irresponsible if not criminally negligent.

More often than not, students' first responses to questions about why young people's media consumption should be supervised, or why violent offenders should be monitored in the community, are of the 'it should just be that way', 'it's common sense', variety. Pressed for a more detailed explanation, like the rest of us, they tend to draw on biographical experience and combine this with culturally dominant ideas about childhood, adolescence, minority and majority, citizenship, and the law. Regarding legal markers for consumption of alcohol, sexual consent, school leaving, and adopting children they recognise from experience that such borders are simply proxies for assumptions about competence and that many people will not abide by them, but they nonetheless agree these should exist. While disagreements are had over the right age to legislate for adoption, or over how parents should manage their children's media consumption, it is common sense that these things should exist and occur. Through elucidating their implicit values and reasoning processes, my students can recognise that common sense is both an expression of the people's collective will in open, democratic societies, but also a potentially antidemocratic force, foreclosing debate, discrediting expertise with home-spun truths, and thwarting the critical attitude of modernity.

Geertz (1983, p. 92) notes the impossibility of cataloguing 'common sense [as] a cultural system' because it is 'wildly heterogeneous'. We cannot simply outline the contents of common sense: 'One has to proceed instead by the peculiar detour of evoking its generally recognized tone and temper, the untraveled side road that leads through constructing metaphorical predicates – near notions like "thinness" – to remind people of what they already know' (Geertz 1983, p. 92). An equal folly would be to frame common sense as either good or bad, either the answer to, or the problem for, difficult questions about governing relations between minors and pleasure. Common sense is a problem where it encapsulates rhetorical justifications by government of the 'too hard' variety, disregarding competing perspectives and forms of knowledge. Child protection discourses sometimes operate this way. Around such issues it might be more productive to think in terms of 'limitations' rather than protection, because limitation requires justification developed through negotiation between multiple parties with as much information as possible about potential harms *and* benefits. Such limitations are also outcomes of common sense, but as reasoning that draws on experiences and other available evidence, and which is operationalised through negotiation to establish temporary, 'good enough' commitments and arrangements. Such temporary, malleable arrangements are clearly appropriate to the dynamic situation of 'growing up'.

In saying this, I am also arguing that cultural studies of youth should take common sense more seriously, as more than the hegemonic discourse established by our enemies, or as clichés that signal shallow thinking which we look to expose or displace. In the pragmatist conception grounded in the work of writers like John Dewey, common sense does not depend on its relation to 'truth' – conceived as some objective reality – but upon its ability to bind people together – to structure social relations such that actors behave with expectations about shared and predictable practices and meanings, knowing that circumstances and the categories required to make sense of them will eventually change. In both fields, drawing on the conception of common sense outlined in this chapter, we should aim for more than an approach that critically outlines the productive effects of regulation in terms of the harmful effects to minors of child protection interventions. We should question what active exclusions take place in the production and reproduction of common sense, but also be attuned to the situated contexts in which common-sense reasoning is utilised to establish temporary limitations that function 'well enough' until further experience and evidence is incorporated to rework them.

Finally, social and cultural analysis of youth might also aim to outline our own field's normative commitments regarding minors – in terms of competency, capacity, development, autonomy, participation, and citizenship – considering the extent to which our scholarship is oriented by the shared interests of common sense. While cultural studies of youth in particular typically takes an equivocal position on evaluating pleasures of any kind, citing contingency and specificity as grounds for a characteristic form of moral relativism, this does not mean it escapes the critical presuppositions that install child protection as a form of basic common sense. Investments in normative models of sexual development, the importance of rights discourse, the role of government, conceptions of the good community, and our obligation to engage, directly or otherwise, with matters of law and policy, remain integral to the contemporary humanities and social sciences. Such normative clarity is also important when considering the extent to and means by which we include minors in discussions concerning their own government – effectively, their inclusion in common sense.

Notes

1 For analyses of these developments, see Arnold (2010), Marx and Steeves (2010), and Rooney (2012).
2 Throughout the coverage of Ferguson, we were regularly reminded that 'People like Ferguson have to live somewhere' (see Green 2005; Corbett 2009).
3 An online ad for FiLIP, a brand of wearable watches and phones for children with location tracking capabilities, claims that 'The world used to be a little simpler ...

Kids ran free and returned at dinnertime, and parents didn't worry so much. But today, parents are under more pressure than ever ... FiLIP has a simple mission – to help kids be kids again, while giving parents an amazing new window into their children's lives' (in Shulevitz 2013).
4   See ALRC (2012, p. 83) and Griffith (2002, p. 10) for a brief discussion of how the 'reasonable adult' test is used in Australian law.
5   Yaron Ezrahi (2012, p. 100) argues that 'common sense realism' is in fact a modern development related to the emergence of democracy and new modes of reasoning about causality following the abandonment of theistic explanations for worldly phenomena.
6   Thanks to Timothy Laurie who developed a previous version of this activity.

References

ALRC 2011, 'National classification scheme review: issues paper', Australian Law Reform Commission, Sydney.
ALRC 2012, 'Classification – content regulation and convergent media', Australian Law Reform Commission, Sydney.
Amossy, R. 1982, 'The cliché in the reading process', *SubStance*, vol. 11, no. 2, pp. 34–45.
Archard, D. 1993, *Children: rights and childhood*, Routledge, London and New York.
Arnold, B. 2010, 'Digital handcuffs or electronic nannies: children, privacy and emerging surveillance technologies', conference: Watch this space: children, young people and privacy conference, Melbourne.
Bennett, T. 1998, *Culture: a reformer's science*, Allen & Unwin, Sydney.
Berlant, L. and Warner, M. 1998, 'Sex in public', *Critical Inquiry*, vol. 24, no. 2, pp. 547–566.
Bourdieu, P. 1993, 'Youth is just a word', in *Sociology in question*, Sage, London, pp. 94–102.
Brewer, J. 1984, 'Competing understandings of common sense understanding: a brief comment on 'common sense' racism', *British Journal of Sociology*, vol. 35, no. 1, pp. 66–74.
Calhoun, C. 2005, 'Public', in T. Bennett, L. Grossberg, and M. Morris (eds), *New keywords: a revised vocabulary of culture and society*, Blackwell, Malden, MA, pp. 282–286.
Common Sense Media 2014, 'Our mission', viewed 24 January 2017, www.commonsensemedia.org/about-us/our-mission.
Corbett, J. 2009, 'He must live somewhere', *Newcastle Herald*, 17 September.
Dewey, J. 1948, 'Common sense and science: their respective frames of reference', *Journal of Philosophy*, vol. 45, no. 8, pp. 197–208.
Driscoll, C. and Grealy, L. 2013, 'International media classification and minority', in M. Rodrigues-Gomes (ed.), *Communication and control: notes on freedom, control and interdicted expression*, Intercom, São Paulo, pp. 61–82.
eBay2014, 'Should parents spy on their kids?', viewed 24 January 2017, www.zdnet.com/debate/should-parents-spy-on-their-kids/10129276.
Ezrahi, Y. 2012, *Imagined democracies: necessary political fictions*, Cambridge University Press, Cambridge.
Faulkner, J. 2011, *The importance of being innocent: why we worry about children*, Cambridge University Press, Melbourne.

Foucault, M. 1984, *The history of sexuality: an introduction*, Penguin, Harmondsworth.
Foucault, M. 1988, 'Sexual morality and the law', in L. Kritzman (ed.), *Michel Foucault: politics, philosophy, culture. Interviews and other writing, 1977–1984*, Routledge, London and New York, pp. 271–285.
Frow, J. and Morris, M. 1996, 'Australian cultural studies', in J. Storey (ed.), *What is cultural studies?*, Arnold, London, pp. 344–367.
Garland, D. 2003, 'The rise of risk', in R. Ericson and A. Doyle (eds), *Risk and morality*, University of Toronto Press, Toronto, pp. 48–86.
Geertz, C. 1983, *Local knowledge: further essays in interpretive anthropology*, Basic Books, New York.
Gramsci, A. 1992, *Prison notebooks*, trans. J. Buttigieg and A. Callari, Columbia University Press, New York.
Grealy, L. 2011, 'Inappropriate powers under the Housing Amendment (Registrable Persons) Act 2009 (NSW)', *Current Issues in Criminal Justice*, vol. 23, no. 3, pp. 459–468.
Grealy, L. 2013, 'Reorienting the Henson debate: child pornography, consent and the masturbating adolescent', *Continuum*, vol. 27, no. 1, pp. 67–79.
Grealy, L. 2014, 'Menacing Dennis: representing "Australia's most hated man" and popular protests for policy change', *Crime, Media, Culture*, vol. 10, no. 1, pp. 39–57.
Grealy, L. 2016, 'Cliché, gossip and anecdote as supervision training', *Review of Education, Pedagogy, and Cultural Studies*, vol. 38, no. 4, pp. 341–359.
Grealy, L. and Driscoll, C. 2015, 'The plastic adolescent: classification and minority', in M. Watkins, G. Noble, and C. Driscoll (eds), *Cultural pedagogies and human conduct*, Routledge, Oxon. and New York, pp. 63–77.
Green, G. 2005, 'Pedophiles and public rage', *Courier-Mail*, 3 February.
Griffith, G. 2002, 'Censorship in Australia: regulating the Internet and other recent developments', Briefing Paper No. 4/02, NSW Parliamentary Library Research Service, Sydney.
Hacking, I. 1990, *The taming of chance*, Cambridge University Press, Cambridge.
Haggerty, K. 2003, 'From risk to precaution: the rationalities of personal crime prevention', in R. Ericson and A. Doyle (eds), *Risk and morality*, University of Toronto Press, Toronto, pp. 193–213.
Hall, S. 1986, 'Gramsci's relevance for the study of race and ethnicity', *Journal of Communication Inquiry*, vol. 10, no. 5, pp. 5–27.
Hall, S., Lumley, B., and McLennan, G. 1977, 'Politics and ideology: Gramsci', in Centre for Contemporary Cultural Studies (ed.), *On ideology*, Hutchinson, London, pp. 45–76.
Hartley, J. 2003, *A short history of cultural studies*, Sage, London.
Hebenton, B. and Seddon, T. 2009, 'From dangerousness to precaution: managing sexual and violent offenders in an insecure and uncertain age', *British Journal of Criminology*, vol. 49, no. 3, pp. 343–362.
Hogg, R. and Brown, D. 1998, *Rethinking law and order*, Pluto Press Australia, Annandale.
Kelly, P. 2001, 'Youth at risk: processes of individualisation and responsibilisation in the risk society', *Discourse: Studies in the Cultural Politics of Education*, vol. 22, no. 1, pp. 23–33.
Kincaid, J. 1998, *Erotic innocence: the culture of child molesting*, Duke University Press, Durham, NC.
Mannin, E. 1947, *Commonsense and the child: a plea for freedom*, Jarrolds, London.

Marx, G. and Steeves, V. 2010, 'From the beginning: children as subjects and agents of surveillance', *Surveillance & Society*, vol. 7, no. 3/4, pp. 192–230.

Morris, M. 2013, 'Transnational glamour, national allure: community, change and cliché in Baz Luhrmann's *Australia*', *Storytelling: critical and creative approaches*, Palgrave Macmillan, Basingstoke, pp. 83–113.

Paine, T. [1776] 2010, *Common sense*, Belknap Press of Harvard University Press, Cambridge, MA.

Rooney, T. 2012, 'Childhood spaces in a changing world: exploring the intersection between children and new surveillance technologies', *Global Studies of Childhood*, vol. 2, no. 4, pp. 331–342.

Rosenfeld, S. A. 2011, *Common sense: a political history*, Harvard University Press, Cambridge, MA.

Rousseau, J. J. 1979, *Emile, or on education*, trans. A. Bloom, Basic Books, New York.

Rousseau, J. J. 1987, *On the social contract*, trans. D. A. Cress, Hackett, Indianapolis.

Shulevitz, J. 2013, 'Big mother is watching you. Technology now lets you spy on your kids all the time. Why you shouldn't', *New Republic*, viewed 11 February 2015, www.newrepublic.com/article/115347/parental-surveillance-creepy-new-ways-spy-your-kids.

Simon, J. 2005, 'Reversal of fortune: the resurgence of individual risk assessment in criminal justice', *Annual Review of Law and Social Science*, vol. 1, pp. 397–421.

SMH 2009, 'Pedophile Ferguson evicted from Sydney property', 24 September, viewed 11 February 2015, www.smh.com.au/national/pedophile-ferguson-evicted-from-sydney-property-20090924-g4gz.html.

Taylor, A. 2010, 'Introduction', *Common sense*, Belknap Press of Harvard University Press, Cambridge, MA, pp. vii–xiv.

Turner, G. 2003, *British cultural studies: an introduction*, Routledge, London and New York.

Warner, M. 2002, 'Publics and counterpublics', *Public Culture*, vol. 14 no. 1, pp. 49–90.

Williams, R. 1958, *Culture and society 1780–1950*, Columbia University Press, New York.

Williams, R. [1961] 1975, *The long revolution*, Penguin, London.

Willis, P. 1990, *Common culture: symbolic work at play in the everyday cultures of the young*, Open University Press, Milton Keynes.

Wyn, J. and White, R. 1996, *Rethinking youth*, Sage, London.

Zedner, L. 2003, 'The concept of security: an agenda for comparative analysis', *Legal Studies*, vol. 23, no. 1, pp. 153–176.

Zedner, L. 2007, 'Preventive justice or pre-punishment? The case of control orders', *Current Legal Problems*, vol. 60, no. 1, pp. 174–203.

3 Regulation beyond government
Weber, Foucault, and the liberal governance of media content

Terry Flew

Introduction: content regulation and the dilemmas of freedom

One of the recurring dilemmas that arises in considering media regulation generally, and content regulation in particular, is the ambiguous status of freedom. Our most common understanding of freedom comes from liberal political philosophy, where freedom is equated with the setting of limits to the arbitrary exercise of governmental power. John Stuart Mill, in his 1859 essay *On Liberty*, proposed that 'the only purpose for which power can be rightfully exercised over any member of a civilized community, against his will, is to prevent harm to others' (Mill 2011 [1859], p. 68). Mill also proposed that 'the only freedom which deserves the name is that of pursuing our own good in our own way, so long as we do not attempt to deprive others of theirs or impede their efforts to obtain it' (2011 [1859], p. 72). Further, Mill proposed that, for individuals, 'independence is, of right, absolute ... over himself, over his own body and mind, the individual is sovereign' (2011 [1859], p. 69).

Nikolas Rose describes this as the 'negative' conception of freedom where:

> Freedom was imagined as the absence of coercion or domination; it was a condition in which the essential subjective will of an individual, a group or a people could express itself and was not silenced, subordinated or enslaved by an alien power.
>
> (1999, p. 1)

This is the liberal definition of freedom as the absence of compulsion, coercion, and intimidation, sometimes referred to as *negative freedom* or, as F. A. von Hayek and his followers would have it, positive liberty. But this definition of freedom coexists with a second notion of *positive freedom*, or the need to enable all members of a society to have the resources and capabilities required to exercise the forms of moral agency associated with civil and political rights. This second notion of freedom enabled the extension of rights discourses from the civil and political spheres to the social and economic spheres, in relation to the welfare state, the rights of workers to collectively bargain through trade unions, universal provision of health and education, and so on (Plant, 2010, pp. 115–120). The debate between the Hayekian or 'minimalist' definition of freedom and the more expansive, 'social justice' conception is, of course, ongoing. Amartya Sen's 'capabilities' approach to development, as outlined in *Development as Freedom* (1999), and for which he received the Nobel Prize in Economics, is one of the more notable recent contributions to this debate.

The third dimension to the question of freedom is its relationship to others, or what lawyers would term third party effects, economists would term externalities, and sociologists would study as the problem of social order. This draws attention to the ambiguities surrounding freedom, and in particular questions of the relationship of the individual to the social, and who is included and excluded from the exercise of freedom. The difficulty is that, while freedom is defined in a legal sense as a property that one has or lacks in different degrees, it exists 'only as a social relation ... a quality pertaining to a certain difference between individuals ... [and] makes sense only as an opposition to some other condition, past or present' (Bauman 1988, p. 7). If 'the free individual, far from being a universal condition of humankind, is a historical and social creation' (Bauman 1988, p. 7), then we need to consider the relativity of different dimensions of freedom, that have been based historically on gender, class, income, race, and citizenship status (Fraser 1989). Of particular relevance in this chapter is the distinction made on the apsis of age, where the distinction between adults and children has been central to establishing the freedom of one group (adults) as being framed around constraints being placed upon another (children). The idea that young people are not 'reasonable' on the basis of not being adults is a legal fiction that has been central to framing contemporary media censorship and classification discourses.

This element has been particularly important in media and communications law, as it has provided the basis for restricting access to particular forms of media content, most notably forms of sexually explicit material (pornography) and content displaying levels of violence deemed to be excessive. In the United Kingdom, for example, the Communications Act (2003) requires the Office of Communication (Ofcom), under section 319(4) of the Act, to consider whether particular content in radio and television programmes may cause 'harm and offence', and to require that the holders of broadcasting licences give due weight to the factors (e.g. audience size and composition) relevant to determining the degree of harm and offence that such material may cause (Hargrave and Livingstone 2009, pp. 276–277). In Australia, the Classification (Publications, Films and Computer Games) Act (1995) requires that consideration be given to 'the standards of morality and decency and propriety generally accepted by reasonable adults' (s. 11[a]). The Australian Broadcasting Services Act (1992) has among its objects (s. 3) the requirements 'to encourage providers of broadcasting services to respect community standards in the provision of program material' (s. 3 [h]), and to ensure that providers of broadcasting services place a high priority on the protection of children from exposure to programme material which may be harmful to them (s. 3 [i]), as well as 'to restrict access to certain internet content that is likely to cause offence to a reasonable adult' (s. 3 [l]) and to protect children from exposure to internet content that is unsuitable for children (s. 3[m]). In the United States, where there is a general constitutional protection of freedom of expression, there are also laws against obscenity, indecency, and profanity set out and enforced by the Federal Communications Commission (FCC), which restrict what content can appear on free-to-air broadcasting (Index on Censorship 2013).

This chapter draws upon the history and institutional practices of media content classification in Australia to identify the degree to which classification can be understood as a form of governmentality, as espoused by Michel Foucault (1991) in his study of the origins of political liberalism as a rationality of government. This involves consideration of the moral *persona* of the classifier, noting the degree to which they are expected to engage in a form of rule-governed pragmatism, which I refer to as *casuistry*, in their decision-making practices. It will then consider the devolution of responsibility for media content classification from government agencies to industry bodies, analysing the resulting regimes of co-regulation and 'enforced self-regulation', with particular reference to the Australian Law Reform Commission's review of the National Classification Scheme undertaken in 2011–2012, as well as recent work by the Australian Communication and Media Authority on adaptive regulation. I conclude that these hybrid forms of regulation move Australian media content regulations closer to new modes of governmentality associated with broader global trends towards 'multi-stakeholderism', where non-government organisations as well as industry are increasingly engaged in both the design and implementation of regulations (Bauer 2014; Burris et al. 2015). At the same time, transformations within governmental regulatory processes now increasingly coexist with 'algorithmic governance' as practised by Internet-based companies themselves. Given the global nature of the companies and platforms involved (Google, Facebook, Twitter, etc.), this will have an impact upon classification systems worldwide, although policy responses will in practice be framed through specific national historical–institutional frameworks, as they are with media more generally (Flew and Waisbord 2015; Saurwein et al. 2015).

Censorship, classification, and governmentality

In the classical accounts of the decline of censorship in Western liberal democracies, the 1960s and early 1970s are commonly identified as marking a significant turning point, at least in terms of changes to laws. The *R* v. *Penguin Books Ltd* case, which concerned whether Penguin Books was in breach of the UK Obscene Publications Act (1959) in its decision in 1960 to republish D. H. Lawrence's *Lady Chatterley's Lover* (first published in 1928), is seen to constitute a watermark, at least in the English-speaking world. In finding against claims that the novel had the capacity to 'deprave or corrupt', the case introduced several critical elements into censorship law, which remain in most countries to this day. These include:

- *Context*: discussion of any individual element of a work needed to place it in the context of the work as a whole. The testimony of cultural theorist Richard Hoggart was critical to the case in this regard.
- *Merit*: the Obscene Publications Act (1959) contained a public good provision under section 4, whereby the public circulation of a work could be justified with reference to this being 'in the interests of science, literature, art or learning, or of other objects of general concern'.
- *The 'reasonable person'*: implicit to the question of whether a work can 'deprave or corrupt' is a question as to the character of the person involved. This, in turn, leads to distinctions about audience type that can appear arbitrary (e.g. the audience at a film festival or an art exhibition as compared to the general public), as well as questions about whether the work is likely to be available to a large audience or a more limited one. It also points to a distinction between adults and children, which remains central to most censorship and classification law.

In Australia, the landmark 1968 *Crowe* v. *Graham* case saw the concepts of 'obscene' and 'offensive' that existed under indecent publications legislation in the state of New South Wales challenged in the High Court of Australia. In the High Court's judgment, and in related cases, a 'community standards' test was proposed, as an alternative to the common law test of a 'tendency to deprave or corrupt' that had been applied based on legal precedents dating back to 1868. Subsequent to *Crowe* v. *Graham*, reforms enacted by Gough Whitlam's federal government in 1972 saw the Australian approach shift from a closed and highly interventionist model of censorship into a more open, liberal, and accountable regime, with classification as the norm and banning of material as the exception, based upon what has come to be known as the 'community standards' test. Gareth Griffith (2002, p. 3) has observed that 'whereas censorship is suggestive of public order and an idea of the public good, classification is associated with the facilitation of informed choice in a community of diverse standards'.

Related to the shift away from censorship and towards classification in Australia was the enunciation of the liberal principle that 'adults should be able to read, hear and see what they want', which has remained a core principle of Australia's National Classification Code to this day. In practice, however, this principle has always been qualified by two other principles: (i) that 'minors should be protected from material likely to harm or disturb them'; and (ii) that 'everyone should be protected from exposure to unsolicited material that they find offensive' (Classification Board 2015). The Classification Act 1995 added the additional principle of 'the need to take account of community concerns about: (i) depictions that condone or incite violence, particularly sexual violence; and (ii) the portrayal of persons in a demeaning manner'. So, freedom as it arose out of the anti-censorship campaigns of the 1960s and 1970s has always coexisted with, and been qualified by, other principles. Moreover, the movement is not a historically linear one. Christina Spurgeon (1999) has made the point that there was considerably more sex and nudity on Australian television in the 1970s, as seen with serial dramas such as *Number 96*, than was the case in the 1990s, when there was controversy about screening of the programme *Sex/Life* in a prime-time viewing period.

Rather than telling the story of this policy field in terms of the turn from censorship to freedom – or, inversely, from freedom to ever-greater regimes of censorship – a different way of approaching these apparent paradoxes of the relationship of freedom and government is through Michel Foucault's concept of *governmentality* (Foucault 1991; 2008). In identifying how political liberalism sought to set limits to government and 'reason of state' (*raison d'état*), it opened up the space for the limits to government arising out of governmental practice itself, and the application of 'critical governmental reason', which turns on 'the rationality of governmental practice' and the question of 'how not to govern too much' (Foucault 2008, pp. 12–13). This is not an absolute divide between the domain of freedom and that of governmental action, but rather a shifting space arising out of the politics of government policy itself:

> One will not try to determine a division within subjects between one part that is subject to governmental action, and another that is definitively, once and for all, reserved for freedom ... this governmental reason does not divide subjects between an absolutely reserved dimension of freedom and another dimension of submission that is either consented to or opposed. In fact, the division is ... in the very domain of governmental practice itself, between the operations that can be carried out and those that cannot, between what to do and the means to use on the one hand, and what not to do on the other.
>
> (Foucault 2008, pp. 11–12)

Summarising the governmentality perspective on public policy, Mitchell Dean and Barry Hindess (1998, p. 8) observed that:

> Government is approached neither as a definite and uniform group of institutions nor as the realization of a certain set of political or constitutional principles. It is approached, rather, as an inventive, strategic, technical and artful set of 'assemblages' fashioned from diverse elements, put together in novel and specific ways, and rationalized in relation to specific governmental objectives and goals.

From this perspective, the shift from censorship to classification in Australia can be seen, not as a once-and-for-all shift from restrictions to freedom, although it did considerably enhance the freedom of adults to access a wider range of media content in the first instance. Rather, it can be seen as enabling a more effective governmentalisation of the regulatory space for media content, by minimising the amount of actual banning of materials (and with it, the familiar paradox of censorship, which is that banning something only serves to make it more attractive), but at the same time rendering the scope to apply the tools of media content classification more widely. The potential for censorship does not of course disappear under this regime of liberal governmentality, as it establishes one end of a spectrum of policy responses. The governmentality perspective enables us to shift an understanding of censorship and classification from the binary opposition between freedom and repression, towards a more nuanced and historicised understanding of how the actions of government, or technologies of power, are being employed towards the content in question, and underlying assumptions about both the producers and consumers of such media content. In this way, as Nicole Moore (2013, p. 61) has observed, evaluation of regimes of censorship turn less upon questions of the freedom or otherwise of the human subject, and instead come to be associated with 'an attempt to identify the limits and effects of regulatory power as such', as applied across a much wider array of social, cultural, and communicative spaces.

Governing content: casuistry and its critics

The other major consequence of the governmentalisation of media content regulation is that it seeks not only to censor except as an exception to the rule but also to establish such regulation as a normal component of public administration, taking it out of the realm of the law, the police, and the courts. As Ian Hunter (1994, p. 151) has observed, with regards to education, this entails establishing the government bureau as an administrative centre driven by 'the deployment of techniques of quantitative calculation and of procedural decision-making in a particular domain'. This in turn requires the bureaucratisation of classification decision-making, characterised by 'the separation of person and office' (Gorski 2005, p. 269), and where the classification agency becomes what Max Weber (1978, pp. 957–959) termed a particular form of 'office', staffed by 'bureaucrats ... "personally" committed to the ethos and purposes of their distinctive office even though that ethos lies outside of their own personal (i.e. individual) moral predilections or principles' (in du Gay 2009, p. 150). This particular personal comportment expected of media classification officers requires, among other things, 'the pragmatic rejection of principled politics' in making decisions, and 'the capacity to detach governmental decisions from personal loyalties and ... passions' (Hunter 1994, pp. 151, 155), and the 'construction of a buffer between civic comportment and personal principles' (du Gay 2009, p. 152).

With the 'de-dramatisation' and 'routinisation' of classification decisions, then, came attempts to 'demoralise' the field, and uncouple classification decisions from questions of personal morality, belief structures, and politics.

Classification becomes an element of the 'government of the social' through the application of expertise and the codification of knowledge associated with liberal forms of governmentality (Dean 2010, pp. 152–154). Decisions are intended to be based upon a close reading of media content in order to assess its compliance with particular guidelines and codes. A member of the Australian Classifications Board, for instance, is required by law to give consideration to such factors as:

a the standards of morality, decency and propriety generally accepted by reasonable adults; and
b the literary, artistic or educational merit (if any) of the publication, film or computer game; and
c the general character of the publication, film or computer game, including whether it is of a medical, legal or scientific character; and
d the persons or class of persons to or amongst whom it is published or is intended or likely to be published (Classification (Publications, Films and Computer Games) Act 1995, s. 11).

We can note that the adult–child distinction permeates these criteria, as there is a binary opposition implicit in the category of 'reasonable adult', with minors not being guaranteed the freedoms associated with the 'reasonable adult'. In that respect, the potentially vulnerable minor becomes more important to a classification-based regime than they are to one based primarily upon censorship. Whereas censorship involved prohibiting access to certain forms of content to all citizens, and is therefore primarily a judgement upon the content itself, classification aims to regulate access to such content based upon certain ethico-moral judgements about the character of the person. The capacity to be 'reasonable' and discerning, for instance, is deemed to be held by adults and not by children. As was noted earlier, other forms of judgement about the moral capacities of individuals are often made, such as certain types of films being given approval to be screened at film festivals, but not made available for general exhibition in cinemas. Such classificatory judgements have typically complemented the physical and technological infrastructure, such as cinema attendants being able to ask for proof of age, or the 'watershed' applied to broadcast TV content that can only be screened after certain times in the evening, premised upon the idea that children go to bed earlier than adults.

Three further elements are critical to such a classification regime. First, in order to get additional control over decisions being governed by 'community standards' rather than personal values, it is a requirement of the Australian Classification Board that its membership be 'broadly representative of the Australian community' (Classification Board 2015). This has been an ongoing source of tension in classification regimes worldwide, as expertise is not considered a sufficient guarantee of decisions meeting 'community standards', meaning that there are different techniques used to engage the public in decision-making processes. In the United States, the Classification and Ratings Administration (CARA) has a rating board made up of parents who nominate to be on the board, with their authority to make informed decisions deriving from their status as parents. Second, the bases on which decisions are made in Australia must be publicly available, through the Board's website and by other means. Third, there must be avenues for appeal by affected parties, meaning that the Classification Board's decisions can be appealed and be subject to the deliberations of another government entity, the Classification Review Board.

But an additional factor that comes into play, particularly in the absence of any clear yardstick on what 'community standards' might be, is what is known in legal terms as case-based reasoning, or the concept of *casuistry* (from the Latin *casus*). The concept of casuistry can be found in Catholic moral thought, associated with the work of Jesuit theologians in the sixteenth century who grappled with the need to assess traditional morality in light of changing reality, as well as the moral challenges arising from the private confession of sins and questions of conscience. It placed an emphasis upon the detailed documentation of how general principles were applied in particular cases, providing guidance to those involved in the training of priests in pastoral pedagogy, based upon analysis of practical examples. Its significance declined from the seventeenth century, as both Protestant theologians and Enlightenment thinkers associated it with the problem of what Blaise Pascal termed 'laxism', that 'served to endow immoral acts with the token appearance of morality' (Stone 2005, p. 271). But casuistry has returned to significance in recent years in debates in fields such as bioethics (Jonson and Toulmin 1988), where either/or moral judgements are often difficult, and where such case-based reasoning can 'provide a dialectical form of exchange between, on the one hand, what appears to be the facts of a particular case and, on the other, one or more generally accepted moral principles which appeared to be relevant to this case' (Mahoney 2000, p. 98).

The merit of such an approach as an alternative to deductive reasoning based upon general moral principles is said to lie in its ability to identify commonalities between new cases and those that have appeared previously, enabling the latter to provide precedents that can assist in identifying new moral principles based upon a particular class of cases. In relation to classification, casuistic reasoning may emerge in a context where conflicting moral principles are in play, such as freedom of expression and protection of children. It also reflects the need for guidance on particular cases being provided to some degree by past decisions, in the absence of an overarching set of ethical principles that can be drawn upon. Community standards, as a surrogate set of benchmarks are clearly subject to change over time, are not the subject of consensus in increasingly diverse societies, and are rarely subject to detailed empirical evaluation. Their relevance could be disputed in any case, if one adheres to an ethical principle that overrides the need for community consensus on the matter, as with some forms of freedom of speech advocacy, or ethical judgements based on particular religious norms and beliefs.

At the same time, the risk is that such casuistic reasoning ends up satisfying no one. Seeking to depoliticise issues associated with moral conscience runs the risk of being at odds with all sides of a debate. The resulting balancing act undertaken by entities such as the Australian Classification Board in practice may satisfy none of the stakeholders who engage regularly with these debates. Free speech advocates, Internet activists, sexual libertarians, gamers, morals campaigners, children's rights advocates, and feminist critics of 'Big Porn' can all find fault with the governmental practices through which the classification and regulation of media content occurs. Moreover, as the Protestant theologians noted in the seventeenth century, it may appear to simply be a pragmatic accommodation to those interests in power, which is a perennial risk for those involved in media classification roles under government jurisdiction. There are also the potential charges that those involved in such decisions are not broadly representative of the community – a charge to which they are almost certain to be found guilty, given the vagueness of the injunction – and that these are inappropriate public interventions into matters of private judgement and morality.

While moral absolutism is one alternative to casuistry, another has revolved around attempts to establish a 'scientific' basis to classification decisions. This has played out in the long history of media effects research, as applied to media such as films, television and video games over a period going back to the 1930s. Often commissioned by public agencies responsible for making decisions about content regulation, and occasionally by the industry groups impacted upon by such decisions, media effects research has marked an ongoing intervention by social science researchers into the vexed question of whether exposure to certain kinds of media content leads to particular forms of antisocial behaviour. The most researched set of questions have been around whether violent media content triggers aggression and desensitisation to the consequences of violent acts. But while such research may appear to be ethically neutral as it is based upon scientific reasoning rather than personal morality, it has its own problems. Willard D. Rowland (1983) argued that a symbiotic relationship had evolved in the United States between the effects research community and its public patrons, which enabled funding to continue for such projects in spite of the recurring inconclusiveness of the research findings. In an overview of fifty years of research on media violence, Barrie Gunter (2008 p. 1113) concluded that 'certain forms of media violence can exert certain kinds of effects on some consumers some of the time', but that the significance of other intervening variables was such that the evidence base made it difficult to make clear policy recommendations. For the flaws identified in casuistic reasoning, then, it has not been replaced by a 'scientific' alternative, which could displace the need for broad moral judgements to be made around classification decisions.

Self-regulatory and co-regulatory regimes: diminished state capacity or 'soft law'?

The gradual displacement of censorship by classification in Australia, at the same time as the scope of what can and should be classified has expanded, can be captured to some degree by the changing names of the government agencies involved. What was the Film Censorship Board from 1956 to 1987 became the Office of Film and Literature Classification in 1988, which in turn became the Australian Classification Board in 1996. At the same time, key elements of the classification process were devolved to industry bodies. With the passing of the Broadcasting Services Act (1992), the classification of radio and television content provided by commercial broadcasters became the responsibility of industry classifiers working within the networks, as part of devolved responsibility for the development of guidelines, decisions about the classification of individual programmes, and the handling of complaints. This process has been overseen and managed through a co-regulatory framework, where relevant industry bodies such as Free TV Australia and the Australian Subscription Television and Radio Association (ASTRA) registered industry codes of practice with the Australian Communication and Media Authority (ACMA) as the relevant government agency.

Policy developments such as industry co-regulation and self-regulation are sometimes presented as being indicative of a neo-liberal turn in media policy, where 'decision making and regulatory powers have been subcontracted out' to industry, in the name of '"slimmed-down" government and less interventionist regulation' (Freedman 2008, p. 51). But they can also be read as possessing an underlying continuity with earlier forms of liberal governmentality, in that what Mitchell Dean (2010, p. 263) terms the 'concern of the art of government' remains one of searching 'for a norm that will allow one to define the proper scope and limits of government, how much governing the state should do and how much should be left up to, or in partnership with, other agencies'. In this way, as Foucault (2008) anticipated, the focus shifts from 'too much' or 'too little' government, to 'one of getting the balance right between governing and not governing, state and civil society, state and market' (Dean 2010, p. 263).

Analyses of the turn to co-regulation in UK media policy (Lunt and Livingstone 2010) and the European Union (Held 2007) have emphasised the vitally important ongoing role of the state in such frameworks. While the state is devolving discretionary power to non-state regulatory agencies, it is doing so in a context where there is a legal connection between these non-state actors and the state regulator, and where the state uses regulatory resources to influence outcomes of the regulatory process. The Pan-European Games Initiative (PEGI) is an example of a non-state entity with quasi-legal standing that classifies video games across twenty-five member states of the European Union, with its decisions accepted by industry and governments. At the launch of PEGI in 2003, the European Commissioner for Education and

Culture explicitly acknowledged the multi-stakeholder as well as cross-national dimensions of PEGI in stating 'The fact that PEGI has been designed to meet varied cultures' standards and attitudes across the participating countries and that society representatives such as consumers, parents and registered groups were involved in the set up of the PEGI system is of utmost importance' (in ALRC 2012, p. 166).

In his review of contemporary regulatory practice, Arie Freiberg (2010) argues that the benefits of a turn from command-and-control regulation towards self-regulation or co-regulation are not simply economic. They are generally seen as having advantages in terms of the proximity of the self-regulatory organisations themselves to detailed and current industry information, with fewer procedural and due process hurdles than those facing government regulators. There is also the potential to promote greater corporate social responsibility or 'good corporate citizenship' on the part of regulated firms and industries (Freiberg 2010, pp. 29–30). Their risks, which are well known, include the potential for conflicts of interest to exist, resulting in inadequate sanctions and under-enforcement of rules, and a relative lack of transparency and accountability (Freiberg 2010, pp. 30–31). Self-regulatory and co-regulatory practices are part of a wider regimen of 'soft law' arrangements, identified by Freiberg (2010, p. 186) as being 'at the borderline between the public and the private [and] between law and non-law'. 'Soft law' has its roots in international law and governance, where there is typically not a single international agency capable of enforcing norms and rules between nation states. Freiberg (2010, p. 186) makes the point that 'where it is produced by non-state actors and where it is only enforced by non-state actors, it is truly "soft"': in order to have regulatory 'teeth', it typically requires the capacity of the state to act at some level in the enforcement of rules and norms.

Peter Lunt and Sonia Livingstone observed that, for the new convergent media regulators, such as Ofcom in the UK and the ACMA in Australia, a vitally important component of their role is that of informing, engaging, and empowering the broader civil society, whether as citizens in a democracy, as consumers in a fast-changing media marketplace, or as representatives of interest groups engaged with the regulatory process. This is because innovation in governance is no longer simply a matter of the balance between government agencies and regulated industries: it also needs to manage and, if necessary, redirect information flows in such ways as to 'create more access to governance networks for the weak, and for weaker players to learn to use more effectively the methods perfected by the powerful' (Burris et al. 2008, p. 33). This is a necessary countervailing force to greater industry self-regulation and co-regulation, and one which has the potential to strengthen – rather than weaken – regulatory capacities, as it promotes civil society groups and organisations as being the monitors of potential regulatory capture between regulated industries and those agencies responsible for their regulation (Christensen 2011; Flew 2014). In the case of film classification, Martin Barker (2009, p. 59) has discussed how the British Board of Film Classification sought to 'relegitimate itself with politicians, with public opinion formers, and with the general public', by broadening its public opinion research activities, including more cultural studies-based approaches to film reception in its commissioned research along with the long-established effects-based approaches, and conducting public consultations and roadshows to make its decision making processes more readily understood by the public.

Assessing media content governance regimes: the Australian case

In Australia, as in most other countries – the United States tending to be the main exception in terms of direct government involvement – there are three broad regimes of media content classification and regulation:

1 The *government regulatory framework* applied to media content classification through the National Classification Code, with its origins in censorship policies. This framework applies to films, some publications, and to video and computer games. It is administered by the Classification Board and through the Attorney-General's Department, and it has significant legal sanctions for breaches of the Code, as well as a strong emphasis on accountability and transparency.
2 The *co-regulatory regime* for broadcasting applied by the industry itself, overseen and enforced by the ACMA. This framework applies to radio, television, and – at least notionally – to Internet content. The code is applied by the broadcasters themselves, and administered by industry representative bodies subject to the jurisdiction of the ACMA, as part of the Department of Communication.
3 The self-regulatory approaches applied by digital content providers and service platforms, including Google/YouTube, Apple iTunes, Facebook, and many others. These entities all manage various forms of content regulation and management, although relatively little is known about how such guidelines work in practice, and levels of accountability and transparency are typically low. The providers would argue that the sheer volume of content they deal with, the speed at which decisions have to be made, and the global reach of these platforms, would make it difficult to apply classification in a different way.

In March 2011, the then Attorney-General of Australia, Robert McClelland MP, asked the Australian Law Reform Commission (ALRC) to inquire into and report on the framework for classification of media content in Australia, and to recommend reforms to the National Classification Scheme. The ALRC was required to consider the extent to which the Classification (Publications, Films and Computer Games) Act 1995 and related laws continued to provide an effective framework for the classification of media content in Australia, and what changes were required to this regulatory framework. Among the factors the ALRC was required to consider were technological and media convergence, community expectations about content regulation, the scope to reduce regulatory burdens and apply existing laws more effectively, and the future development of the Australian media and digital content industries (Flew 2012).

In the course of receiving over 2,500 public submissions in twelve months, and conducting over sixty consultations with industry, community and other stakeholders, the ALRC found that while there was general support for some form of media content classification, the clear message indicated there was a need for fundamental reform to the National Classification Scheme, rather than incremental changes to existing legislation. This was a particularly strongly held view among industry participants, with the Australian Publishers Association describing the current scheme as 'an analogue piece of legislation in a digital world', and the Special Broadcasting Service calling for 'a framework that applies across platforms in a consistent and equitable manner' (in ALRC 2012, pp. 59–60). The digital media giant Google argued that 'the existing classification regime was developed in an age where the media landscape was characterised by technologically distinct vertical media silos', and was ill-equipped to deal with a converged media environment where 'vertical media silos have been replaced by a horizontal, converged landscape of platforms, content providers and users, facilitated by communications networks' (in ALRC 2012, pp. 60).

The ALRC proposed a principles-based approach for reform as the basis for a new National Classification Scheme that could respond to changing community needs and expectations, be more effective and consistent in its application, and be adaptive in the face of technological change and media convergence. This would mean, for instance, that the principle that 'Australians should be able to read, hear, see and participate in media of their choice', would coexist with a principle that 'communications and media services available to Australians should broadly reflect community standards, while recognising a diversity of views, cultures and ideas in the community' (ALRC 2012, pp. 80–83). It proposed that 'classification regulation should be kept to the minimum needed to achieve a clear public purpose', and that 'classification regulation should be focused upon content rather than platform or means of delivery' (ALRC 2012, pp. 57–58). The final point meant that there would be one legislative regime establishing obligations to classify or restrict access to content across media platforms, with a single Commonwealth regulatory agency having responsibility, and that its focus would be on so-called 'higher-level' content (in terms of sexual explicitness, violence, etc.), with much of the more general media content classification being undertaken by industry itself, with the development of classification codes subject to oversight by a convergent media regulator (ALRC 2012, pp. 24–29).

While principles-based regulation would appear to be at odds with the casuistry-based approach discussed earlier, the two are in fact reliant upon one another. Precedent-based reasoning is not a sufficient basis for classification decision-making, because it cannot adequately account for technological changes or changes in community attitudes, and it also relies upon an underlying legislative foundation to give decisions legitimacy. At the same time, if principles-based regulation is to avoid becoming a set of dogmas that are enforced regardless of local circumstances, then expert judgement is required for deliberation over hard cases. In the Australian context, the need for legal clarity surrounding classification decisions has intensified as progressively more of the content subject to classification is online, and as there is a transfer of classification responsibilities from the Australian Classification Board to the ACMA. In October 2015 the Australian Classification Board was transferred from the Attorney-General's portfolio to that of the Department of Communication and the Arts. A Review of the ACMA, which issued a discussion paper in May 2016, has been actively considering whether the remit of the ACMA should be expanded to include the functions of the Classification Board and the Classification Review Board. Such a move would be consistent with the ALRC's recommendation for a single national scheme for classifying content across all media platforms.

The ALRC Review of the National Classification Scheme took place alongside the Department of Broadband, Communications and the Digital Economy's Convergence Review of communications legislation, and both reviews shared the observation that:

> Australia's policy and regulatory framework for content services is still focused on the traditional structures of the 1990s – broadcasting and telecommunications. The distinction between these categories is increasingly blurred and these regulatory frameworks have outlived their original purpose.
>
> (ACMA 2011, p. vii)

In the media content classification field an example of the subsequent 'broken concepts' that the ACMA (2011) has referred to is in the area of computer games. If games are purchased as physical objects in a store, they are taken to be akin to a publication, and hence subject to the Classifications Act. If such games content is online, however, it is Internet content, and therefore subject to the provisions of the Broadcasting Services Act. If it takes the form of an app, downloadable from Apple iTunes, Google Play, or other equivalent sites, its status in terms of Australian government classification is unclear, although it is widely acknowledged that such sites are extensively curated by the companies themselves, with Apple seen as being particularly diligent in terms of ensuring a 'family-friendly' app store. Moreover, consumers can set their devices to screen content based on the classification rules of Australia or many other territorial jurisdictions. The ACMA (2015, p. 6) has identified mobile apps as an ongoing regulatory challenge as 'the development of the one device, one platform environment was bringing together a number of previously distinct sectors – telecommunications, radio communications, broadcasting, computing, publishing and financial services'. Such developments 'pose challenges to traditional approaches to regulation where apps are not reflected in existing legislative or regulatory concepts' (ACMA 2015, p. 6). The ALRC (2012, pp. 159–163) recommended that responsibility for games classification should shift from the Classification Board to industry self-classification under an agreement with a relevant government regulator. In September 2014, the Classification Act was amended to enable certain content to be classified using online classification tools that deliver automated decisions, thus moving the Australian games classification system closer to that of the PEGI approach and that of the Entertainment Software Review Board (ESRB) in the US.

The ACMA's approach to media content governance is important to note, as it envisages its own role diminishing over time. Perhaps more accurately, it aims to devolve regulatory responsibilities through its provision of an evidence base that can 'build capability among our stakeholders to make communication and media work in Australia's public interest' (ACMA 2015, p. 1). Drawing upon the insights of regulatory theorists, such as Malcolm Sparrow (2000, 2008), this approach is less about controlling a space in order to make it capable of being subject to regulatory techniques by public agencies than it is about 'how a regulator might influence and potentially intervene in the behaviour of industry players and citizens', moving from achieving the full administration of media towards focusing upon the 'mitigation of harms', both real and potential (ACMA 2015, p. 12). Such regulatory practice draws upon the techniques of 'soft law' and the methodologies of behavioural economics and 'nudge theory',[1] to engage in adaptive regulatory practice which the ACMA (2015, p. 23) describes as involving three elements:

- adopting problem-solving approaches;
- breaking down problems into parts with associated measurable tasks; and
- using collaborative partnerships in the design and delivery of adaptive solutions.

The adaptive regulatory practice proposed by the ACMA in this instance marks a turn from governmentality, driven by the rule-governed pragmatism of the Weberian bureaucrat towards hybrid forms of government regulation, industry self-regulation, consumer advice, and citizen engagement. Freiberg (2010, p. 31) refers to such hybrid arrangements by the awkward neologism of 'enforced self-regulation'. In the governmentality literature, Dean (2010; 192–193) notes that these 'advanced liberal' forms of government are based less upon the promise of a 'government of society' – which was subject to the neo-liberal critique of risking 'governing too much' and suppressing social innovation – towards the promotion of a kind of 'responsible freedom' where such freedom can 'act as a principle of a philosophical critique of government while at the same time being an artefact of multiple practices of government'. Suggesting that dominant critiques of neo-liberalism are too economically reductionist to fully capture the dynamics of such changing forms of governmental practice (Barnett 2010), Dean (2010, p. 263) suggests that contemporary concerns with adaptive regulation point towards 'a concern of the art of government ... to search for a norm that will allow one to define the proper scope and limits of government, how much governing the state should do and how much should be left up to, or in partnership with, other agencies'.

Conclusion

I have argued in this chapter that, rather than seeing the history of media content classification as a never-ending struggle between the desire for freedom and the forces of censorship, we can understand it as a case study in evolving modes of governmentality in liberal societies, where ideas of freedom have long coexisted with practices of governance. Using Australian media content classification as a case study, I have drawn upon Michael Foucault's concept of governmentality, as well as Max Weber's work on the ethics of bureaucracy, to argue that the practices of classification can be understood through the concept of casuistry, or applied case-based reasoning based upon a mix of principles and precedents.

I have also proposed that such a framework enables us to better understand the shifting parameters of media content regulation, from direct monitoring by government agencies such as the Classification Board, to co-regulation with government oversight, and the regulator taking a more active role in informing consumer-citizens and industry itself on the requirements of regulation. It is a case study in the turn towards 'soft law' and regulation based upon the mitigation of harms, informed by behavioural economics and nudge theory. Further exploration of this topic would consider how these regulatory regimes – command-and-control, co-regulation, and self-regulation – increasingly coexist with what has been termed 'algorithmic regulation' (Muciani 2013), or governance based upon the management of big data flows, of the sort now being undertaken within the big Internet-based companies themselves.

Note

1 'Nudge theory' refers to the ways in which positive reinforcements and indirect suggestions can be used to reshape the motives, incentives, and decisions of groups and individuals in ways that are predictable and do not rely upon regulation, legislation, or sanctions. Thaler and Sunstein (2008) give as an example of how eating habits can be improved by more prominent display of healthy options such as fruit and vegetables, leading to improved public health outcomes without the need for more direct regulations, such as restrictions on 'junk food'. See Peter John (2011) for its application in behavioural economics.

References

ACMA [Australian Communications and Media Authority] 2011, 'The Australian communications legislative landscape', Australian Communications and Media

Authority, Melbourne, viewed 6 June 2016, www.acma.gov.au/~/media/Office%20of%20the%20Chair/Information/pdf/ACMA_BrokenConcepts_Final_29Aug1%20pdf.pdf.

ACMA [Australian Communications and Media Authority] 2015, 'Evidence-informed regulatory practice – an adaptive response, 2005–15: occasional paper', Australian Communications and Media Authority, Melbourne.

ALRC [Australian Law Reform Commission] 2012, 'Classification – content regulation and convergent media: ALRC report 118', Australian Law Reform Commission, Sydney.

Barker, M. 2009, 'The challenge of censorship: "figuring" out the audience', *Velvet Light Trap*, no. 63 (spring), pp. 58–60.

Barnett, C. 2010, 'Publics and markets: what's wrong with neoliberalism', in S. Smith, R. Pain, S. Marston, and J. P. Jones III (eds), *SAGE handbook of social geographies*, Sage, London, pp. 269–295.

Bauer, J.M. 2014, 'Platforms, systems competition, and innovation: reassessing the foundations of communications policy', *Telecommunications Policy*, vol. 38, no. 8–9, pp. 662–673.

Bauman, Z. 1988, *Freedom*, Open University Press, Milton Keynes.

Burris, S., Drahos, P., and Shearing, C. 2015 'Nodal governance', *Australian Journal of Legal Philosophy*, vol. 30, no. 1, pp. 30–58.

Burris, S., Kempa, M., and Shearing, C. 2008 'Changes in governance: a cross-disciplinary review of current scholarship', *Akron Law Review*, vol. 41, no. 1, pp. 1–66.

Christensen, J.G. 2011, 'Competing theories of regulatory governance: reconsidering public interest theories of regulation', in D. Levi-Faur (ed.), *Handbook of the politics of regulation*, Cheltenham, Edward Elgar, pp. 96–110.

Classification Board 2015, 'Australian classification – national classification code', viewed 30 August 2015, www.classification.gov.au/About/Pages/Classification-Board.aspx

DBCDE [Department of Broadband Communications and the Digital Economy] 2012, *Convergence review: final report*, DBCDE, Canberra.

Dean, M. 2010, *Governmentality: power and rule in modern society*, 2nd edn, Sage, London.

Dean, M. and Hindess, B. 1998, 'Introduction: government, liberalism, society', in M. Dean and B. Hindess (eds), *Governing Australia: studies in contemporary rationalities of government*, Cambridge University Press, Cambridge, pp. 1–19.

Flew, T. 2012, 'Media classification: content regulation in an age of convergent media', *Media International Australia*, no. 143, pp. 5–15.

Flew, T. 2014, 'Convergent media policy', in P. Dearman and C. Greenfield (eds), *How we are governed: investigations of communication, media and democracy*, Cambridge Scholars, Newcastle, pp. 10–30.

Flew, T. and Waisbord, S. 2015, 'The ongoing significance of national media systems in the context of media globalization', *Media, Culture & Society*, vol. 37, no. 4, pp. 620–636.

Foucault, M. 1991, 'Governmentality', in G. Burchell, C. Gordon, and P. Miller (eds), *The Foucault effect: studies in governmentality*, Harvester Wheatsheaf, Brighton, pp. 87–104.

Foucault, M. 2008, *The birth of biopolitics: lectures at the Collège de France 1978–1979*, ed. M. Senellart, trans. G. Burchell, Palgrave Macmillan, Basingstoke.

Fraser, N. 1989, *Unruly practices: power, discourse and gender in contemporary social theory*, Polity, Cambridge.
Freedman, D. 2008, *The politics of media policy*, Polity, Cambridge.
Freiberg, A. 2010, *The tools of regulation*, Federation Press, Sydney.
du Gay, P. 2009, 'Max Weber and the ethics of office', in P. S. Adler (ed.), *The Oxford handbook of sociology and organization studies*, Oxford University Press, Oxford, pp. 146–173.
Gorski, P. 2005, 'The Protestant ethic and the bureaucratic revolution: ascetic Protestantism and administrative rationalization in early modern Europe', in C. Camic, P. Gorski, and D. Trubek (eds), *Max Weber's economy and society: a critical introduction*, Stanford University Press, Stanford, CA, pp. 267–296.
Griffith, G. 2002, *Censorship in Australia: regulating the Internet and other recent developments*, NSW Parliamentary Library Research Service, Sydney.
Gunter, B. 2008, 'Media violence: is there a case for causality?', *American Behavioral Scientist*, vol. 51, no. 8, pp. 1061–1122.
Hargrave, A. M. and Livingstone, S. 2009, *Harm and offence in media content: a review of the evidence*, Intellect, Bristol.
Held, D. 2007, 'Co-regulation in European Union member states', *Communications*, no. 32, pp. 415–422.
Hunter, I. 1994, *Rethinking the school*, Allen & Unwin, Sydney.
Index on Censorship 2013, 'United States: free expression constrained by cultural and political factors', viewed 6 June 2016, www.indexoncensorship.org/2013/08/united-states-free-expression-constrained-by-cultural-and-political-factors.
John, P. 2011, *Nudge, nudge, think, think: using experiments to change civic behaviour*, Bloomsbury, London.
Jonsen, A. and Toulmin, S. 1988, *The abuse of casuistry: a history of moral reasoning*, University of California Press, Berkeley, CA.
Lunt, P. and Livingstone, S. 2010, *Media regulation*, Sage, London.
Mahoney, J. 2000, 'Casuistry', in A. Hastings, A. Mason, and H. Pyper (eds), *The Oxford companion to Christian thought*, Oxford University Press, Oxford, pp. 98–100.
Mill, J. S. 2011, *On liberty*, S. Shaw-Miller (ed.), Yale University Press, New Haven, CT.
Moore, N. 2013, 'Censorship is', *Australian Humanities Review*, no. 54, pp. 45–65.
Muciani, F. 2013, 'Governance by algorithms', *Internet Policy Review*, vol. 2, no. 3, viewed 23 January 2017, https://policyreview.info/articles/analysis/governance-algorithms.
Plant, R. 2010, *The neo-liberal state*, Oxford University Press, Oxford.
Rose, N. 1999, *Powers of freedom: reframing political thought*, Cambridge University Press, Cambridge.
Rowland, W.D. 1983, *The politics of TV violence: the policy uses of communication research*, Sage, Los Angeles, CA.
Saurwein, F., Just, N., and Latzer, M. 2015, 'Governance of algorithms: options and limitations', *info*, vol. 17, no. 6, pp. 35–49.
Sen, A. 1999, *Development as freedom*, Oxford University Press, Oxford.
Sparrow, M. 2000, *Regulatory craft: controlling risks, solving problems and managing compliance*, Brookings Institution Press, Washington, DC.
Sparrow, M. 2008, *The character of harms: operational challenges in control*, Cambridge University Press, Cambridge.

Spurgeon, C. 1999. 'The "digital/life" moral panic', *Media International Australia*, no. 92, pp. 43–54.

Stone, M. W. F. 2005, 'Casuistry', in M. C. Horowitz (ed.), *New dictionary of the history of ideas*, Thomson Gate, Detroit, MI.

Thaler, R. and Sunstein, C. 2008, *Nudge: improving decisions about health, wealth, and happiness*, Yale University Press, New Haven, CT.

Weber, M. 1978, *Economy and society*, University of California Press, Berkeley, CA.

4 Classifying adulthood

A history of governing minority in media classification

Rachel Cole, Catherine Driscoll and Liam Grealy

Minority and adulthood in classification

The now highly visible and remarkably consistent international field of media classification constitutes a form of cultural governance but also, and simultaneously, a form of cultural production. Media classification involves state-sanctioned mechanisms that permit and limit the distribution of cultural forms and practices, typically dividing these into categories stratified by age. This chapter focuses on *film* classification – as the medium with the longest history of such systems – and centrally on the changing conceptions of 'adult content'. The problem of defining and managing that content is always concerned with the governance of minors, and here we emphasise the difficulty of classification practices keeping pace with the shifting cultural expectations they are supposed to represent. Nevertheless, changes in categories, policies, and processes belie the consistency of this governmental endeavour, where media classification is a central technology for the production of both minority and adulthood.

This chapter considers minority and adulthood aware that these are not a natural pair, and that minority–majority or childhood–adulthood might appear more appropriate combinations. We employ the legalistic term 'minority' to signify the restricted access to content shared by children and teenagers, as well as their exclusion from the citizenly status of the reasonable person. We have developed this concept elsewhere as 'minoritised adolescence', focusing on the developmental ideas articulated in classification categories (see Grealy and Driscoll 2015). The premise of all media classification is protection from disturbing content, but this encompasses several related ideas, including that audiences are differentiated by their capacities for discernment, and that minors require protection because they lack adult capacities for judgement and contextualisation. Checks are deemed necessary on what should circulate among *immature* audiences, as determined by experts whose judgement is mature enough to stand in for all reasonable adults and thus as proxy for those less reasonable and less adult.

We employ 'adult' because it is consistently used by classification systems to name rating categories corresponding to (usually national) ages of majority.

This is true even if adults are themselves subject to limits on available content deemed to risk disrupting the social status quo. The idea of adulthood deployed in classification defines 'adult' in three ways: as a group of consumers; as an adjudicating perspective; and as a field of restricted content.

Media classification systems are continually shifting parameters to keep pace with available evidence of popular tastes and expectations and erecting categorical distinctions to cover the valid social uncertainties exposed by such change. While regulatory bodies internationally have tended, across the twentieth century, towards greater segmentation into categories describing the experience and capacity of minors, the category of 'adult' appears to be the endpoint of such developmentally organised ladders of capacities; the obverse of immaturity. The adult category is not subject to continual revision like the age-based categories developmentally preceding it, but it is nevertheless a space of negotiating changes to what is deemed appropriate for adults.

Drawing on archival research and in two main parts, this chapter considers how the ideas of minority and adulthood on which media classification depends are represented and evaluated together. First, it examines how the British Board of Film Classification (BBFC) has established and revised its idea of minority, focusing on the significance of Steven Spielberg's films to such changes in the 1980s and 1990s. Second, the chapter turns to Australia, to examine the limits on adult consumption through shifts in ideas about the adult category and reasonable representations of youth sexuality. Across these case studies we consider specific public controversies, the impact of technological developments, and longer-term changes in how minority, sexuality, and risk have been understood. We argue that the *motility* of ratings categories – by which they not only respond to social pressures but often absorb them – is central to the pragmatics of media classification and its continuation, despite questions now frequently raised about how such national systems could govern internationally distributed digital content.

'I begin to feel I may be wrong': classifying immaturity at the BBFC

Since its first film examinations in 1913, classification under the BBFC has involved a constantly re-evaluated map of dominant ideas about the protection of minors and acceptable forms of citizenship. Close consideration reveals the extent to which BBFC classification processes are shaped by popular ideas about childhood, youthful development, and adulthood, as they appear in public debate but also film texts. An overview of changes to the BBFC's ratings categories suggest the adult category's comparative stability (see Table 4.1).

These changing categories use concepts like Universal, Adult, Parental Guidance, and Advisory as well as specific age limits to signify different relations to maturity, and a presumption of completed maturity thus appears to consistently close this developmental schema. The idea of an unrestricted because mature adulthood is key to the schema's legibility in the same way

Table 4.1 Changes to the BBFC's ratings categories

BBFC classification categories							
1913	U	A					
1932	U	H	A				
1950	U	A	X				
1970	U	AA	A	X			
1982	U	PG	15	18	R18		
1985	U	UC	PG	15	18	R18	
1989	U	UC	PG	12*	15	18	R18
2009	U	PG	12A*	15	18	R18	

*12 for cinema only, extended to video in 1994; renamed 12A for cinema in 2002.

that the relative positions of 'AA' and 'UC' in such developmental ladders imply their meanings. Nevertheless, the apparent stability of the adult category is disrupted by continual changes to its description, the content signified, and its relation to concomitant categories.

Although the 'C' in BBFC stood for Censorship from 1912 to 1984, this was always a *classification* system in which films were differentiated according to appropriate audiences (see Lamberti 2012a). While no age was attached to the first categories by legislation or regulation – U meant 'universal' and A meant either 'adult' or 'advisory', depending on the document – these categories were always clearly directed to distinguishing content for adults only. The 1932 introduction of an 'H', for horror, category also meant unsuitable for children, with the additional advice that such films were for adults who would enjoy horror themes. This modification by taste importantly represents adulthood as heterogeneous. A taste-based distinction between A and H was maintained until 1950, when the BBFC changed its sign for Adult from A to X. Local Councils satisfied with the existing distinctions resisted this change, and the debate clarified that in practice local regulations interpreted both A and H certificates to mean 'over 16'. The London Metropolitan Council, which governed the largest number of picture theatres and largely led the complaint, worried that X was an unclear label because it did not obviously signify adults.

Elsewhere, including the US and Australia, an X label has also been trialled for signifying mature audiences but often abandoned as easily confused with signifiers of pornography – a conception of 'adult' but not a synonym for mature judgement. The BBFC used an X label from 1950 to 1982, when it was replaced with the more denotative labels 18 for an adult audience and R18 for films determined to need a stronger warning for violent or sexual content. In the US, the Motion Picture Association of America (MPAA) used an X category to signify adult content from 1968 to 1990, but always accompanied by the less restrictive category 'R'. The R label, signifying 'Restricted' as opposed to 'eXplicit', was applied to films that minors could only attend when accompanied by an adult. In the US, the age limit denoted by X shifted from 16 to 17 in 1970, and the category was renamed 'NC17' in 1990 ('no children under 17'). In Britain, also in 1970, the age limit denoted by X shifted from 16 to 18, and was eventually replaced by the more literal '18' in 1982. As our examples below suggest, this coincidence should be tied to changes in popular sentiment, including that expressed in film, as much as to exchange in regulatory policy. Moreover, this apparently straightforward increase in the age of film-going maturity involved a reconceptualisation of what that maturity involved, and how it was achieved.

The 1970 BBFC reform also included the introduction of an adolescent category. The single age specified as separating general from adult audiences (16) was replaced by a ladder of maturing viewership, with an 'AA' category now specifying films suitable for those over 14 years of age. This refigured the general U category as referring to 'family' appropriate films rather than 'all ages', as it had been understood in 1950, and positioned the adolescent AA audience as in-training for mature film-viewing; capable of understanding new kinds of content without adult guidance. All subsequent changes to BBFC categories maintain the divided A/X adult audience but further refine the rungs in the developmental ladder that both protects and tests a maturing audience.

Media classification systems strive to keep pace with changing social contexts that mean, for example, that 16 no longer credibly suggested an adult sensibility in 1970, and that childhood was presumed capable of a relatively higher degree of frightening pleasure by the late 1980s. As an enlightening sequence of cinematic examples surrounding the BBFC's introduction of PG in 1982 and 12 in 1989 we want to consider Spielberg's *Indiana Jones and the Temple of Doom* (*IJTD*, 1984), Joe Dante's *Gremlins* (1984, produced by Spielberg's Amblin Entertainment), and Spielberg's *Jurassic Park* (1993).[1] This list's emphasis on Spielberg highlights how classification category changes proceed through dialogue that involves media producers as well as regulators and audiences. Although Spielberg is credited with considerable influence over the transformation of MPAA classification categories in the 1980s, as we will discuss, here he indicates that the role played by producers is not confined to broad industrial agreement but involves idiosyncratically specific perceptions of changing popular attitudes and negotiations of film taste.

The BBFC files sometimes represent *IJTD*, and sometimes *Gremlins*, as *the film* that inspired the creation of the new MPAA PG-13 category which appeared in 1984. In the US this divided the parental guidance warning into forms for older and younger children, distancing the MPAA system from the BBFC's at a time when family- and youth-oriented films were overwhelmingly being produced in the US. In 1984, the BBFC had five categories available. The adolescent category AA (over 14) had shifted to '15' in 1982, accompanied by a new PG category. These changes responded to new film genre blends but also technological advancement such as the rapid emergence of a home video market, further emphasising the care required of adults charged with deciding which movies were for which viewers at home. Peter Kramer situates Spielberg films of this time as 'family adventure movies', a genre he sees emerging 'since the late 1970s', to broaden the core cinema audience beyond 'teenagers and young adults' (1998, pp. 294–295). He draws on Robin Wood's argument that Spielberg (and George Lucas) films are centrally 'children's films conceived and marketed largely for adults' (Wood quoted in Kramer 1998, p. 295). While for Wood this centrally involves 'films that construct the adult spectator as a child, or, more precisely, as a childish adult' (p. 295), for the BBFC these films were a classification problem because they clearly addressed and invited child viewers (Kramer 1998, p. 296), whatever they also had to say to adults. The BBFC was particularly concerned with what Kramer and others perceive as 'the severity and realism' of a 'treatment of childhood experiences' (Kramer 1998, p. 298) that connects Spielberg's *E.T.* and *Jurassic Park* with Disney's *The Lion King* and Lucas's *Star Wars*.

Questions about whether existing BBFC ratings could successfully categorise Spielberg films appear repeatedly in the files dealing with his films. Assessing *IJTP* (Lamberti 2012b), all examiners identified violent content as an issue, but some focused on the conjunction of violence and horror, others on violent humiliation, and some on the problem of violence inflicted on the young secondary hero, Short Round. The correspondence with Amblin Entertainment, Spielberg's production company, conveys concern that a cultural difference in what the *British* public thought minors should be protected from was at stake, but this is part of a broader emphasis on distinguishing adult and minor audiences. James Ferman, BBFC Secretary from 1975 to 1999, travelled to Hollywood to directly discuss a British edit. This edit excised only fragments of the scene where a heart is removed from a living boy, which had concerned many examiners and later complainants, and significantly cut the final fight scenes, including the soundtrack, to make them less impactful. However, the film still exemplified what one examiner called 'the old dilemma of a large age range at "PG" and how to protect the younger end of the range from real fear and disturbance while allowing the older range a wonderfully rich and exciting experience' (BBFC 30/4/1984). The PG certificate thus came with a warning – a special advisory label indicating that some children might find some scenes disturbing.

The 'familiar Spielbergian elements' (BBFC 22/8/1984), blending childhood fantasy and adult anxiety in a heavily merchandised blockbuster, were also the key problem with *Gremlins*. Combined with the deflation of comforting child-oriented images of Christmas and familial safety the BBFC could offer no way to resolve the problem of this film with editing guidelines. Some examiners saw *Gremlins* as a clear 15 while others argued for PG with cuts. One argument for PG acknowledged that 'We seem to have been mightily exercised recently by the category challenges thrown to us by directors whose concept of childish tolerance is less bounded than ours' (BBFC 22/6/1984). Another argument for 15 felt that

> Whether it can or should be turned into a 'PG' horror movie, as the Company is asking on resubmission, is another question. To deal with the policy question first of whether we should expand the Ferman School of Creative Cutting – fruitful though it is, depends primarily on JF himself but also on the effect benign cutting will have on future standards.
> (BBFC 2/7/1984)

Publicly, Ferman remained categorical, stating that 'Horror films in Britain are reserved either to teenagers of 15 and over or for adults, and there is no doubt in anyone's mind that this film falls into the modern horror genre' (BBFC 12/7/1984). The form letter responding to complaints about the rating, many from children excluded by it, stressed reports of 'furor' in the US, despite Amblin's insistence that 'Unlike INDIANA JONES, there is no controversy over the rating at all' (BBFC 12/7/1984). At the BBFC, *Gremlins* became a touchstone for discussion of category revision. Neither adult nor mature was the right conceptual label for *Gremlins* and the desire to maintain the existing broad PG as 'more authentic, particularly for British kids' (BBFC 22/6/1984) was visibly strained by both the difficulty of the decision and the substantial level of objection. The file contains several references to the possibility of a new category. One of the examiner's reports arguing for PG, with slight cuts to remove dangerous imitable behaviour, shifts position part way through:

> now that I've read about all the hoo-ha in the States (where kids are expected to be tough) I begin to feel I may be wrong, and perhaps English kids might be terrified out of their wits by the *Gremlins* ... Thinking ahead (especially about what Spielberg may do to Peter Pan) perhaps we should follow the US lead and start re-considering a new '11+' category for these films?
> (undated)

The BBFC did refine its PG category in 1985, strengthening the PG warning for home video by adding a 'UC' category to label films suitable for children to watch without an adult present. UC was most directly a product of the Video Recordings Act 1984 (UK), and the BBFC's new legislated role in monitoring content available for home viewing (Petley 2012, p. 30). But as the *IJTD* case suggests, the stress UC placed on adults making informed choices on behalf of immature viewers also helped clarify that PG was a warning label. On both counts the problem of unguided domestic viewing stressed the need to recognise differentiated autonomy among 'child' audiences. The impossibility of cutting *Gremlins* for a British PG helped craft space for the

'12' category which was added in 1989, but the problem of distinguishing what kinds of cinematic pleasures are appropriate to children, youths, and adults was not solved by this change. Although they now had a mature parental guidance category, BBFC examiners were still prepared for *Jurassic Park* to pose a problem.[2] Not only was it another Spielberg 'family' film but, like *Gremlins*, *Jurassic Park* arrived for examination surrounded by a heavy marketing campaign. U and PG-rated trailers were speedily added to videos on sale for Christmas 1992 and widely screened in theatres during the months before submission in May 1993.

Rating *Jurassic Park* took only weeks and the PG certificate issued was predicted from the beginning. The initial screening report states 'No way "12" or cuts for PG, yes way PG', but nevertheless predicts difficulties: 'a strong warning at the top of the film would not be amiss. This is obviously going to be big and we don't want to contribute towards the quota of nightmares among toddlers' (BBFC 26/5/1993). Controversy also fuelled by reports of Spielberg's statement that he wouldn't take his own young children to see the film, because the BBFC's PG was unusually *less* restrictive than the MPAA's rating, which used the PG-13 category developed at least partly in response to those earlier Spielberg films (Doherty 2002 p. 207). The decision involved an intense period of discussion, including a test screening with children (accompanied by their teachers) and all examiners.

If the problem home video raised for film classification affected adjudication of Spielberg films in the mid 1980s, *Jurassic Park* was examined in the context of an international expansion of research into the relation between children and media violence. This was spurred by a range of factors, including debates about new videogame genres in the US, the James Bulger murder in the UK, and the proliferation of new academic approaches to popular media. The collected examiner reports from the test screening are neither unanimous nor simplistic, providing considered ethnographic and critical engagement with questions concerning immaturity and film consumption. One examiner's critique of *Jurassic Park* is whimsically recorded on the questionnaire decorated with dinosaurs that was distributed to children at the end of the screening, while another cites recent academic research (Wilson 1993) to suggest that realistic visual effects were the key problem, given that young children would not realise this was fantastic danger of which they should not be afraid themselves. The majority opinion, however, sided with a report that concludes 'Let curmudgeons wheel out their bilious theories and options. For once, let fun triumph' (BBFC 9/6/1993).

The examiners watched the children watching *Jurassic Park* for signs that the film did not require more sophistication than they could bring to its consumption. Numerous comments thus focus less on the sample audience's questionnaire responses than the audience itself. One examiner is reassured to find that

> a large number of the children had made a previous bid to be recognised as adolescents: lipstick on several of the girls, often a strut in the walk

and post-pubertal fashion sense. For me it was something of a relief to see them so diverted by this essentially childish form of entertainment, making the case for cuts or a higher category look more than a little anomalous.

(BBFC 09/06/1993)

As media classification requires the adult be not only a group of consumers but also an adjudicating perspective, these signs of sophistication needed to be matched by a self-consciousness that would moderate the impact of the film's reality effects. This case is made, for example, by one examiner's report on the viewing experience of 'Wayne', a boy who

> did not like being scared. As T-Rex attacked the kids in the car, he disappeared behind the seat. 'Don't watch!' shouted his class mates. 'I'm not!' shouted Wayne from his huddle ... 'This film should be "12" or "15"' said Wayne, repeatedly – even though his classmates told him to shut up. This classification he stoutly maintained until the kids were being chased by the raptor in the kitchens whereupon he couldn't keep his eyes off the screen. He clapped when the T-Rex which had previously so frightened him, chomped the raptor in mid-leap. 'This film should be "PG" or "12"' declared Wayne. And after, his feeling was that 'I really enjoyed it. There were some people who were a bit scared, but I enjoyed it.' I think Wayne enjoyed surviving being scared.

(BBFC 09/06/93)

Wayne's capacity to remain anchored in the social network of his viewing peers and their judgements, and remain in dialogue with the task of evaluating the film for other viewers, demonstrates here the nascent critical perspective appropriate to PG.

Supported by such evidence, in addition to a special advisory warning, *Jurassic Park* became the BBFC test case for new detailed advisory labels which subsequently became standard practice (although the content has changed). The examiner who wanted fun to triumph suggests the following 'explanatory words':

> Language; mild
> Sex; none
> Nudity; none
> Violence; occasionally strong, frightening
> Theme; Monsters.

(BBFC 9/6/1993)

This new level of explanation gave governmental substance to the idea of 'parental guidance' by filling the category more explicitly with questions about maturity. All subsequent changes to BBFC categories – such as refiguring 12 as '12A', with the A signifying that under-12s can also see these movies if 'accompanied' by an adult – have furthered this emphasis.

Changing cultural expectations seem to impact media classification most visibly when content once off limits for a particular audience category becomes possible – such as monster movies for children. But the fact that classificatory categories themselves are open to modification means that even content which seems to stay in one place is subject to the indeterminacy of distinctions between childhood, adolescence, and adulthood and the implications of changes in one category for all others. Ratings categories thus manifest the problem of the young audience as a liminal zone in which the idea of maturity is constantly monitored for how it divides minority from adulthood. Because such division can never be categorical, classification makes the uncertainties that underpin such categories visible by continually evaluating what they popularly (rather than categorically) mean.

The Australian 'R' rating: maturity and genre

The second half of this chapter turns to the specification and management of 'adult' film, but we want to first reiterate that 'adult content' is key to defining youthful minority by opposition. Adult content is that which puts minors at risk and defines minority as at-risk. Our examples shift from the BBFC to the Australian film classification system now managed by the Australian Classification Board (ACB), also established in the public interest, and with an increasingly explicit charge to protect minors. We trace the classificatory definition of 'adult' in Australia here not only to emphasise continuities between systems but to throw into sharper relief the simultaneous difficulty and importance of defining adulthood through media content. The mutually dependent concepts of 'adult content' and the 'reasonable adult' consumer persist in the face of important changes to what they describe, and the Australian case makes it clear that while concepts like 'governmentality' helpfully situate classification among the 'regimes of practices' that define appropriate citizenly attitudes (Foucault 1994), closer analysis demands more attention to relations between governance and aesthetics. Film classification defines not only appropriate standards of adult behaviour and attitudes but also appropriate visual and narrative standards for representing the borders of adulthood.

The capacities of the reasonable adult have long concerned the organisations that have managed censorship and classification on behalf of Australian government.[3] Since 1917, a set of national statutory and non-statutory bodies have found themselves accountable for public anxieties over technological developments in media consumption, encompassing literature, film, television, and most recently digital media. We are interested here in film, not only for continuity but also because film makes particularly visible some of the ways the state governs ideas about adulthood by setting limits around the representation of adolescence. Through the history of the Restricted 'R18+' rating we illustrate how continuing expectations related to age are upheld by media classification in the representations of minors made available to adults rather than to minors themselves. We consider the R18+ rating in terms of its own generic tendencies, its conventional approaches to semiotic and syntactic content, and its assumed relations between texts and audiences. In this way, the R18+ age-based boundary is important for consolidating the distinction between 'minoritised adolescence' and the 'reasonable adult' (Grealy and Driscoll 2015), where the latter functions as an arbiter of social and sexual norms.

Australian age-based film categories have changed numerous times (see Table 4.2).

Since 1930, films deemed suitable for viewing by children have been rated G for 'general exhibition' (Commonwealth Film Censorship Board [CFCB] 1930, p. 5). The A rating indicating 'Not suitable for exhibition before children under 16' (or 'Suitable for Adults') arrived with less fanfare, having been introduced in 1928 for Commonwealth censorship of films distributed in the state of Victoria but gradually becoming more widely used. Due to pressure from exhibitors during the Depression, the Victorian Censorship of Films Act that had created a clause to exclude audiences between 6 and 16, was repealed in 1932 (Strickland 1977, p. 206). The basic categories of G and A thus remained advisory until the onset of the contemporary system with R18+ implemented as a legal category in the 1970s.

Until all Australian states authorised the federal censor to act on their behalf in the 1940s, the legal capacity to enforce classification decisions clearly lay outside the CFCB's jurisdiction and was enabled by a 'gentleman's agreement' with distributors and exhibitors only legislated in Victoria (CFCB 1940, p. 5).[4] The limitations of this system in practice led to harsher censorship of films in Australia than elsewhere. J. O. Alexander, Chief Censor from 1942 to 1957, believed the Adult category included films of low production value, and the absence of a category equivalent to the BBFC's 'H' rating meant the horror genre was effectively banned for twenty years in Australia

Table 4.2 Changes to Australian ratings categories

Australian Film classification categories						
1930	G	A				
1943	G	A	H*	X**		
1971	G	NRC	M	R18+		
1984	G	PG	M	R18+	X18+	
1993	G	PG	M	MA15+	R18+	X18+

*Note: Horror category for advertising only; **X category for advertising only to denote 'not for General Exhibition' (Victoria only).

from 1948, including for adults (Harris and Dutton 1970, p. 54). Alexander had used Regulation 14 of the Customs Act 1901 to define horror films as 'undesirable in the public interest' (CFCB 1960, p. 1) and to skew Australian censorship towards films for General exhibition. But according to an internal Censorship Board document from 1959, 'mature and adult' themes became more prevalent in Australian cinemas from the late 1950s. The Board reasoned declining cinema audiences were attributable to both television's development and a widely held belief that cinema was 'crude, vulgar and immature' (CFCB 1960, p. 1). A resolve to return adults to cinemas thus produced a more pronounced focus on sex and on everyday adult problems (CFCB 1960, p. 1). Citing a contemporary US magazine, the Board felt that 'maturity has suddenly become a fetish' (*Saturday Review* in CFCB 1960, p. 1). Determining what makes content 'mature', however, involves judging both the content itself and how it is approached.

Many factors combined to produce the liberalised Australian system of media classification which we date at the introduction of the R18+ rating in 1971. Among them, the rise of the 'adult film' was key (Stockbridge 1996, p. 124).[5] The 'Restricted' or R18+ rating was a legally enforceable adult category, while others, such as NRC ('Not Recommended for Children under 12') were only advisory. As in the UK, the Australian adult category was always key to other categories' motility. For example, NRC was changed to PG ('Parental Guidance recommended for children under 15 years') in 1984 following a public perception that 'Not recommended' was restrictive rather than advisory (Wright 1987, p. 4). NRC became unclear when it lost the clause of 'under 12' in advertising and was not only perceived as a higher category than the Mature rating used to denote adolescent viewing (Wright 1987, p. 4), but undermined the need for an adult as adjudicating perspective on content for the adolescent age range signalled by the category.

Discontinuing NRC in 1984 corresponds with the new emphasis on parental guidance categories in other countries. As elsewhere, Australia's new PG rating established a need for public education in the interests of parental guidance. Also in line with the discussion of the UK above, the term 'adult themes' became part of the classification system lexicon when consumer advice was implemented alongside the ratings categories in the early 1990s, and still appears on media rated above G ('General'). The implementation of such labels coincided with a nationwide advertising campaign on media classification called 'What to see before you see a movie' (Office of Film and Literature Classification [OFLC] 1990–1991, pp. 1, 18, 32–33).

The meaning of the R18+ rating was also widely misunderstood, though not replaced. In 1987, Andree Wright, a member of the Film Censorship Board, stated the R18+ rating had earned a 'dubious reputation because it [was] often incorrectly equated solely with softcore porn and violence exploits', with distributors and exhibitors preferring the M ('Mature') rating open to wider audiences (Wright 1987, p. 4). The difficulty of capturing multiple versions of 'adult' within the R18+ category is also apparent in the films assigned this rating. The period 1971–1989 is also the one in which 'Australian New Wave' cinema emerged, describing a resurgence of Australian films for an adult audience, focused on taboo themes such as sexuality and drugs (Conway and Crawford 2016, p. 91). And in the 1990s R18+ films continued to be popular and profitable in Australia despite controversy over suitable content for adults (Huntley 1995). These changes highlight conceptions of maturity and citizenship in negotiation with both moral judgements and aesthetic regimes.

In Australia, the tie between new technological developments and controversy over domestic consumption became particularly prominent in the mid 1990s, and centred on debates about pay-TV, videogames, and the Internet. The federal Senate Select Committee on Community Standards Relevant to the Supply of Services Utilising Electronic Technologies, running from 1991 to 1997, is a key site for these debates. The Committee recommended the R18+ category be banned on pay-TV, despite an Australian Broadcasting Authority survey finding that 82 per cent of Australians supported access to restricted material on pay-TV (ABA 1994) and debated 'the lack of clarity of the R classification which permits an excessively broad range of material to be permitted within its definition' (Senate Hansard 1995). These discussions drew on debates about media effects and community concern with media violence, especially sexual violence and realistic and demeaning or exploitative sexual material, and its recommendations called for an 'overhaul' of the adult category so that audiences could presume uniformity in classification and 'ensure its appropriateness in the home environment' (Senate Hansard 1998).

In the wake of such debates the Australian R18+ rating gradually transformed until it could be tacitly separated into two categories: one that dealt with adult content and one that acknowledged some adults were open to 'sophisticated' themes and/or 'arthouse' content that challenged social norms. This distinction cannot be formally acknowledged within classification categories given the homogeneous conception of adult at the heart of 'community standards'. Instead it is conveyed in consumer guidance, such as 'some R18+ material may be offensive to sections of the adult community' (ACB 2018. This echoes the qualifications attached to family viewing of Spielberg films in the UK, and the BBFC's implicit acknowledgement of taste distinctions among adult audiences. In Australia, second-order consumer warnings that guide either parental or adult judgement denote taste-based variations in what counts as adult, mature, or moral. We suggest that such distinctions cannot be entirely defined by specific content, so that claims to artistic merit can but will not always signal 'sophisticated' content. The fine line between the two interpretations of R centrally relies on education through the use of aesthetic cues, and this is an easily missed element of how film classification has moved beyond the 'prohibition model' of censorship (Flew 1998, p. 96).

As noted by the 1990s Senate Committee, what constitutes an adult film is open to interpretation. The current Classification Code (2005) defines R18+ films as: 'films (except RC [Refused Classification] films and X 18+ films) that are unsuitable for a minor to see'. However, *all* classification decisions are made on the following principles:

a   adults should be able to read, hear and see what they want;
b   minors should be protected from material likely to harm or disturb them;
c   everyone should be protected from exposure to unsolicited material that they find offensive;
d   the need to take account of community concerns about:

  i   depictions that condone or incite violence, particularly sexual violence;
  ii the portrayal of persons in a demeaning manner.

(Classification Code 2005)

Together, these demonstrate a broadly liberal approach to media governance constrained by restrictions on representations of risky behaviour and the protection of children.

However, limits on representation are never clear-cut, and the content deemed appropriate for an R18+ rating depends on both anticipated audiences and modes of presentation. In *Film/Genre* (1999), Rick Altman examines the musical genre – to which spontaneous singing and dancing are integral – as generating forms of expectation that do not correspond with real life. That is, generic regimes contain their own rules and norms recognisable to audiences. Steve Neale (1990, pp. 45–47) understands such versions of 'realism' as distinguishing 'generic verisimilitude' from 'cultural verisimilitude' which could apply to the real world. We suggest that media classification employs ratings categories with similar generic effect. The R18+ rating summarises broad limits on content at the upper (refused classification) end, while simultaneously representing the maturity required to access 'adult' material without specifying the content of such material. Altman's broader account of genre is useful here (1999, p. 14), understanding genre both 'as *contract*, as the viewing position required by each genre film of its audience' and 'as *blueprint*, as a formula that precedes, programmes and patterns industry production'.

Kevin S. Sandler (2002) makes a similar argument regarding the MPAA's R ('Restricted – under 17 requires accompanying parent or adult guardian') category. This rating emerged as a sign for maturity but eventually came to label mature intergenerational family entertainment, especially after the appearance of PG-13 in 1984 for younger 'family' films, and the X category's revision as NC-17 ('No one [formerly "children"] 17 and under admitted') in 1990. Sandler (2002, p. 208) suggests that this newly specific R category was shaped by both aesthetic and economic conceptions of 'responsible entertainment'. Centrally, it named films that represented sex in ways the MPAA deemed appropriate for family viewing. In Australia, the semantic and syntactic content available under the R18+ rating offers portrayals of sex, violence, and risky behaviour tailored to a mature majority. While not coherent enough to form a genre, such categories draw on and elicit audience expectations as genres do, offering both a contract as to what provocations should be expected and a blueprint for a particular evaluation of maturity, particularly, as Sandler has argued, in relation to sexual experience. An adult rating establishes expectations about film content, including aesthetic codes and preferred interpretations. The R18+ rating thus establishes the representational territory of maturity, at the same time as it interpellates mature citizens and institutions to police those borders.

It seems easy to miss the importance of aesthetics in determining what requires an R18+ rating and, in effect, how mature audiences should understand that content. Two films directed by Larry Clark and written by Harmony Korine provide useful examples for this point in the Australian context. Child sexuality is a theme closely monitored by classification policy, operating as a key limit on the representations in which adults can acceptably take pleasure. And the depiction of adolescent sexuality is also closely governed, reinforcing the tight conventionality of the 'teen movie' genre and spurring the proliferation of ratings that dissect adolescent audiences (Driscoll 2011, pp. 121–134). The Clark/Korine films exemplify how public and governmental negotiations concerning depictions of child and adolescent sex depend on both the anticipated audience and aesthetic choices made in representing such content.

A focus of international controversy, *Kids* (1995) follows a group of unsupervised teenagers in New York City as they engage in sex and other risky and illegal behaviours. A predicament builds when the 15-year-old male protagonist, who openly enjoys casual, unprotected sex – as often as possible with virgins – is found to have HIV by one of his female conquests. *Kids* deliberately exploits concern over HIV and the sexual lives of minors. In Australia, it was given an Australian R18+ rating with little debate, whereas in the US controversy surrounded the film's pre-release rating of NC-17, usually thought to severely limit box office potential. Stressing the film's realism, the production company surrendered the rating amid wide publicity and circulated it unrated. In Australia, *Kids*'s realism and its status as a 'serious' film were consolidated in media coverage highlighting its documentary-style camera work, the age of 19-year-old writer Korine (Schembri 1995), and the use of untrained young people among the actors (Driscoll 2011, p. 116). If the film's risky, imitable content ensured an R18+ rating and the consumer advice labels warning of 'adult themes', 'sexually explicit language', and 'drug use', its artful cinematography, soundtrack, and morally open ending reified the viewer's subject position as 'reasonable adult'. Rating *Kids* R18+ indicates state endorsed norms for citizenship by simultaneously displaying a problem – adolescent sexuality and drug use – and implying a solution – increased adult management of adolescence and monitoring of protection measures. The R18+ classification as well as publicity framing the film as 'a wake-up call to the modern world', strengthen rather than undermine an association between adolescent sexuality and risk and thus the requirement for both individual and institutional adult intervention. The rating signals the role of media classification in the mature citizen's pedagogical and protective responsibilities in the management of minors (Grealy 2013).

While rarely described as a censor today, the ACB retains a 'Refused Classification' (RC) category. We have argued that R18+ both relies on and helps define collective understandings of the mature and reasonable adult, but the RC category draws another significant line between adult and unreasonable content. This is clear in the case of Clark and Korine's next film, *Ken Park* (2003), which was refused classification in Australia. *Ken Park* portrays multiple adolescent protagonists in dysfunctional relationships with their parents or guardians. Claude is forced to inhabit his father's highly masculine, heterosexual expectations; Peaches must perform religious piety to her father and, in some cases, substitute for her dead mother; Sean is having an affair with his girlfriend's mother; and Tate engages in autoerotic asphyxiation symbolically linked to his eventually murdering his caregiver grandparents. Thematically, the film challenges assumptions about the favourable influence of adult guidance on adolescent development. While *Kids*'s 'wake-up call' was acceptable because it emphasised the dangerous conjunction of sexuality and immaturity, *Ken Park* centrally focuses on the sexuality and immaturity of parents and of the world of adult responsibility these young people will inherit. Eschewing the figure of the 'reasonable adult' shifts the film's generic address to one antagonistic to the liberal perspective on developing 'maturity'.

Ken Park was refused classification in Australia due to scenes and themes deemed 'high' and 'very high' impact. When, in June 2003, the organisers of the Sydney Film Festival resubmitted the film, the Classification Review Board (CRB) report noted the 'cumulative impact' (CRB 6/6/2003) of these scenes and themes which it felt could not be resolved by editing: 'Whilst these themes of themselves would not necessarily warrant an "R" classification, they add to the overall impact of the film ensuring ... the film is very confronting' (CRB 6/6/2003). Quoting the Classification Code, the CRB determined that *Ken Park* fell into that category of films which 'depict sex and violence in a way that offends standards of morality, decency and propriety accepted by reasonable adults' and should therefore be rated RC (6/6/2003). This judgement depended on *Ken Park*'s stylistic realism as much as its content, with special focus paid to a sex scene between Peaches, Claude, and Sean that dominated the film's conclusion and advertising. The ACB determined that this scene involved 'actual sex' based on criteria including extent of nudity and supposed gratuitousness, but also the generic cues involved in soundtrack and lighting, and the invisibility of any choreography. The ACB and CRB chose the more restrictive options at many points where judgement was called for in applying the code. When Sean touches Peaches' labia minora, for example, this is identified as 'actual digital penetration' and therefore 'real sex'. And in the scene where Claude's father attempts to fellate

Claude while he is asleep, the CRB identified 'child sexual abuse material'. In the same way, fetishes such as auto-erotic asphyxiation can always be refused classification, but this is not always the determination.

Our point is not to claim excessive censoriousness but to draw attention to what grounds these choices. The non-classification of *Ken Park* turns on the importance of adult competency, specifically in relation to the governance and consumption of minority. The ACB and CRB's rulings were contested by protesters, who organised a Sydney screening but were stopped by police. The organisers were questioned and cautioned for attempted exhibition of RC material. Unlike possession of child sexual abuse material, possession of RC material is not a criminal offence, except in Western Australia. Despite the CRB's characterisation of *Ken Park* as containing 'child sexual abuse material' there is no evidence they considered the film to require criminal attention by police consistent with that label. Instead, in this context the phrase distinguishes *Ken Park* from other films representing teen sex and fetishism, such as *American Pie* (Weitz and Weitz 1999), based on its tone, cinematography, degree of nudity, explicitness of sex, and its absence of diegetic adult moral guidance. Refusing classification effectively consolidates an R18+ 'blueprint' (Altman 1999) for representing acceptable adolescent sex on-screen.

Binoy Kampmark (2006 p. 352) contends that anxieties integral to the 'media effects' discourse convey a distaste for 'reality', alongside which censorship 'renders the representation of reality obscene; it proliferates as its own regime against realistic representations'. Although this is a much stronger claim that we would make ourselves, we want to emphasise the significance of 'realism' to classification in all the forms by which fiction (or fantasy) can act as a powerful educative tool. Realism and reality are not identical, as is clear in the Clark/Korine examples, and this may be even more pointedly true with regards to sexual experience, with its special relation to fantasy for adults as well as minors. However, generic cues signifying realism have important effects on classification decisions. While particularly clear when applied to images of child and adolescent sexuality, realism is more broadly an interesting touchstone for classification decisions, extending from the fear children have not yet unlearned through exposure to popular genre and special effects in the BBFC evaluations of Spielberg films to the ambivalent role played by realism in distinguishing Australian R, X, and RC categories as ways of representing maturity and reasonable content.

Conclusion

Media classification represents an intricate interplay between policy, content, and individual conduct. This chapter has argued that media classification is a governmental technology aimed at managing the relationship between minoritised adolescence and cultural objects. Media classification consolidates cultural meanings for both minority and adulthood, and the relations between them, and it makes specially visible the mobility and ambiguity of the apparently clear opposition between these terms, which is so fundamental to liberal governance. Our historical examples not only show that the ages associated with the highest (typically restricted) classification categories have varied across history and context. Those individuals able to access restricted content, and deemed de facto mature and thus able to act as adjudicating authorities in relation to consumption by minors have also ranged in age, and the types of content they adjudicate has changed too, in ways that cannot be simply described as increased freedom or increased restriction. While those nominated adult by such systems share the right to access mature content, they are also not a homogeneous group, encompassing differences of taste and judgement that allow for cinematic pleasures that might offend or alarm 'sections of the adult community'.

While an adult category consistently closes the developmental ladder used by most classification systems, the content of its referent cannot be straightforwardly assumed. We argue that this is not simply a matter of categories being 'mutually constitutive', and instead want to emphasise that the presence of multiple categories, and the possibility of additions and removals, is what makes media classification functionally possible, and inevitably open to policy reformulation. We have also sought to show how such reworking frequently follows the emergence of cultural objects (such as films) that challenge prevalent categories and approaches. New films, whether those of Spielberg or Clark/Korine, require ongoing evaluation of questions concerning maturity in the absence of any objectively verifiable demarcations grounding regulation. This is practically discerned by regulatory authorities in various ways, ranging from public protests over refused classification material to their observation of children watching *Jurassic Park* for evidence of their capacity to distinguish reality from fantasy. But we have also argued that aesthetics plays a central role in governmental determinations over mature content, from the role played by music and sound in making a sex or a fight scene realistic to the use of editing to intervene in realism. Together, the mechanisms for discerning mature, adult, and prohibited content draw attention to what quickly became the central premise of media classification in the historical development of these systems around the world: that adulthood is defined by a critical capacity that also makes adults responsible for the management of minor viewers.

Notes

1 With more space we would begin this list with Peter Brook's *Lord of the Flies* (1963) and its relationship to the AA category that appeared in 1970. The history of rating and re-rating Brook's film exemplifies the historical production of classification categories, the challenge of representing violence involving children for minor audiences, and the significance of claims to pedagogical and artistic value for texts that cross over youth and adult audiences.
2 For an official summary of the file and a representative report see http://bbfc.co.uk/case-studies/jurassic-park.

3 Whereas the British film censorship and classification functions can neatly fit into the acronym 'BBFC' this is not the case for Australia where the relevant statutory body has changed name and structure many times.
4 A complex network of lobbying between governmental agencies and debate in legislative houses obscures the impact of Commonwealth agreements with the states in 1927 (Victoria) and 1946 (all other states) which meant Australian censorship was a national system in practice at least by 1949 despite the NSW legislature refusing age-specific screening times in 1948.
5 Sally Stockbridge (1996, p. 126) outlines other factors, including the increased popularity of arthouse and foreign films, a 1969 Australian Labour Party conference which proposed an anti-censorship regime for over-18s, and emphasis on 'community standards' in updated obscenity law.

References

ABA [Australian Broadcasting Association] 1994, *R classified programs on Pay TV: report to the Parliament of Australia*, ABA, Sydney.

Altman, R. 1999, *Film/genre*, British Film Institute Publishing, London.

Clark, L. 1995, *Kids*, motion picture, Independent Pictures, Killer Films and Shining Excalibur Films, USA. Produced by C. Konrad, C. Vachon, G. Van Sant and C. Woods.

Clark, L. and Lachman, E. 2002, *Ken Park*, motion picture, Kasander Film Company Cinéa, France and Netherlands. Produced by K. Kasander and J. L. Piel.

Classification (Publications, Films and Computer Games) Enforcement Act 1995 (NSW) viewed, 12 July 2016, www.austlii.edu.au/au/legis/nsw/consol_act/cfacgea 1995596.

Commonwealth of Australia, Senate, 2 July 1998, *Community standards committee report: government response*, pp. 4766–4768.

Commonwealth Film Censorship Board 1929–1960, *Report by the chief censor*, CFCB, Sydney.

Conway, S. and Crawford, L. 2016, 'Games for grown-ups? A historical account of the Australian classification system', in S. Conway and J. DeWinter (eds), *Video game policy: production, distribution, and consumption*, Routledge, New York and London, pp. 85–97.

Dante, J. 1984, *Gremlins*, motion picture, Amblin Entertainment, USA. Produced by M. Finnell.

Department of Communications and the Arts, Australian Classification Board (2011–2015) ACB, Sydney, viewed 25 January 2017, www.classification.gov.au.

Doherty, T. 2002, *Teenagers and teenpics: the juvenilization of American movies*, Temple University Press, Philadelphia, PA.

Driscoll, C. 2011, *Teen film: a critical introduction*, Berg, Oxford and New York.

Driscoll, C. and Grealy, L. 2013, 'Media classification and parental guidance (Classificacao etaria e orientacao parental)', in M. R. Gomes (ed.), *Comunicacao e controle: observacoes sobre liberdade, controle e interdicao de expressao (Communication and control: notes on freedom, control and interdicted expression)*, Intercom, São Paulo, pp. 83–102.

Flew, T. 1998, 'From censorship to policy: rethinking media content regulation and classification', *Media International Australia*, vol. 88, no. 1, pp. 89–98.

Foucault, M. 1994, 'Governmentality', in J. D. Faubion (ed.), *Michel Foucault: power*, Penguin, London, pp. 201–222.

Grealy, L. 2013, 'Reorienting the Henson debate: child pornography, consent, and the masturbating adolescent', *Continuum*, vol. 27, no. 1, pp. 67–79.

Grealy, L. and Driscoll, C. 2015, 'The plastic adolescent: classification and minority', in M. Watkins, G. Noble, and C. Driscoll (eds), *Cultural pedagogies and human conduct*, Routledge, New York and London, pp. 63–77.

Harris, M. and Dutton, G. 1970, *Australia's censorship crisis*, Sun Books, Melbourne.

Huntley, R. 1995, 'Censuring Salò: the unbanning of Pier Paolo Pasolini's Salò', BA, dissertation, UNSW, viewed 23 February 2016, libertus.net.

Kampmark, B. 2006, 'A wowseristic affair: history and politics behind the banning of *Ken Park, Baise-moi* and other like depravities', *Continuum*, vol. 20, no. 3, pp. 345–361.

Kramer, P. 1998, 'Would you take your child to see this film?: The cultural and social work of the family-adventure movie', in S. Neale and M. Smith (eds), *Contemporary Hollywood cinema*, Routledge, London, pp. 294–311.

Lamberti, E. (ed.) 2012a, *Behind the scenes at the BBFC: film classification from the silver screen to the digital age*, British Film Institute and Palgrave Macmillan, London.

Lamberti, E. 2012b, 'Indiana Jones and the Temple of Doom', in E. Lamberti (ed.), *Behind the scenes at the BBFC: film classification from the silver screen to the digital age*, British Film Institute and Palgrave Macmillan, London, p. 124.

National Classification Code 2005, Commonwealth Government of Australia, Canberra, viewed 2 March 2016, www.comlaw.gov.au/Details/F2013C00006.

Neale, S. 1990, 'Questions of genre', *Screen*, vol. 31, no. 1, pp. 45–66.

Office of Film and Literature Classification 1990–1991, *Report on activities*, AGPS, Canberra.

Petley, J. 2012, 'Head-on collisions: the BBFC in the 1990s', in E. Lamberti (ed.), *Behind the scenes at the BBFC: film classification from the silver screen to the digital age*, British Film Institute and Palgrave Macmillan, London, pp. 127–142.

Sandler, K. 2002, 'Movie ratings as genre: the incontestable R', in S. Neale (ed.), *Genre and contemporary Hollywood*, British Film Institute, London.

Schembri, J. 1995, 'What New York kids get up to?', *The Age*, Melbourne, 29 December.

Senate Hansard 1995, *Senate Select Committee on Community Standards. Codes of Practice in the Television Industry*. 18 May. http://parlinfo.aph.gov.au/parlInfo/search/display/display.w3p;db=COMMITTEES;id=committees%2Fcommsen%2Frcomd950518a_scs.out%2F0001;orderBy=_fragment_number;query= ((Dataset3Acommsen)%20SearchCategory_Phrase%3A%22committees%22)%20Parliament Number%3A%2237%22%20CommitteeName_Phrase%3A%22senate%20select%20committee%20on%20community%20standards%22%20Questioner_Phrase%3A%20 22chair%22; rec=4.

Senate Hansard 1998, *Community Standards Committee Report: Government Response*. 2 July. http://parlinfo.aph.gov.au/parlInfo/search/display/display.w3p;db=CHAMBER;id=chamber%2Fhansards%2F1998-07-02%2F0136;query=Id%22chamber%2Fhansards%2F1998-07-02%2F0000%22.

Spielberg, S. 1984, *Indiana Jones and the Temple of Doom*, motion picture, Lucasfilm Ltd., USA. Produced by R. Watts.

Spielberg, S. 1993, *Jurassic Park*, motion picture, Amblin Entertainment, USA. Produced by K. Kennedy and G. Molen.

Stockbridge, S. 1996, 'Cultural policy regulation, technology and discourse: regulatory agendas and research paradigms – film regulation from the 1970s to the 1990s', *Culture and Policy*, vol. 7, no. 2, pp. 123–140.

Strickland, J. 1977, 'How Australian film censorship works', *Cinema Papers*, no. 11, pp. 206–208 and 280.

Weitz, P. and Weitz, C. 1999, *American Pie*, motion picture, Summit Entertainment, USA. Produced by C. Weitz, P. Weitz, C. Moore, W. Zide, and C. Perry.

Wilson, B. J. 1993, 'What's wrong with the ratings?', *Media and Values*, vol. 63, pp. 13–15.

Wright, A. 1987, 'R wars', *Filmviews*, vol. 32, pp. 2–7.

Part 2
Young people and technologies: ethical research and sexting

5 Ethical issues in qualitative research addressing sensitive issues with children and young people

Catharine Lumby, Kath Albury, Alan McKee and Sky Hugman

Introduction

This chapter is written for researchers who are preparing to conduct qualitative research with young people about sensitive topics such as sexuality and members of ethics committees who must evaluate proposals for such research. Research institutions routinely require researchers to seek permission from an ethics committee or similar body before they can undertake research with human subjects. The history of the evolution of ethics regimes in their current form places a strong emphasis on biomedical approaches to ethics – which commonly favour quantitative research methods. This has led to criticisms that formal ethical provisions for qualitative researchers are inadequate because they have been 'generalised far beyond the context in which they were formulated' (Gallagher 2009, p. 13). This is particularly so when the standards for what constitutes 'useful' research can differ markedly between disciplines. For instance, qualitative research methods can provide data that is equally – and, for some purposes, even more – valuable as that produced using quantitative approaches. This is the case even – and perhaps particularly – when the research in question is studying young people, and addressing sensitive issues such as sexuality.

While there is a strong and varied tradition of academic research into this issue (including the authors we discuss in this chapter), it has not been made available in a form that is useful for academics preparing to conduct qualitative research with young people into sensitive issues, nor for those academics who sit on ethics committees and may be required to make judgements on projects whose methods are far removed from their own training. For this reason, we outline best practice research ethics and methods for qualitative research into sensitive issues with young people under or 18 years of age. Under the label of sensitive issues, we include topics such as sexuality, bullying, suicidal ideation, and drug use. These are topics where 'common-sense' public discourses about children's 'innocence' and assumed vulnerability render research that listens to young people's views controversial. Nevertheless, recent trends in academic writing, as we show in this chapter, insist that it is important to listen to young people's perspectives on these issues, and to allow them to contribute to the process of making sense of these aspects of their lives. In this chapter we take the case study of sexuality, and how young people's perspectives on this topic might ethically be researched, to illustrate the complexity of these issues. We hope that this chapter will be of practical use for everyone who engages with the ethics processes of research institutions in relation to these issues.

'Young people', agency, and research

Social attitudes towards children and young people are closely linked to the way they are approached in research and research ethics (Morrow and Richards 1996; Greig and Taylor 1999, p. 3). Traditional conceptions of young people in ethics procedures have understood them to be 'developing adults'. That is, in their developing state, young people were seen to be fundamentally vulnerable research subjects, lacking the communicative and cognitive abilities to participate properly in research (Birbeck and Drummond 2007, p. 26).[1] Childhood was understood as a knowable, biological state of being best observed through quantitative methods in laboratory settings (Graue and Walsh 1998, p. 3). Young people were 'objects' that research was performed on or done 'to', sometimes resulting in 'guinea pig' studies that severely compromised their rights (for examples of studies that took this approach in the twentieth century, see Lederer and Grodin 1994, pp. 9–11).

A related research framework saw young people as 'innocent' or weak and therefore in need of protection in research (see Sime 2008, p. 67). While researchers who favoured a 'development' paradigm took a dim view of young people's capacities, researchers who favoured a model of young people as 'innocent' were doubtful about their resilience. For both these reasons it was common practice to bypass young people altogether in research that concerned them, particularly about sensitive issues such as sexuality, instead asking adult proxies to report on young people's experiences and opinions.

This is the simplest approach to the issue of research ethics with young people. There might appear to be no ethical issues raised in 'protecting' young people from sensitive issues by not even raising those issues with them. However, over the past two decades researchers have increasingly argued that there are in fact problems with this approach (Powell and Smith 2009; Graham and Fitzgerald 2010; Robinson and Davies 2014) and that it may even be regarded as unethical to silence young people's contribution to research that concerns them. Clearly, excluding the views of young people weakens the depth and breadth of research findings in the field.

There exists no international agreement about the definition of a 'child' or 'young person'. The definition varies on the bases of legislation, common law, and public policy frameworks. These frameworks underpin cultural discourses about the boundaries between childhood, adolescence, and adulthood. Depending on the national and institutional context, a 'young person' can range from birth to 25 years old. In Australia, for example, a person under the age of 18 years of age is defined as a child in all states and territories except in South Australia and in some legislation in New South Wales (Bessant 2006, p. 52). This means that a 17-year-old's status as a 'young person' – and thus their perceived capacity to participate in research – can vary as they cross state borders. In this chapter we therefore use the term 'young person' to refer to participants up to the age of 18 years old, allowing 19-year-olds to be counted as adults for the purposes of research ethics. In other contexts, however, a 19-year-old would still be regarded as a young person, and could thus be caught up in protocols which denied her the right to contribute to research that concerns her.

Recognising that the category of 'young person' is a cultural and legal mode of classification that shifts between contexts, rather than a simple biological fact, frames our ways of thinking about the characteristics of 'young people'. Over the past twenty years, interdisciplinary work under the umbrellas of childhood studies and youth studies has begun to present a very different picture of who 'young people' are in ways that have important implications for research methods and ethics for exploring sensitive issues. Childhood and adolescence are now, and indeed have been for some time, understood as socially constructed, not biologically predetermined (see Ariès 1962; Qvortrup 1994; James and Prout 1997). Recognition of the social context of childhood has been accompanied by an understanding that 'childhood' is not a universal or homogeneous experience. Influential academic researchers have laid the groundwork for understanding young people's agency and have argued that young people are able to make sense of their own experience and articulate it given the right environment and tools (see Duits and van Zoonen 2006; Matthews 2005; Alderson and Morrow 2004; 2011). Researchers taking this approach have critiqued the notion that young people are undeveloped and incompetent to express their views, and argued that they should have agency in contributing to how they are understood by the adult world (Christensen and James 2008, p. 5; James 2007; Lewis 2010). The Ethical Research Involving Children (ERIC) resource (http://childethics.com) has brought together researchers working with children and young people to identify best practice in the area. As Powell et al. (2012) note, the critical issue of young people's voices and the ways they are represented are recurring themes in the literature.

This revised understanding of young people and their agency has been cemented by the recognition that children have human rights. The United Nations Convention on the Rights of the Child (UNCRC) (1989) recognised the civil, cultural, economic, political, cultural, and social rights of those under 18 years of age and has become the most widely ratified human rights convention. Of particular relevance for researchers are Articles 12(1) and 13(1), which stipulate that young people have the right to express their opinions on matters that affect them and the right to be heard. The 2002 UN Special Session on Children reaffirmed the international community's focus on human rights for young people, including their right to be actively involved with all stages of decision making that concern them.

This international commitment is reflected in research that explores the human rights edict that young people have complex human rights and should not be treated as different from adult humans. Michael Ignatieff (2000, p. 108) notes that young people 'have the right not just to be sheltered and cared for and protected from abuse, but also to be treated as moral agents in their own right'. The Australian National Health and Medical Research Council's *National Statement on Ethical Conduct in Human Research* (2007), the standard document on ethical practice in Australia, stipulates that 'researchers must respect the developing capacity of children and young people to be involved in decisions about their participation in research'.[2] Indeed, young people are now widely viewed by researchers as 'subjects' rather than objects in the research process (Tisdall et al. 2009, p. 1). In their comprehensive literature review, Powell et al. (2012) show how recent developments in childhood studies and youth studies have enabled a change in the values and beliefs of researchers working with young people, including the growing focus on situating young people as 'co-researchers'. This view not only impacts on what sorts of research is carried out in terms of a project's focus on what young people think and experience, but also on *how* it is carried out. As Emma Clavering and Janice MacLaughlin (cited in Powell et al. 2012) note, in research practice there is a broad scope to create new research, which results in approaches that focus *on* research rather than *on* young people. It is critical that we document and evaluate participatory approaches that enable young people's opinions to inform both the process and outcomes of research (see Bell 2008, p. 7).

The changing theoretical discourses about young people, and what it means to be young, have challenged existing categories of 'child', 'adolescent', 'youth', and 'adult', making the value of determining a young person's intellectual, social, or ethical competence by reference to their age debatable (Bessant 2006). Debates around ethical issues of consent and participation often treat young people as an undifferentiated and homogeneous group. More recently, researchers problematising concepts of 'being' a child, or 'becoming' an adult (Balen et al. 2006; Uprichard 2008) have argued for a theorisation of young people as 'beings and becomings' (Uprichard 2008, p. 303). This approach addresses the temporality of childhood, framing it as something young people themselves are able to give voice to, while also aiming for a more conceptually realistic representation that is deemed suitable by those working in the field.

These definitions have implications for questions about who should be allowed to speak in research that concerns young people. Taking the sensitive issue of sexuality as an example, Kerry Robinson (2012) raises the issue of 'difficult citizenship' when thinking about the representation of young people's sexuality, young people as sexual subjects, and the sexual norms to which young people are subjected. Like Robinson, we argue that values, identity, bodies, behaviours, sexual health, and well-being are relevant to young people themselves. Any articulation or exploration of young people's lives must consider the 'prevailing relations of power that constitute who they are as subjects' (Robinson 2012, p. 271). For example, in Australian State and Territory law, young people are acknowledged as having capacity to consent to medical procedures from the age of 14, and to body-to-body sexual interaction at age 16 or 17 (Albury et al. 2013). Despite these legal acknowledgements of young people's bodily autonomy with respect to medical and sexual activities they are not afforded the legal capacity to consent to participating in the production of sexual texts or images – indeed sexual images of young people aged under 18 are deemed 'child pornography'.[3] This regulatory discrepancy places young people (particularly 16–17-year-olds) in a liminal zone between childhood and adulthood where they can participate in particular modes of embodied sexuality but may not document their own experiences of these activities (Albury et al. 2010). As ethical researchers, then, it is vital to consider how 'children's difficult citizenship is intensified through the volatile relationship between sexuality and childhood; a relationship that is socioculturally constructed and constantly mobilized not just to regulate children's lives, but also to maintain dominant relations' (Robinson 2012, p. 271).

The value of qualitative research methods for research with young people

The desire to see young people as 'co-participants' (Sime 2008, p. 64) and co-researchers in research that concerns them raises issues about research methods (Kellett 2010; Powell et al. 2012). While quantitative methods are useful in identifying broad trends and issues, for example, the age at which people first have intercourse or the numbers of young people diagnosed with an STD, they do not provide much detail about people's motivations and opinions (see Buckingham and Bragg 2003, p. 19). If we seek to recognise the agency of young people in making sense of their engagement with sensitive issues, qualitative research methods offer a more powerful way of doing this than does quantitative work.

Qualitative research can allow us to understand how young people make meaning out of their practices. For example, much research shows that young people continue to practise unsafe sex, despite being educated about safe sex practices (Steele 1999). Qualitative research begins to explain why this is the case, exploring the vital but nebulous concept of embodied and embedded meaning. Quantitative research often aspires towards linguistic neutrality, implying that words can have objective meanings – assuming that the subjects who fill in surveys will understand the words that are used in just the same way as do the researchers who create the surveys. But qualitative research shows us that this is not often the case. Qualitative research has explored, for example, how teenagers (girls in particular) receive media messages about sexuality as well as how they distribute that information – or variations of it (see Ward et al. 2006). This research demonstrates that young people interact with media, and particularly popular media, in nuanced ways and that meaning is always contingent on the context in which it is received as much as by the content.

Qualitative research allows researchers to explore the complexity of lived experience, which always exceeds representation, and particularly the representation of such slow-moving institutions as academic research. Qualitative research is the best way to identify new practices, including meaning-making practices, in populations: for example, the question of why young people engage in sex messaging (or sexting) on their mobile phones, where and how they do this, and what personal and social issues or repercussions they face in doing so. For example, Abbey Hyde and Etaoine Howlett's wide-scale qualitative analysis of teenage sexuality in Ireland used focus groups to go beyond existing survey data to understand the pressures and problems teenagers face, including their (poor) knowledge of STDs and the gender norms that contribute to their sexual decision-making (Hyde et al. 2005; 2008).

Our understanding of how young people make sense of these issues is enhanced because qualitative research can explore the ways language itself contributes to young people's identities and decision-making practices. For example, research by Paul Flanagan (2010; 2012; 2014) examines the role discourse and narrative play in shaping young people's sexuality in educational and social service settings. Focusing on management policies and practices within schools, he explores how they are used to respond to young people's sexual actions: for example, addressing the questions of when and how sexuality is deemed problematic, exploratory, or playful, and how young people's sexual behaviours come to be seen as such.

In an effort to develop reflexive ethical research processes that incorporate school teaching staff, counsellors, students, and their parents, Flanagan (2014, p. 143) argues for research that enables young people to 'participate freely and fully as active agents that hold some tension of dependence and independence with adults'. This points to perhaps the most important benefit of qualitative research with young people into sensitive issues such as sexuality: it can show researchers the ways young people contribute as agents to the construction of their own sexuality and sexual experiences, and allow them to express themselves when it comes to issues that concern them (Powell and Smith 2009). For example, Judy Orme's (2007) use of drama to research childhood sexuality in 'Project Jump' not only captured the experiences of hard-to-reach young people but provided a creative outlet for them to contribute ideas to the research process. Project Jump participants attended a play depicting a young couple's first sexual encounter, and then engaged in an interactive workshop exploring sexual health and relationships. The research team then utilised a range of strategies (including postcards, short surveys, and small and large group discussions) to include all participants (including those with challenges in terms of concentration, language, and literacy skills) to fully participate in the project evaluation process (Orme 2007, p. 362).

Similarly, Tracey Skelton (2008) discusses the use of participant-led discussions in a study on impoverished teenage girls (14–17 years) in Wales, who not only felt empowered by the research process, but were able to successfully apply for a grant from the European Union to get computer training in their neighbourhood as a result of the responsibility they demonstrated through the project. Indeed, Anne Graham and Robyn Fitzgerald (2010, p. 136) draw attention to current research that shows links between young people's participation in qualitative research and their well-being. They also argue that young people's participation in research can bring their voices into policy debates (see Tisdall 2009, p. 5). While there are many high-profile (largely biomedical) examples throughout history of harm done to children as the result of research (see Lederer and Grodin 1994), the majority of contemporary research carried out with children has been 'sensitive' and beneficial (Greig and Taylor 1999, p. 2). Indeed, Trudi James and Hazel Platzer (1999) argue that researchers have a 'moral duty' to conduct research on vulnerable groups in order to improve their place in society (see Hesse-Biber 2004).

Ethical considerations in qualitative research with young people about sensitive issues

Ethical research standards require us to scrutinise how we apply qualitative methods with young people to research sensitive issues. We note above that qualitative research methods offer the potential for research subjects to demonstrate agency in ways that are simply not possible with quantitative research. However, theoretical work on the notion of power and language insists that we must not ignore the power that is present in all knowledge-gathering relationships. Qualitative research may allow subjects to challenge the power held by researchers, but it does not simply allow them to express themselves transparently. For example, Lesley-Anne Gallacher and Michael Gallagher (2008) observe that participatory methods are no less ethically ambiguous than any other research method. The way power relations with adults shape children's voices and the situated nature and limits of children's voices is discussed by Spyros Spyrou (2011). Giving children a voice and accessing their views in ways that adequately represent their version of life remains complicated (Powell et al. 2012). Powell et al. (2012, p. 12) also argue that, while there is a large body of literature that discusses children's participation rights in a general way, there is less published about children's participation rights in relevant academic research. In this context we explore a number of ethical issues that have been identified as arising in the practice of qualitative research with young people about sensitive issues.

1. Young people are the same as adults and young people are different from adults

A key area of debate is whether or not young people should be regarded as 'similar or different' from adults (Morrow and Richards 1996, p. 270; Punch 2002). Current consensus suggests that they are in fact both: young people are just as competent as adults in their own way (the same) but also in need of particular care (different). Greig and Taylor (1999, pp. 2–3) argue that young people deserve to be treated differently to adults – on account of the future role they will play in adult society, their diversity and vulnerability – and that research about young people should be approached with special attention. They also note that young people are not 'mini adults' and do not always see the world in the same way or approach issues with the same values. Researchers have cautioned against superimposing adult-based ethical frameworks onto young subjects as young people can have different notions of concepts such as privacy, harm and benefit to the adults conducting the research (see Edwards and Alldred 1999; Skelton 2008; Gallagher 2009, p. 17).

In ethical terms, some researchers still regard young people as a vulnerable or marginalised group (Nyamathi 1998, p. 65; Liamputtong 2007). While this echoes traditional conceptions of the child as innocent or incompetent and contemporary concerns about risk, in this context it is used as a means to protect, not discount, young people in research. Linda Moore and Margaret Miller (1999, p. 1034) acknowledge the difficulty of defining vulnerability but argue it is characterised by a limited ability to 'make personal life choices, to make personal decisions, to maintain independence, and to self-determine'. Using this definition, Samantha Punch (2002, p. 323) argues that young people are particularly vulnerable in an adult-dominated society that marginalises them through unequal power relations. Vulnerability raises particular ethical concerns. If vulnerable participants are not adequately informed throughout a research process, and asked to reflect upon stressful or painful things without adequate support, research can 'reinforce' vulnerability or marginalisation rather than address it (Connolly 2003).

Ethical approaches to qualitative research with young people about sensitive issues therefore require a delicate balancing act between minimising harm while respecting the need to learn about young people's experiences and hear their voices (see Grodin and Glantz 1994). Indeed, there is a 'growing awareness that ethical issues with child research bring their own special considerations' (Hopkins and Bell 2008, p. 2).

2. Power imbalance

Differences in psychological, physical, and political power between adult researchers and the young people they study pose a range of ethical problems (Graue and Walsh 1998, p. xiv; Valentine 1999; Hill et al. 2004). These differences can lead to situations of abuse of power, most easily with regards to informed consent – a key component of ethical research. It is possible for adults (as researchers, guardians, or gatekeepers) to inadvertently coerce a young person into participating in a study or to prevent them from participating when they would have agreed to it on their own terms (see Gallagher 2009, p. 16).

3. Confidentiality

Young people are the subject of greater surveillance than most other groups, with their practices – particularly in relation to sensitive issues such as sexuality – the focus of intense scrutiny. Qualitative research with young people can involve discussions about their personal lives and opinions on topics such as relationships, family, school, drug use, and sex (see for example, France 2000). In some cases, legislative instruments define all activity in these areas by young people – even if it is consensual – as abuse. Because researchers are required to report abuse to relevant authorities, the confidentiality of the young person can be compromised. For researchers, it is an ethico-legal quandary: do they honour the trust participants place in them or their duty of care as adults according to the legal system within which they are working?

To ameliorate difficulties raised by confidentiality, some researchers advocate explaining to participants at the outset that if instances of abuse or harm (as defined by relevant laws) are reported during the research process they are required by law to inform relevant authorities, thereby giving young participants control over whether they disclose. Allan France et al. (2000) used this approach when investigating the health beliefs of children and young people, as did Margaret Melrose (2002) in her study of young prostitutes in England and Wales. Similarly, the Young People and Sexting in Australia Project provided participants with information regarding relevant laws and followed confidentiality protocols recommended by the Australian National Children and Youth Law Service (Albury et al. 2013). If reportable information is disclosed, some researchers have discussed *how* they will report information with participants, providing them with greater control over the consequences of their disclosure (for examples see Barbovschi et al. 2013).

4. Harm minimisation

Protecting young people from physical, psychological, or emotional harm is at the forefront of any ethics committee's consideration of research proposals that involve them. As Priscilla Alderson (2005, p. 27) notes, there may be a distinctive character to risk involved in qualitative research with young people about sensitive issues – small risks can have serious consequences for a young person. However, while benefits and risks are often easily identifiable in a clinical setting, the impact of qualitative research is often difficult to predict, both in terms of what it will mean for broader society and the individuals who participate in the study. Priscilla Alderson and Virginia Morrow (2011, p. 27) argue that risks in social research are more likely to include things like distress, embarrassment, loss of self-esteem, and anxiety rather than physical harm. Concepts of harm and risk in social research may also not be as clear-cut as they are in clinical studies (Powell et al. 2012, p. 2). There is a chance that research will cause pain, embarrassment, or suffering to young people who might be required to talk about uncomfortable or sad events in their lives or who might experience something confronting, unpleasant, or unforeseen in the research process (Alderson 1995). Shame and social stigmas may also be reinforced through clumsy report writing or media coverage of research (NSW Commission for Children and Young People, 2005) and this is also of particular concern for research into vulnerable or marginalised populations of young people.

Creating safe spaces for young people to participate

Two major approaches have been identified to address the particular ethical issues of gathering qualitative data from young people about sensitive issues. The first is the use of data-gathering methods that create a research environment where young people are comfortable participating or withdrawing (Hopkins and Bell 2008, pp. 2–3). One way to do this is to use the skills that children may be 'expert in', such as painting, drawing, and recording for data gathering (see Borland et al. 2001). Shirley Prendergast (cited in Hallowell et al. 2005) made use of the drawing method via a 'visual lifeline' for research on young, homeless LGB people. Prendergast used coloured textas and butcher paper to plot key events in the subjects' lives to enable them to reflect positively on their past, present, and future. Authors have also discussed the utility of methods that diffuse the power of the researchers – including group interviews and 'task' versus 'talk'-centric activities (Hood et al. 1996). In their study of sexualised goods aimed at children in Scotland, David Buckingham et al. (2010) relied upon drawing and group discussions to give primacy to participants' voices (aged 9–17 years old), ensuring an open-ended and non-threatening research environment.

Anne Greig and Jayne Taylor (1999, p. 6) also note the importance of studying children in neutral settings that do not signify adult power, as opposed to settings such as laboratories or schools (see Buckingham et al. 2010). A recent study of young gay and lesbian people's experiences in the UK consciously chose not to interview participants at school or at home, as these are places where they may have already felt marginalised or unsupported (see Skelton 2008). Instead, the study made use of familiar voluntary sector spaces in which participants were comfortable. Other studies have made use of focus groups where adults are outnumbered by young people. In Hyde et al.'s (2005) study of sexuality among schoolchildren in Ireland, the use of focus groups allowed peers to challenge each other and bring their fears and concerns to the surface of the research in a non-confrontational manner. And Richard Hessler et al. (2003) removed the 'adult' from the research process through the use of online journals and emails to research young people engaging in risky behaviours. Hessler (2003) has noted this provided a familiar and informal means for the young people to communicate, providing far richer data than was obtained for a similar study conducted face to face in 1998.

Reflexive research methods to address ethical issues

A second important element of ethical qualitative research with young people on sensitive issues is a self-reflexive approach (Guillemin and Gillam 2004; Horton 2008; Skånfors 2009; Flanagan 2014). Gallagher (2009, p. 26), for example, argues that 'ethical process could be seen as an ongoing process of questioning, acting and reflecting, rather than straightforward application of general rules of conduct'. Reflexive approaches reject the idea that every element of a project's research method can be locked down before data gathering begins. Rather, all elements of a research method – including the size and make-up of the cohort, the process for gaining consent, the processes for gathering data, the process for analysing data, the process for distributing results, and even the research questions themselves – are taken to be provisional, and open to the possibility of change depending on the feedback of the young people involved in the research (Tisdall 2009). Indeed, some studies have gone so far as to include young people on the research team: in Jill Clark's (2001) study of young refugees and asylum seekers, a small group of young adults (16–21 years old) were included on the research team at all stages of the process.

Conclusion

Researchers intending to engage in qualitative research with young people about sensitive issues, and the ethics committees who have to deal with proposals to do such research, often find themselves attempting to assess the ethical implications of approaches and subjects that are not familiar to them. In this chapter we have argued, first, that although qualitative approaches may on the surface appear to raise more challenging ethical issues than traditional quantitative research methods, an emerging literature proposes that such research can in fact be *more* ethical as it allows for the agency of young people to be recognised, and allows for their voices to be heard in relation to issues that affect them. A philosophical movement away from seeing young people as helpless and innocent, and instead recognising and valuing their emerging agency, supports this perspective.

We have noted that there are particular challenges with regards to the ethics of qualitative research with young people about sensitive issues: the fact that young people are both the same as adults, and different from them; that differences in power can be particularly stark in these situations; that legal requirements to report particular behaviours by young people can cause problems for confidentiality; and that young people may be particularly vulnerable to harm from apparently small risks in research. However, the literature has proposed two important ways to address these risks. The first is to create safe spaces for young people, for example by using forms of data gathering that respect their expertise, by avoiding formal spaces for data gathering, or by ensuring that young people's control of the process is emphasised. The second is to employ self-reflexive methods that are open to the possibility of change based on the feedback of young people involved in the research.

We hope that we have shown that, in reviewing the ethical framework for qualitative research with young people into sensitive issues, it is useful for researchers to understand ethical practice in the area, and it is our intention that this chapter will provide a useful starting point for this. Similarly, for members of ethics committees assessing proposals to conduct qualitative research with young people into sensitive issues, the evaluation of ethical frameworks can acknowledge prior evidence about the methods and the situations in which young people, at different ages, feel supported and safe in participating in such research. Methods and protocols may differ in qualitative research from the methods and protocols that are appropriate in biomedical and related fields. Again, we hope this chapter will provide a useful starting point for understanding this tradition. Researchers increasingly understand that young people, while they are in some ways different from adults, in other ways are developing their own agency and voice in relation to issues that concern them. Qualitative research can provide a route for supporting and recognising this process. This chapter strives to provide information to help researchers and members of ethics committees as they address the ethical specificities of this work.

Notes

1 The notion that children are incomplete can be seen in Jean Piaget's theory of intellectual development and Lawrence Kohlberg's theory of moral development (Birbeck and Drummond 2007, p. 23).
2 Young people's participation and protection in research is also reinforced by domestic legislation, which includes background checks on those who work with young people. In NSW, The Children and Young Person's (Care and Protection) Act 1998 requires those working with young people to provide for their safety and well-being. The participation principle (s. 9b) stipulates that 'wherever a child or young person is able to form a view on matters concerning their safety, welfare and wellbeing, they must be given an opportunity to express these views freely'.
3 For an overview of Australian Commonwealth, State and Territory laws regarding young people, sexuality, and media, see Tallon et al. (2012).

References

Albury, K., Crawford, K., Byron, P., and Mathews, B. 2013, 'Young people and sexting in Australia: ethics, representation and the law', April 2013, ARC Centre for Creative Industries and Innovation/Journalism and Media Research Centre, University of New South Wales, Sydney.

Albury, K., Funnell, N., and Noonan, E. 2010, 'The politics of sexting: young people, self-representation and citizenship', July 2010, Australian and New Zealand Communication Association Conference: Media, Democracy and Change, Canberra.

Alderson, P. 1995, *Listening to children: children, ethics and social research*, Barnardo's, London.

Alderson, P. 2005, 'Designing ethical research with children', in A. Farrell (ed.), *Ethical research with children*, Open University Press, Milton Keynes and New York, pp. 27–36.
Alderson, P. and Morrow, V. 2004, *Ethics, social research and consulting with children and young people*, Barnardo's, London.
Alderson, P. and Morrow, V. 2011, *The ethics of research with children and young people*, Sage, London.
Ariès, P. 1962, *Centuries of childhood: a social history of family life*, Jonathan Cape, London.
Balen, R., Blyth, E., Calabretto, H., Fraser, C., Horrocks, Christine, and Manby, M. 2006, 'Involving children in health and social research: "human becomings" or "active beings"?' *Childhood*, vol. 13, no. 1, pp. 29–48.
Barbovschi, M., Green, L. and Vandoninck, S. 2013, 'Innovative approaches for investigating how children understand risk in new media. Dealing with methodological and ethical challenges', EU Kids Online, London School of Economics and Political Science, London.
Bessant, J. 2006, 'The fixed age rule: young people, consent and research ethics', *Youth Studies Australia*, vol. 25, no. 4, pp. 50–57.
Bell, N. 2008, 'Ethics in child research: rights, reason and responsibility', *Children's Geographies*, vol. 6, no. 1, pp. 7–20.
Birbeck, D. and Drummond, M. 2007, 'Research with young children: contemplating methods and ethics', *Journal of Educational Enquiry*, vol. 7, no. 2, pp. 21–31.
Borland, M., Hill, M., Laybourn, A. and Stafford, A. 2001, *Improving consultation with children and young people in relevant aspects of policy-making and legislation in Scotland*, Stationery Office, Edinburgh.
Buckingham, D. and Bragg, S. 2003, 'Young people, media and personal relationships', Research project funded by the Advertising Standards Authority, the British Board of Film Classification, the BBC, the Broadcasting Standards Commission, and the Independent Television Commission, London.
Buckingham, D., Willett, R., Bragg, S., and Russell, R. 2010, *Sexualised goods aimed at children: a report to the Scottish Parliament Equal Opportunities Committee*, Scottish Parliament Equal Opportunities Committee, Edinburgh.
Christensen, P. and James, A. 2008, *Research with children: perspectives and practices*, 2nd edn, Routledge, London and New York.
Clark, J. 2001, *Young people as researchers: possibilities, problems and politics*, National Youth Agency, Leicester.
Clavering, E. and McLaughlin, J. 2010, 'Children's participation in health research: from objects to agents?', *Child: Care, Health and Development*, vol. 36, no. 5, pp. 603–611.
Connolly, P. 2003, *Ethical principles for researching vulnerable groups*, Office of the First Minister and Deputy First Minister, London.
Duits, L. and van Zoonen, L. 2006, 'Headscarves and porno-chic: disciplining girls' bodies in European multicultural society', *European Journal of Women's Studies*, vol. 13, no. 2, pp. 103–117.
Edwards, R. and Alldred, P. 1999, 'Children and young people's views of social research: the case of research on home–school relations', *Childhood*, vol. 6, no. 2, pp. 261–281.
Flanagan, P. 2010, 'Making molehills into mountains: adult responses to child sexuality and behaviour', *Explorations: An E-Journal of Narrative Practice*, vol. 1, pp. 57–69.

Flanagan, P. 2012, 'Ethical review and reflexivity in research of children's sexuality', *Sex Education: Sexuality, Society and Learning*, vol. 12, no. 5, pp. 535–544.

Flanagan, P. 2014, 'Ethical beginnings: Reflexive questioning in designing child sexuality research', *Counselling and Psychotherapy Research: Linking Research with Practice*, vol. 14, no. 2, pp. 139–146.

France, A., Bendelow, G., and Williams, S. 2000, 'A "risky" business: researching the health beliefs of children and young people', in A. Lewis and G. Lindsay (eds), *Researching children's perspectives*, Open University Press, Buckingham, pp. 150–162.

Gallacher, L. and Gallagher, M. 2008, 'Methodological immaturity in childhood research? Thinking through "participatory methods"', *Childhood*, vol. 15, no. 4, pp. 499–516.

Gallagher, M. 2009, 'Ethics', in K. Tisdall, J. Davis, and M. Gallagher (eds), *Researching with children and young people: research design, methods and analysis*, Sage, London and Thousand Oaks, CA, pp. 11–28.

Graham, A. and Fitzgerald, R. 2010, 'Children's participation in research: some possibilities and constraints in the current Australian research environment', *Journal of Sociology*, vol. 46, no. 2, pp. 133–147.

Graue, M.E. and Walsh, D. J. 1998, *Studying children in context: theories, methods and ethics*, Sage, London and Thousand Oaks, CA.

Greig, A. and Taylor, J. 1999, *Doing research with children*, Sage, London and Thousand Oaks, CA.

Grodin, M. A. and Glantz, L. H. 1994, 'Preface', in M. A. Grodin and L. H. Glantz (eds), *Children as research subjects: science, ethics and law*, Open University Press, New York, pp. vii–ix.

Guillemin, M. and Gillam, L. 2004, 'Ethics, reflexivity, and "ethically important moments" in research', *Qualitative Inquiry*, vol. 10, no. 2, pp. 261–280.

Hallowell, N., Lawton, J. and Gregory, S. 2005, *Reflections on research: the realities of doing research in the social sciences*, McGraw-Hill, Maidenhead.

Hesse-Biber, S.N. 2004, 'Feminist approaches to research as a process: reconceptualising epistemology, methodology, and methods', in S. N. Hesse-Biber and M. L. Yaiser (eds), *Feminist perspectives on social research*, Open University Press, New York, pp. 3–26.

Hessler, R.M., Downing, J., Beltz, C., Pelliccio, A., Powell, M., and Vale, W. 2003, 'Qualitative research on adolescent risk using e-mail: a methodological assessment', *Qualitative Sociology*, vol. 26, no. 1, pp. 111–124.

Hill, M., Davis, J., Prout, A., and Tisdall, K. 2004, 'Moving the participation agenda forward', *Children and Society*, vol. 18, no. 2, pp. 77–96.

Hood, S., Kelley, P., and Mayall, B. 1996, 'Children as research subjects: a risky enterprise', *Children and Society*, vol. 10, no. 2, pp. 17–28.

Hopkins, P. and Bell, N. 2008, 'Editorial: interdisciplinary perspectives, ethical issues and child research', *Children's Geographies*, vol. 6, no. 1, pp. 1–6.

Horton, J. 2008, 'A "sense of failure"? Everydayness and research ethics', *Children's Geographies*, vol. 6, no. 4, pp. 363–383.

Hyde, A., Drennan, J., Howlett, E., and Brady, D. 2008, 'Young men's vulnerability in constituting hegemonic masculinity in sexual relations', *American Journal of Men's Health*, vol. 3, no. 3, pp. 238–251.

Hyde, A., Howlett, E., Brady, D. and Drennan, J. 2005, 'The focus group method: insights from focus group interviews on sexual health with adolescents', *Social Science and Medicine*, vol. 61, no. 12, pp. 2588–2599.

Ignatieff, M. 2000, *The rights revolution*, House of Anansi Press, Toronto.
James, A. 2007, 'Giving voice to children's voices: practices and problems, pitfalls and potentials', *American Anthropologist*, vol. 109, no. 2, pp. 261–272.
James, A. and Prout, A. 1997, *Constructing and reconstructing childhood: contemporary issues in the sociological study of childhood*, Falmer Press, London.
James, T. and Platzer, H. 1999, 'Ethical considerations in qualitative research with vulnerable groups: exploring lesbians' and gay men's experiences of healthcare – a personal perspective', *Nursing Ethics*, vol. 6, no. 1, pp. 73–81.
Kellett, M. 2010, 'Small shoes, big steps! Empowering children as active researchers', *American Journal of Community Psychology*, vol. 46, no. 1–2, pp. 195–203.
Lederer, S. E. and Grodin, M. A. 1994, 'Historical overview: pediatric experimentation', in M. A. Grodin and L. H. Glantz (eds), *Children as research subjects: science, ethics and law*, Open University Press, New York, pp. 3–28.
Lewis, A. 2010, 'Silence in the context of "child voice"', *Children and Society*, vol. 24, no. 1, pp. 14–23.
Liamputtong, P. 2007, *Researching the vulnerable*, Sage, London and Thousand Oaks, CA.
Matthews, H. 2005, 'Rising four: reflections on the state of growing-up', *Children's Geographies*, vol. 3, no. 3, pp. 271–273.
Melrose, M. 2002, 'Labour pains: some considerations on the difficulties of researching juvenile prostitution', *International Journal of Social Research Methodology* vol. 5, no. 4, pp. 333–351.
Moore, L.W. and Miller, M. 1999, 'Initiating research with doubly vulnerable populations', *Journal of Advanced Nursing*, vol. 30, no. 5, pp. 1034–1040.
Morrow, V. and Richards, M. 1996, 'The ethics of social research with children: an overview', in K. W. M. Fulford, D. L. Dickenson, and T. H. Murray (eds), *Healthcare ethics and human values: an introductory text with readings and case studies*, Wiley-Blackwell, Malden, MA, pp. 270–274
NSW Commission for Children and Young People [NWCYP] 2005, *Participation: count me in: involving children and young people in research*, Sydney.
Nyamathi, A. 1998, 'Vulnerable populations a continuing nursing focus', *Nursing Research*, vol. 47, no. 2, pp. 65–66.
Orme, J., Salmon, D., and Mages, L. 2007, 'Project jump: young people's perspectives on a sexual health drama project for hard to reach young people', *Children and Society*, vol. 21, no. 5, pp. 352–364.
Powell, M. A., Fitzgerald, R., Taylor, N. J., and Graham, A. 2012, *International literature review: ethical issues in undertaking research with children and young people*, report for the Childwatch International Research Network, Southern Cross University, Centre for Children and Young People, Lismore NSW and University of Otago, Centre for Research on Children and Families, Dunedin.
Powell, M. and Smith, A. B. 2009, 'Children's participation rights in research', *Childhood*, vol. 16, no. 1, pp. 124–142.
Punch, S. 2002, 'Research with children: the same or different from research with adults?', *Childhood*, vol. 9, no. 3, pp. 321–341.
Qvortrup, J., Bardy, M., Sgritta, G., and Wintersberger, H. 1994, *Childhood matters: social theory, practice and policy*, Aldershot, Avebury.
Robinson, K. 2012, '"Difficult citizenship": the precarious relationships between childhood, sexuality and access to knowledge', *Sexualities*, vol. 15, no. 3–4, pp. 257–276.

Robinson, K. and Davies, C. 2014, 'Doing sexuality research with children: ethics, theory, methods and practice', *Global Studies of Childhood*, vol. 4, no. 4, pp. 250–253.

Sime, D. 2008, 'Ethical and methodological issues in engaging young people living in poverty with participatory research methods', *Children's Geographies*, vol. 6, no. 1, pp. 63–78.

Skånfors, L. 2009, 'Ethics in child research: children's agency and researchers' "ethical radar"', *Childhoods Today*, vol. 3, no. 1, pp.1–22.

Skelton, T. 2008, 'Research with children and young people: exploring the tensions between ethics, competence and participation', *Children's Geographies*, vol. 6, no. 1, pp. 21–36.

Steele, J.R. 1999, 'Teenage sexuality and media practice: factoring in the influences of family, friends, and school', *Journal of Sex Research*, vol. 36, no. 4, pp. 331–341.

Spyrou, S. 2011, 'The limits of children's voices: from authenticity to critical, reflexive representation', *Childhood*, vol. 18, no. 2, pp. 151–165.

Tallon, K., Choi, A., Keeley, M., Elliott, J., and Maher, D. 2012, *New voices/new laws: school-age young people in New South Wales speak out about the criminal laws that apply to their online behavior*, National Children's and Youth Law Centre and Legal Aid NSW, Sydney.

Tisdall, K., Davis, J., and Gallagher, M. 2009, 'Introduction', in K. Tisdall, J. Davis, and M. Gallagher (eds), *Researching with children and young people: research design, methods and analysis*, Sage, London and Thousand Oaks, CA, pp. 1–10.

Uprichard, E. 2008, 'Children as "being and becomings": children, childhood and temporality', *Children and Society*, vol. 22, no. 4, pp. 303–313.

Valentine, G. 1999, 'Being seen and heard? The ethical complexities of working with children and young people at home and school', *Ethics, Place and Environment*, vol. 2, no. 2, pp. 141–155.

Ward, L. M., Day, K. M., and Epstein, M. 2006, 'Uncommonly good: exploring how mass media may be a positive influence on young women's sexual health and development', in L. Diamond (ed.), *Rethinking positive female adolescent sexual development: new directions for child and adolescent development*, Jossey-Bass, San Francisco, CA.

6 Sexting pleasures

Young people, fun, flirtation, and child pornography

Thomas Crofts, Murray Lee, Alyce McGovern and Sanja Milivojevic

Introduction

Public, media, and political concern has escalated in recent years over the practice of young people using new media technologies to digitally upload, send, or distribute sexually suggestive or explicit images of themselves to friends and others, a practice described as 'sexting'. The term 'sexting' is somewhat problematic in that it is evolving and amorphous and used to cover a wide array of behaviours, motivations, and emotions. These can range from the consensual sharing of an intimate image for pleasure or fun to the non-consensual sharing of that once consensually shared image to brag or to harass, bully or groom a young person (Parliament of Victoria 2013; Crofts et al. 2015). It is also not a term that is used by young people, who tend to regard it as a term used by 'out-of-touch' adults (Crofts et al. 2015). Yet, it is a term in common usage in academic and public discourse and therefore we use it throughout this chapter being mindful of the various behaviours it describes and thus the varied legal and non-legal responses it may require.

There are various laws that apply to sexting in Australia but the main laws which have caught media, public, and academic attention are child pornography offences. While it seems that in Australia police mainly use their discretion to divert young people from prosecution the potential for conviction under these offences has fuelled much debate over whether it is ever appropriate to apply such laws to young people, who engage in sexting (see Crofts et al. 2015). This stems partly from a concern about the severe consequences that can follow such a conviction but also from a questioning of whether the behaviour of young people fits the rationale for these offences. Such debates about how the law should respond to sexting are not limited to Australia but are facing communities across the globe (see Moran-Ellis 2012; Schmitz and Siry 2012; Slane 2013; Thompson 2014). This chapter adds to the debate about whether such a criminal response is necessary by exploring young people's sexting behaviours and how these align with the law. It examines this issue by presenting the rationales for a tough legal response to sexting and contrasting these with the motivations of young people who engage in sexting. Reporting on data from a large-scale survey of young people and their perceptions of and motivations for sexting, this chapter explores the notion that young people engage in sexting for reasons that are outside of the remit of child pornography laws. By giving a voice to young people it demonstrates how the framing of young people's lack of sexual agency around 'sexting' – often constructed in terms of risk, abuse, and pathology – generally ignores the lived experiences and complexities of young people's sexual communications. This leads us to argue that there needs to be transition away from the dominant politico-legal discourse that conceptualises sexting as child pornography and towards the development of other legal and non-legal methods to address sexting, which listen and respond to the voices of young people. The chapter concludes by suggesting that both the legal and sociocultural frameworks through which sexting is currently understood need rethinking if the harms associated with the practice are to be minimised or appropriately responded to.

Discourses on sexting

The public and the media have a long-running fascination with the behaviours of young people. There are countless examples across history of panics driven by the media about the way that young people conduct themselves, particularly in relation to crime and deviancy, either as perpetrators or victims or both (Cohen 1973; Taylor 1999). Unsurprisingly, young people's engagement with new technologies and social media has been the cause of much recent concern (Burke 2008; Mascheroni et al. 2010)[1] – and sexting has been central to this. As Heidi Vanderbosch et al. (2013, p. 99) argue, 'the news media pay considerable attention to stories on internet-related risks and children, especially those involving sex and aggression'. Stories of young people engaging in sexting fulfil a number of 'news values', evoking the newsworthy elements Steve Chibnall (1977) has described as titillation, personalisation, simplification, dramatisation, and others identified by Yvonne Jewkes (2015) such as children and risk. More generally, many of the discourses that have emerged around young people and their use of new technologies to take and share sexually suggestive or explicit images of themselves have tended to focus on the risks, harms, and consequences associated with the practice.

In Australia, the 'problem' of young people's sexting first came to light around 2009 to 2010 in media reports that discovered (or indeed invented) this new 'problem'. Such reports in turn fed public and political anxieties, connecting sexting with cyberbullying and the 'pornification' of society[2], and highlighting its associated negative reputational damage for young girls in particular who may suffer from 'digital mistakes' (Fineran 2010, p. 5). According to such scenarios, even where images are taken and distributed with consent, young people risk feelings of regret, shame, and low self-esteem, as well as potential cyberbullying victimisation (Parliament of Australia 2011, [4.60]). Further, these risks were seen to be compounded by the distribution of these images without consent – a practice some media commentators such as Susan McLean (2011)[3] have argued is ubiquitous, but with little empirical evidence to support such claims. Indeed, reports variously claimed that 'sexting is a form of child pornography' (Mather 2009, p. 1), and 'children posting sexual images of themselves on the internet put them in considerable danger' (Gregg 2009, p. 9). As a US study by Nora Draper (2012, p. 226) similarly noted, there is a trend in the media to 'conflate concerns regarding a perceived increase in teen sexuality brought on by the seductive powers of digital media with a yearning for an idealized past'. When it comes to sexting, such concerns simply perpetuate long-held concerns over the sexuality of young people. Youthful sexual expression (or exploitation) is certainly not a new phenomenon (Fishman 1982) and taking a genealogical perspective, there is a continuity in the anxieties about childhood sexuality and telecommunications technologies (Lee et al. 2013).

The association made between sexting and negative outcomes features not only in media reports and public discourse but is also reinforced in education campaigns directed at young people and at parents. As we have explored elsewhere (Crofts et al. 2015), the way in which young people are educated about sexting very often follows a 'zero tolerance' model of practice; that is, young people are told to simply refrain from sexting as the most appropriate method to avoid these negative risks.

This was seemingly backed up by media also reporting that 'the recent "sexting" craze has resulted in several young people across Australia facing serious offences after sending raunchy images' (Crowe 2009, p. 11). Following such sensationalist and often unsubstantiated reports of young people being prosecuted for child pornography offences (see Hasinoff 2013; Podlas 2014) the dominant themes in media discourse around 2011 to 2012 was the need to do something to address the perceived risks of sexting in regard to both harms to reputation, but also the harms of prosecution.

Despite the prevailing negative associations made between sexting and young people, the nature of the discourse and the focus of panics around the risks facing young people engaging in sexting has shifted – or at least been joined by another, sometimes competing discourse. This draws on the negative legal consequences of the criminalisation of teen sexting. From 2012 onwards a key focus of media discourse was law reform and a questioning of whether such draconian legal responses were necessary and appropriate (see Podlas 2014, p. 139 for a similar shift in focus in the US). For example, in 'One student call shouldn't turn a kid into a criminal', Clem Newton-Brown (2013) argues that 'the stigma associated with being a child sex offender would destroy your life' and that new approaches to dealing with sexting would protect 'our kids from punishment for engaging in activity that is unwise but should not be illegal'.

If a central theme from the shifting discourses around sexting and young people is to be identified it is one of risk and fear:

> [F]ear initially that young people might actually be sexting, then fear that young people may be at risk of exploitation or that they are being sexualised too early. The concerns then lead to fears over the consequences – legal or otherwise – of sexting for young people.
>
> (Crofts et al. 2015, p. 38)

Finally, what is clear from the media and public discourse around teen sexting is that it has been adults expressing these concerns: prominent are the voices of government officials, parents, teachers, and criminal justice agents. These are not the voices of the young people engaging in the practices; young people are rarely heard in these debates. Indeed, privileging the voices of adults (parents and experts) has helped facilitate the development of paternalistic laws and policies (Thill 2015), which may cause significantly more harm than the behaviours they seek to address. This makes it vitally important to listen to the voices of children because '[c]hildren, like adults, are social agents, who make sense of their lives' (Tangen 2008, 158). Thus, listening to young people's experience acknowledges that they are also 'experts in their own lives' (Langsted 1994, p. 35).

Child pornography offences

The need to protect young people from all forms of sexual exploitation is expressed in Article 34 of the United Nations Convention of the Rights of the Child:

> States Parties undertake to protect the child from all forms of sexual exploitation and sexual abuse. For these purposes, States Parties shall in particular take all appropriate national, bilateral and multilateral measures to prevent ... [t]he exploitative use of children in pornographic performances and materials.

The most evident rationale to prosecute child pornography is the direct harm to the young person involved as the subject of that material. As the Attorney-General's Department of the Australian Government (Attorney-General's Department (Cth) 2009, [238]) notes:

> Offences directed at possession and distribution should recognise the sexual exploitation which such images represent. Dealing in child pornography or abuse material fuels market demand, thereby increasing the incidence of actual abuse of children. It reflects varying scales of harm involving the initial abuse of the child (from images taken of an unknowing child playing naked on the beach, to images of serious rape/ torture) and varying scales of harm relating to the subsequent exploitation (from private access within the home to large-scale commercial exploitation).

Such rationale was also identified in *New York v Ferber*, 458 US 747, 774 (1982) where the court found that the use of children in images was harmful to their 'physiological, emotional and mental health' (at 756–758). This harm is exacerbated by the fact that this permanent record of the abuse may be circulated, thus haunting the young person for years to come. As Shouvlin (1981, p. 545) notes:

> Pornography poses an even greater threat to the child victim than does sexual assault or prostitution. Because the child's actions are reduced to a recording, the pornography may haunt him in future years, long after the original misdeed took place. A child who has posed for a camera must go through life knowing that the recording is circulating within the mass distribution system for child pornography.

A further perceived harm is the risk that child pornography may be seen to whet the appetite of child abusers, and entice other children to participate in child pornography. These concerns were evident in the US decision of *Osborne* v. *Ohio* (1990, 495 US 103), where the court referenced evidence suggesting that child pornographic materials are used to entice young people into sexual behaviour (at 111). In the Canadian case *R* v. *Schultz* (2008) 450 AR 37, it was found that harms beyond direct exploitation and abuse include: distorting a person's view to understand child abuse as normal; fuelling fantasies of paedophiles; using existing material to groom young people and thus facilitating the production of new material; and causing an attitudinal change in society at large. Attitudinal harm 'is manifested in the reinforcement of deleterious tendencies within society' through degrading or dehumanising representations or treatment of the subject (*R* v. *Sharpe* [2001] 1 SCR 45 at [160]).

The growth of new technologies has further fuelled these anxieties about child pornography. New technologies have become important platforms for the exchange of child pornography and have made child pornography more readily and widely available. They are also thought to exacerbate the exploitation of children by increasing demand for 'ever greater levels of depravity' and 'through the repeated distribution of the image, or images, through international networks' (Attorney-General's Department (Cth) 2009, [245]). Recognition of the need for international cooperation to combat such harms led to the United Nations adopting an Optional Protocol on the Sale of Children, Child Prostitution and Child Pornography in 2000, which entered into force in 2002. This Optional Protocol was designed to strengthen international cooperation and improve law enforcement at the national level as called for at the First World Congress Against the Sexual Exploitation of Children held in 1996 in Stockholm. It employs a definition of child pornography that includes 'any representation ... of a child engaged in real or simulated sexual activities or any representation of the sexual parts of a child for primarily sexual purposes' (Article 2[c]). The Protocol does not define the age at which a person should be considered a child for the purposes of child pornography. The Council of Europe Convention on Cybercrime is an example of a treaty which has set an age level at 18, while allowing a state to have a lower age level, but not lower than 16 (2001, Article 9[3]).

Taking these obligations seriously, the Australian Commonwealth Government has adopted 'an important leadership role in this area', reforming Commonwealth offences to 'provide a springboard to a national approach to this issue' (Slipper 2004, 32036). In 2004 the Commonwealth Criminal Code Act 1995 was amended to include 'a range of important new measures dealing with the use of the Internet to facilitate or exploit the sexual abuse of children' (Slipper 2004, 32035). In recognition of the difficulty in precisely defining the sorts of images that should be classified as child pornography (Makki 2005, p. 1), the Crimes Legislation Amendment (Telecommunications Offences and Other Measures) Act (No. 2) 2004 (Cth) amended the Commonwealth Criminal Code Act 1995 in an effort to clearly detail what material is subject to prohibition. Child pornography is defined in the Commonwealth Criminal Code Act 1995, section 473.1 to include not only an image which shows a person under 18 actually or apparently involved in or witnessing a sexual pose or a sexual act but also images which show as a dominant characteristic, for a sexual purpose, the sexual organ, anal region, or breasts (of a female).[4] In all these instances the depiction or representation must be done 'in a way that reasonable persons would regard as being, in all the circumstances, offensive'. Commonwealth offences cover using a carriage service (service for transmitting communications, i.e. telephone, mobile telephone, internet) to access, transmit, or make available child pornography (section 474.19). The Commonwealth Criminal Code also includes the preparatory offences of possessing, controlling, producing, distributing, or obtaining child pornography with the intent to place it on the Internet (section 474.20). Doing these things in terrestrial space is also an offence in Australia (section 273.5). All Australian states and territories also have provisions to criminalise child pornography, variously defined, with some jurisdictions closely following the Commonwealth definitions.

It should be noted that, alongside child pornography, there are other criminal offences that may be applied to sexting practices, including prohibitions against encouraging indecent acts, publishing indecent material, exposing young people to indecent material, harassment, and stalking. For instance, in *DPP* v. *Eades* [2009] NSWSC 1352, the accused was charged with possessing child pornography (now termed child abuse material) and also inciting an act of indecency after he persuaded a girl to send him photos of herself naked.[5] Civil law, particularly actions for defamation and breach of confidence, may be used to provide redress in certain instances of sexting (see Svanesson 2011; Crofts et al. 2015). Civil law actions must be activated by the aggrieved party and therefore would generally only provide redress where there has been a non-consensual distribution or use of the images. Furthermore, civil law measures lack the censuring function that is central to criminal law. As

Andrew Ashworth and Jeremy Horder (2013, p. 1) note '[i]t is the censure conveyed by criminal liability which marks out its special social significance'. The focus of this chapter is on child pornography offences because the aim of these laws, which is to protect children from abuse and exploitation, has a tendency to override other interests, such as the child's right to sexual expression (Albury et al. 2010; Kimpel 2010). As such, these offences can and do apply even where the child is the creator of the image and consents to its distribution.

While there are reported cases of young people being prosecuted under child pornography offences in the US for sexting, the exact extent to which these offences are applied to young people in Australia remains relatively unclear. The media have provided conflicting reports about the number of young people prosecuted, with some reports suggesting that numbers are high (Feeney 2013) while others suggest that numbers are low and that young people are generally diverted from formal proceedings (Bita 2012). Accounts from police (e.g. Paterson 2012, p. 13) suggest that the latter is probably more accurate and that young people are rarely prosecuted under child pornography laws and only where there are aggravating factors involved (such as exploitation and/or other offences). While prosecutions may be rare, the point is that in most Australian jurisdictions young people are exposed to the threat of prosecution under such laws, with the range of severe consequences that may follow, such as entry on the sex offender register. In many jurisdictions there is little to legally prevent such prosecution and much relies on police discretion not to pursue prosecution (Crofts et al. 2015). This leaves young people in a vulnerable position where prosecutorial policies may be subject to change and individual decisions are difficult to review. Only a few jurisdictions provide defences for young people to child pornography charges, which generally apply where the images do not depict a sexual offence (i.e. it depicts consensual sexual conduct between young people over the age of consent).[6] Rather than provide a defence to offences under the Commonwealth Criminal Code Act 1995 the preferred reform was to insert a requirement that the permission of the Attorney-General is sought before prosecution of an under 18-year-old is pursued (Crimes Legislation Amendment (Sexual Offences Against Children) Act 2010 (Cth) inserted sections 273.2A and 474.24C into the Criminal Code Act 1995 (Cth)). A further cultural consequence of the threat of prosecution is the 'educative' or censuring effect of law and the message it sends or moral claim it makes about the wrongfulness of the behaviour. This contrasts, and conflicts, with many young people's perceptions of sexting and risks sending a harmful message. Amy Kimpel (2010, p. 332) argues that criminalising behaviour, which if undertaken by consenting adults would not amount to an offence, could damage the development of young people's intimate citizenship.

In the following section we draw on our own empirical research on young people and sexting to argue that the motivations of young people for sexting rarely fit the rationales for prosecuting child pornography and therefore show that prosecution under child pornography laws is not an appropriate response to the perceived problem.

Young people's motivations for sexting

While there has been much social, political, and legal discourse on sexting by and between young people little attention has been paid to the voices of the subjects of that discourse: young people themselves. Understanding young people's motivations, experiences, and perspectives is in our view important if appropriate and effective legal and non-legal strategies are to be developed to address concerns about sexting. In order to address this gap, we conducted an internet-based survey, directed primarily at 13–18-year-olds, to canvass information about how they understand their practices and also their perceptions of sexting. The survey discussed here, which consisted of 34 items, was a self-selection-style survey, administered through the University of Sydney Law School using the Survey Monkey platform. It was made available online between July 2013 and October 2013 and promoted through a range of sources, including social media (Facebook, Twitter), radio programmes (youth radio station Triple J's 'Hack' programme), University webpages (University of Sydney, Western Sydney University, and University of New South Wales), as well as a large range of youth service providers. The data captured was statistically analysed using the SPSS program.

Sample of respondents

The survey was attempted by 2,243 respondents, with 1,416 completing every question (63.1 per cent completion rate). The sample cohort consisted of 48 per cent males and 52 per cent females, with <1 per cent of respondents (0.5 per cent) identifying as 'other'. In terms of age breakdown, 28 per cent of respondents were aged 13–15; 42 per cent were aged 16–18; 9 per cent were aged 19–21; 7 per cent were aged 22–25; and 13 per cent were aged 24 and above. This spread of age groups allowed us to make some comparisons between different groups of young people, and between young people and adults. While 36 per cent of respondents were from the state of New South Wales, respondents were spread across all Australian states and territories. They lived mainly in urban areas, with only 15 per cent of respondents residing in rural areas. The majority of respondents were born in Australia and of Anglo-Saxon origin, however, respondents identified as belonging to fifteen different ethnic groups. Reponses on religious background also revealed the majority of respondents did not identify with any religion (57 per cent), with a significant number identifying with Christianity (28 per cent). As our survey indicated, almost all young people use some form of social media; 98.4 per cent of our respondents reported having a social media profile.

Experience of sexting

We defined sexting relatively narrowly as 'the sending and receiving of sexual pictures/videos', with specific questions dealing with whether the images were of oneself or others. This definition could possibly include sexual images that would not contravene the current legal definitions of 'child pornography material'. However, it was agreed – with the input of the young people with whom we consulted prior to the completion of survey design[7] – that this was the most accurate way in which to capture sexting by young people that, in Australian jurisdictions at least, could be criminalised.

Prevalence

Research suggests that 'Sexting has become "normalised behaviour" in adolescent culture' and that 'Australia now has a generation of people who have never been without online access and have integrated it fully into their lives' (Parliament of Australia 2011, [4.54]; [1.33]). Our survey confirms this, with 38 per cent of young people between 13 and 15 years of age, and 50 per cent of those between 16 and 18 years of age reporting that they have sent a sexual image of themselves. The rate at which respondents report receiving a sexual image are higher, at 67 per cent across the cohort of respondents. These figures indicate that the practice of sexting is more widespread in Australia than much of the existing Australian and international research indicates. However, these raw prevalence figures need to be interpreted with care. They also hide the fact that while many young people have sent and received images, most do not do this often or with many partners – as we will explain below.

Motivations

Much research claims that young people engage in sexting due to pressure, particularly gendered pressure, with girls feeling pressured or coerced into sexting by boys (see Lee and Crofts 2015). We asked respondents what they thought were the reasons *others* sent sexual images or videos, as well as asking what motivated *them* to send (if indeed they reported sending). When reporting on their perceptions of why they thought others might sext, the responses would appear to justify the claims that young people sext due to pressure or coercion. Indeed, when respondents were asked to choose three possible reasons why they *thought* young women sent sexual images the most popular answers were that it was 'to keep a girl or guy's attention' (with 65 per cent of males and 54 per cent of females choosing this), 'a boyfriend or girlfriend pressured them to do it' (46 per cent of females, 42 per cent of males), 'to try to get a guy or girl to like them' (33 per cent of females), or 'as a sexy present for a boyfriend or girlfriend' (38 per cent of males). These responses contrasted quite markedly from respondents' perceptions as to why young males sent sexts, for which 'getting noticed and showing off' ranked the highest

(43 per cent of females and 54 per cent of males), and 'get or keep a guy/girl's attention' (37 per cent of females and 34 per cent of males) ranked second. Significant differences in male and female responses were apparent with the third most popular choice for male respondents being 'because he received one' (31 per cent) and for female respondents 'as a sexy present' (27 per cent) (see Crofts et al. 2015 for a more detailed account).

When asked to identify the three reasons why respondents themselves sent a sexual image or video from a list of possible motivations, however, a very different picture emerged; pleasure or desire were identified as the driving motivations for those who actually engaged in the sending of images or videos. The top three responses by teenage women were (in order): (1) to be 'fun and flirty' (21 per cent); (2) 'as a sexy present' (18 per cent); and (3) to 'feel sexy and confident' (15 per cent). This was very closely followed by 'because I received one' (14 per cent). Teenage boys' responses differed slightly: (1) 'to be fun and flirty' (23 per cent); (2) 'because I received one' (23 per cent); and (3) 'as a sexy present' (16 per cent). Respondents thus generally positively framed their motivations for their sexting behaviours but tended to negatively frame the motivations of others. Only small numbers of respondents reported being motivated by pressure or coercion across the respondent cohort. Nonetheless, for younger females, when compared to their male and older counterparts, a more mixed pictured emerged, with around 13 per cent endorsing a range of responses that could be interpreted as pressure. This reinforces some gender disparity in relation to levels of pressure.

From a list of possible selections respondents were also asked to nominate which three reasons might discourage them from sending sexual images or videos. Young males reported that the risk of 'getting in trouble with the law' was a primary factor that would discourage them, and while young females reported 'damage to their reputation' as the most popular reason for not sexting, they also identified 'getting in trouble with the law' in high numbers. This suggests that young people are generally aware of the legal implications for sexting. This is further exemplified by contrasting these responses to those of the adult cohort of our sample, who are much less likely to be criminalised under existing laws and were perhaps less concerned with this as a risk. This data also reinforces the gendered double standard in responses to sexting where young women (rightly) report being far more concerned about reputation than do young men (Lee and Crofts 2015).

Sending pictures to third parties

As well as attempting to understand perceptions and practices of sexting, the survey sought to understand the redistribution, or sharing, of personal sexual images and videos. The vast majority of respondents to our survey believed that 'personal pictures/videos usually end up being seen by more than the people they were sent to' and that images were 'mostly' seen by more people than they were sent to; indeed, 84 per cent of young females strongly agreed with this statement. Such perceptions reflect media and public discourse discussed above, which suggests that one of the biggest risks of sexting is that the images may end up in the hands of someone other than the intended recipient. When our respondents were asked how often such images are *actually* forwarded to third parties, however, we see again that perceptions do not match what was reported. According to our findings, only a very small minority of those respondents who had ever sent or received a picture or video reported ever having sent a picture/video on or shared it digitally (almost 8 per cent had 'ever' forwarded and 6 per cent had 'ever' posted online). It was more common that recipients physically showed the image(s) to someone else, with 22 per cent of respondents who had ever sent or received a picture or video 'ever' physically showing it to a third party.

As noted above, while large numbers of young people reported having sent and received sexts, our data suggests that the majority do not do it often and generally send only to a few sexting partners. Indeed, the majority of young people who had ever sent a sext reported sexting with only a partner or not at all in the previous twelve months (58 per cent of males and females 13–15 years, 56 per cent of males 16–18 years, 70 per cent of females 16–18 years). Most who reported having sent a sext also reported having been in a relationship at the time they sent the image (Crofts et al. 2015, p. 115). Thus, although social media may be saturated with publicly accessible images of young people in sexualised poses we should be wary of jumping to the conclusion that sexting is simply an extension of these public expressions of sexual selfhood. Rather, most (but certainly not all) sexting by young people appears to be for quite a targeted audience, and is very much an expression of life in the private sphere, relationship driven, and motivated by fun and flirtation, or desire.

The need to move away from the child pornography framework

While they no doubt bring associated risks, new technologies provide novel and potentially exciting platforms through which young people can begin to explore their sexuality. The behaviour at the core of most sexting is essentially not new; rather, it is the use of technology associated with the behaviours that recalibrates risks – both positive and negative. Sexting can potentially foster positive risk-taking experiences for young people and reduce the negative risks associated with physical sexual exploration. The online environment can give them a relatively safe (cyber) space within which to explore their sexuality. In this space they can safely adopt and explore certain subject positions, avoiding the dangers of sexual contact in the physical world.[8] As Marsha Levick and Riya Shah argue in their amicus brief to the Third Circuit Court of Appeals in the case of *Miller* v. *Mitchell*, adolescents develop and discover their identities by 'thinking and experimenting with new areas of sexuality' (Arcabascio 2009, p. 7). Brian Simpson (2013, p. 692) also suggests that mobile technologies may allow young people to free themselves from the traditional constraints imposed on their sexuality by adults and to have more freedom to construct their own paradigms of sexual life. Similarly, Emma Bond (2010, p. 590) notes that 'the mobile phone has become embedded in children's social worlds in later modernity' replacing the bike shed as the place where fumbling adventures into sexual and romantic relationships take place.

However, with these positive risks and pleasures also come negative risks and potential harms. Behaviour behind the bike shed is rarely seen by others, and certainly not by an uncontrolled number of people. In contrast, the nature of digital images means that once an image is sent a person also loses control over its dissemination and therefore risks that it will be shared more widely that the initial sender intended in the present and in the future. A person may therefore regret distributing a digital image, and this may lead to negative emotions and experiences – which for young people might include low self-esteem, school avoidance or depression (Parliament of Australia 2011, [4.60]). As already noted, our research suggests that the risk of wide dissemination of images is relatively low and that images tend not to be shared beyond the intended recipients. Further, it should be noted that even non-consensual sharing may not necessarily always be experienced as a negative risk and could be part of the attraction of sexting for some. Forwarded sexts may in some circumstances enhance the status of the forwarder and the subject of the image, despite the gendered double standards evident in attitudes towards sexting. More serious risks are involved in the ways that sexts can be used to bully, harass, and coerce a young person. Such practices, while cause for concern for policymakers, are not the common experience of sexting for those whom we surveyed. Our research and the work of others suggests that young people are aware of incidents of non-consensual sharing, cyberbullying, and harassment either in their immediate circles or via media reports, but that such incidents are not common. For example, as Sonia Livingstone and Peter Smith (2014, p. 635) note:

> Prevalence estimates vary according to definition and measurement, but do not appear to be rising substantially with increasing access to mobile and online technologies, possibly because these technologies pose no additional risk to offline behaviour, or because any risks are offset by a commensurate growth in safety awareness and initiatives.

There is thus a degree of overstating the negative risks associated with sexting, which may contribute to the panicked sense that sexting, new technologies, and cyberbullying are inextricably linked. As some research indicates, cyberbullying may often be a continuation of real-life bullying (Ringrose et al. 2012; 2013), and real-life bullying is more of a concern to young people than cyberbullying (Corby et al. 2014). None of this means that sexting is harmless; however, it is important to remember that it may be inaccurate to conceptualise sexting and cyberbullying and harassment as causally related or motivationally connected.

Most cases of sexting, according to our research, tend to be consensual and are motivated by fun and exploration of sexuality, rather than fear or coercion. There will, however, be cases of the latter or even cases where images are taken of a criminal offence, such as a sexual assault. Sexting has varied motivations, carrying varied pleasures and risks. As such, a single legislative or policy approach is inappropriate and unlikely to be effective. Pursuing the possibility of prosecution under child pornography laws is likely, in most cases, to be an overreaction that could cause disproportionate harm to a young person. Creating new offences to deal with sexting-type behaviours could also be harmful and lead to net-widening by drawing more young people into the criminal justice system (Paterson 2012; Hasinoff 2015). This is because, as noted above, at present police tend to divert young people from formal criminal proceedings unless the sexting involves coercion or exploitative behaviour. A new offence with a label that fits the behaviour involved in sexting and which carries a lower penalty than child pornography may then be seen by police as the appropriate response rather than diversion.

We would argue therefore that the best approach moving forward is to develop and use a range of legal, regulatory, and educational strategies to address the range of behaviours that make up sexting. Where sexting behaviours are part of a consensual exploration of sexuality or playfulness, there is little need for any legal intervention. Indeed, empowering young people through holistic sexual education strategies concerning how to deal ethically with behaviours that include sexting would likely be more productive. The World Health Organization's (2006) definition of what sexual health should be provides a useful blueprint for this:

> Sexual health is a state of physical, emotional, mental and social well-being in relation to sexuality; it is not merely the absence of disease, dysfunction or infirmity. Sexual health requires a positive and respectful approach to sexuality and sexual relationships, as well as the possibility of having pleasurable and safe sexual experiences, free of coercion, discrimination and violence. For sexual health to be attained and maintained, the sexual rights of all persons must be respected, protected and fulfilled.

Our research shows that a significant proportion of young people are sexting and therefore educational campaigns that focus on negative risks and adopt a message of abstinence do not reflect the experience of the majority of those who do sext, and are therefore unlikely to be effective. What is needed are educational campaigns that assist them to ethically negotiate sexting to maximise their pleasure and reduce the negative risks. Indeed, as Julia Hirst (2012) has argued, education campaigns that help young people understand sexual pleasure actually empower them to resist pressure and coercion – on the basis that this reduces the pleasures involved in the encounter. For Hirst (2012, p. 430)

> If pleasure is asserted as a right and continually reinforced through SRE [sex and relationships education] and issues of safeguarding, young people are more likely to feel vindicated in declining pressure to take part in sexual acts or related activities they are not comfortable with, might not enjoy, regret or evoke anxiety.

Indeed, young people themselves have continually called for positive messages to be included in sex education programmes (DiCenso et al. 2002).

Alongside such campaigns it would be appropriate to educate young people about already available civil law measures that may be available for redressing the non-consensual distribution of images. Such actions include breach of confidence, breach of copyright, defamation, nuisance, and sexual harassment. The advantage of civil law is that it can provide a range of measures (such as injunctions) and direct compensation to the affected party. The disadvantage is that it requires action to be brought by the affected party and it does not carry the condemnatory stigmatisation inherent in criminal law. Where a civil law response is inadequate and the behaviour associated with sexting is abusive or exploitative a criminal law response might be necessary; however, this does not mean that the response should be prosecution under child pornography laws. Such a response should only be available for the most exploitative forms of behaviour and/or where the behaviour is motivated either by maliciousness or by a conscious distribution to significantly older adults who may sexualise the image. To improve clarity, it would be better if sexting were not used to describe such behaviours. As the Victorian Law Reform Committee (2013, p. 73) has noted, 'child pornography laws were created for the purpose of protecting children from predatory sexual behaviour ... They were not designed to capture this type of behaviour'. This view is echoed by Elizabeth Ryan (2010, p. 371) who notes that when images are initially taken consensually and free from coercion, direct exploitation has not occurred and, although a young person may later regret taking the image, especially if he or she is faced with consequences if the image is shared, that experience is 'drastically different from victims of traditional child pornography'. Ryan argues that using such laws to criminalise conduct willingly engaged in by minors is contrary to legislative intent.

As our research has found, it will only be in the rarest of cases that young people will engage in sexting for such motivations and therefore mechanisms should be adopted which restrict the application of child pornography offences to only aggravated cases alongside the exploration of whether existing or new offences are appropriate. This could include steps, as taken in Victoria, to create a new offence targeting non-consensual distribution of an intimate image or threat to distribute, as well as developing defences to child pornography offences. On the other hand, where sexting is related to, or the product of, a criminal act (for instance, where the image is taken of a sexual assault), or is used as a tool of cyberbullying a legal (civil or criminal) response may be much more necessary.

Conclusion

The brief overview above of some of our research findings reveals that the child pornography framework that has dominated the legal regulatory approach to sexting is seriously misaligned with young people's practices, motivations, and experiences of sexting. Our research has aimed to give a voice to young people. This provides a strong counter discourse to the media and governmental discourses discussed in the first section of this chapter. We have established that despite perceptions that young people sext mainly due to pressure, the motivations for those who actually sext are mainly to have fun or to flirt, and to provide a sexy gift to a boyfriend or girlfriend. They are largely understood by young people themselves as not being exploitative. And even where pressure or coercion might take place this rarely accords with the motivations of adults who have a sexual interest in children.

Criminalising sexting excludes sexually active 16- and 17-year-olds (in some jurisdictions) from sharing visual representation of their sexual life, even with one another. Kath Albury et al. (2010) question whether this also excludes young people from the rights and forms of citizenship enjoyed by adults. This criminalisation effectively silences the voices of young people as participants in sexual behaviour (Karaian 2012). As Amy Kimpel notes, criminalising behaviour, which if undertaken by consenting adults would not even amount to an offence, could be harmful to the development of young people's intimate citizenship: 'Branding sexually active minors who seek to memorialize their private intimate conduct as criminal delegitimizes the relationships and sexual autonomy of adolescents' (2010, p. 332).

It follows then that there should be a range of legal and non-legal strategies to deal with young people who sext. While the criminal law may be an important tool when coercion and exploitation occur, and most particularly when adults are motivated to share pictures of children for the purposes of child pornography, it is not appropriate in cases where children consensually sext one another, nor where children forward images on without consent from those photographed but without being motivated by some form of bullying. A 'one size fits all' approach to legal responses to sexting clearly does not allow for the diversity of experiences to be captured and, as such, could draw young people into the criminalisation net who might otherwise be dealt with outside of the criminal justice system. A problem with retaining the possibility of prosecuting children for child pornography offences is that much depends on police discretion not to prosecute and this can mean that police selectively apply child pornography laws without clear public criteria guiding which cases are appropriate for prosecution. Given that such practices are unofficial, they are easily changed dependent on public attitudes, political opinion, operational constraints, and so forth. As Kelly Tallon et al. (2012, p. 19) note, 'while this unofficial policy may provide a useful rubric for police, and may have implicit public approval, it does not provide a great deal of certainty or transparency to young people'.

More appropriate in the vast majority of cases would be a suite of realistic education strategies aimed at developing sexual ethics for young people which listen to the voices of young people who have experiences with sexting. Indeed, such education may eliminate the need for criminal justice intervention in many cases. Where bullying or intimidation is involved, forms of caution or diversion should be applied. As we have shown, however, the behaviour is almost never motivated by child pornography per se when sexting occurs between young people. Sexting between young people is a practice that policymakers now have to realistically understand is here to stay. Strategies aimed at prohibiting the practice are likely to fail and, as such, we believe that a much more nuanced approach, both within and outside of the criminal justice system, is required in order to capture the range of experiences, motivations, and appropriate responses to young people's sexting.

Notes

1 Some researchers, for example Drotner (1992) and Draper (2012), argue that such reactions should be seen as a 'media panic', a specific form of moral panic. A media panic model sees that 'the media is both instigator and purveyor of the discussion' around new media and its effects on young people (Drotner 1999, p. 596). In this way, media reaction to the 'issue' sparks further reports in the media on the same phenomenon.
2 This term has entered the debate via commentators, such as Melinda Tankard-Reist (2008), who argue that images, symbols, and ideologies of pornography have become a normal part of popular culture and everyday life.
3 Cited from *60 Minutes* (2011) 'One click from disaster', www.dailymotion.com/video/x2xvuy3.
4 In all of these instances it is also an offence where the person is not under 18 but appears to be.
5 Eades was acquitted of this charge on the basis that there was 'no posing, no objects, no additional aspects of the photograph which are sexual in nature or suggestion' (at [33]). Since this decision the definition of child abuse material has been amended in New South Wales and extended to include material that depicts or describes the private parts (genital or anal area or breasts of a female) of a child in a way that a reasonable person would regard in the circumstances as being offensive (Crimes Act 1900 (NSW), section 91FB). It is therefore possible that under this definition Eades could have been convicted.
6 Examples include the states of Victoria and Tasmania. Alongside introducing defences to child pornography offences, Victoria has established a new offence to deal with the non-consensual distribution of an intimate image or the threat to distribute such an image and South Australia has an offence of distributing an 'invasive' image without consent. The Commonwealth Parliament is currently considering a new offence to cover using a carriage service to convey a private image. For discussion of the appropriateness of such specific offences in the context of sexting by young people see Crofts et al. 2015.
7 The draft survey underwent a significant consultation period. In particular we consulted with the youth advisory group for NSW Commission for Children and Young People.
8 This is not of course to deny that the online world can be used by others to exploit or 'groom' young people.

References

Albury, K., Funnell, N., and Noonan, E. 2010, 'The politics of sexting: young people, self-representation and citizenship', in K. McCallum (ed.), *Media, democracy and change: refereed proceedings of the Australian and New Zealand Communication Association Conference 2010*, viewed, 23 January 2017, www.anzca.net/documents/2010-conf-papers/466-the-politics-of-sexting-1/file.html.

Arcabascio, C. 2009, 'Sexting and teenagers: OMG R U going 2 jail?', *Richmond Journal of Law and Technology*, vol. 16, no. 3, pp. 1–43.

Ashworth, A. and Horder, J. 2013, *Principles of criminal law*, 7th edn, Oxford University Press, Oxford.

Attorney-General's Department (Cth) 2009, *Proposed reforms to Commonwealth child sex-related offences*, Australian Government, Canberra.

Bita, N. 2012, 'Sexting teens risk porn charge', *Courier Mail*, 1 October, viewed 12 December 2014, www.couriermail.com.au/news/national/sexting-teens-risk-porn-charge/news-story/4a5ffc5545de33b91d352d832cbe9a7e

Bond, E. 2010, 'The mobile phone = bike shed? Children, sex and mobile phones', *New Media and Society*, vol. 13, no. 4, pp. 587–604.

Burke, R. 2008, *Young people, crime and justice*, Willan, Devon.

Chibnall, S. 1977, *Law and order news: an analysis of crime reporting*, Tavistock, Abingdon.

Cohen, S. 1973, *Folk devils and moral panics*, Paladin, St Albans.

Corby, E.-K., Campbell, M., Spears, B., Slee, P., Butler, D., and Kift, S. 2014, 'Students' perceptions of their own victimization: a youth voice perspective', *Journal of School Violence*, vol. 15, no. 3, pp. 322–342.

Crofts, T., Lee, M., McGovern, A., and Milivojevic, S. 2015, *Sexting and young people*, Palgrave, London.

Crowe, D. 2009, 'Expert: penalty not appropriate', *Manningham Leader*, 22 July, p. 11.

DiCenso, A., Guyatt, G., Willan, A., and Griffith, L. 2002, 'Interventions to reduce unintended pregnancies among adolescents: systematic review of randomized controlled trials', *British Medical Journal*, vol. 324, no. 7351, pp. 1426–1430.

Draper, N. 2012, 'Is your teen at risk? Discourses of adolescent sexting in United States television news', *Journal of Children and Media*, vol. 6, no. 2, pp. 221–236.

Drotner, K. 1992, 'Modernity and media panics', in M. Skovmand and K. C. Schroder (eds), *Media cultures: reappraising transnational media*, Routledge, London and New York.

Drotner, K. 1999, 'Dangerous media? Panic discourses and dilemmas of modernity', *Paedagogica Historica: International Journal of the History of Education*, vol. 35, no. 3, pp. 593–619.

Feeney, K. 2013, 'Sexting children charged with porn offences', *Brisbane Times*, 25 June, viewed 12 December 2014, www.brisbanetimes.com.au/queensland/sexting-children-charged-with-porn-offences-20130625-2oub3.html.

Fineran, L. 2010, 'Flirty girls send the wrong message', *Gold Coast Bulletin*, 29 November, p. 5.

Gregg, N. 2009, 'Adult imagery sparks calls for stricter control', *Courier Mail*, 2 September, p. 9.

Hasinoff, A. 2013, 'Sexting as media production: rethinking social media and sexuality', *New Media Society*, vol. 15, no. 1, pp. 449–465.

Hasinoff, A. 2015, *Sexting panic: rethinking criminalization, privacy and consent*, University of Illinois Press, Urbana-Champaign.

Hirst, J. 2012, '"It's got to be about enjoying yourself": young people, sexual pleasure, and sex and relationships education', *Sex Education*, vol. 13, no. 4, pp. 423–436.

Karaian, L. 2012, 'Lolita speaks: "sexting", teenage girls and the law', *Crime, Media, Culture*, vol. 8, no. 1, pp. 57–73.

Kimpel, A. 2010, 'Using laws designed to protect as a weapon: prosecuting minors under child pornography laws', *New York University Review of Law and Social Change*, vol. 34, no. 2, pp. 299–338.

Langsted, O. 1994, 'Looking at quality from a child's perspective', in P. Moss and A. Pence (eds), *Valuing quality in early childhood services*, Paul Chapman, London, pp. 28–42.

Lee, M. and Crofts, T. 2015, 'Gender, pressure, coercion and pleasure: untangling motivations for sexting between young people', *British Journal of Criminology*, vol. 55, no. 3, pp. 454–473.

Lee, M., Crofts, T., Salter, M., Milivojevic, S., and McGovern, A. 2013, '"Let's get sexting": risk, power, sex and criminalisation in the moral domain', *International Journal for Crime, Justice and Social Democracy*, vol. 2, no. 1, pp. 35–49.

Livingstone, S. and Smith, P. K. 2014, 'Annual research review: harms experienced by child users of online and mobile technologies: the nature, prevalence and management of sexual and aggressive risks in the digital age', *Journal of Child Psychology and Psychiatry*, vol. 55, no. 6, pp. 635–654.

Makki, T. 2005, 'Foreword', in T. Krone, 'Does thinking make it so? Defining online child pornography possession offences', *Trends and Issues in Criminal Justice*, no. 299Australian Institute of Criminology, Sydney.

Mascheroni, G., Ponte, C., Garmendia, M., Garitaonandia, C., and Murru, M. 2010, 'Comparing media coverage of online risks for children in southern European countries: Italy, Portugal and Spain', *International Journal of Media and Cultural Politics*, vol. 6, no. 1, pp. 25–43.

Mather, A. 2009, 'Mobile menace Tassie children's high use sparks abuse fears', *The Mercury*, 23 November, p. 1.

Moran-Ellis, J. 2012, 'Sexting, intimacy and criminal acts: translating teenage sexualities', in P. Johnson and D. Dalton (eds), *Policing sex*, Routledge, London and New York, pp. 115–131.

Newton-Brown, C. 2013, 'One bad call shouldn't turn a kid into a criminal', *Herald Sun*, 13 December, p. 58.

Parliament of Australia, Joint Select Committee on Cyber-Safety2011, *High-wire act: cyber-safety and the young, interim report*, Commonwealth of Australia, Canberra.

Parliament of Victoria, Law Reform Committee 2013, *Inquiry into sexting: report of the Law Reform Committee for the Inquiry into Sexting*, Parliamentary Paper No. 230, Session 2010–2013, Victorian Government Printer, Melbourne.

Paterson, N. 2012, Acting Commander, Intelligence and Covert Support Department, Victoria police, evidence before the Inquiry into Sexting, Law Reform Committee of Victoria, 18 September.

Podlas, K. 2014, 'Media activity and impact', in T. C. Hiestand and W. J. Weins (eds), *Sexting and youth*, Carolina Academic Press, Durham, NC, pp. 123–151.

Ringrose, J., Gill, R., Livingstone, S., and Harvey, L. 2012, *A qualitative study of children, young people and 'sexting'*, NSPCC, London.

Ringrose, J., Harvey, L., Gill, R., and Livingstone, S. 2013, 'Teen girls, sexual double standards and "sexting": gendered value in digital image exchange', *Feminist Theory*, vol. 14, no. 3, pp. 305–323.

Ryan, E. 2010, 'Sexting: how the state can prevent a moment of indiscretion from leading to a lifetime of unintended consequences for minors and young adults', *Iowa Law Review*, vol. 96, no. 1, pp. 357–383.

Schmitz, S. and Siry, L. 2012, 'Teenage folly or child abuse? State responses to "sexting" by minors in the U.S. and Germany', *Policy and Internet*, vol. 3, no. 2, pp. 1–26.

Shouvlin, D. P. 1981, 'Preventing the sexual exploitation of children: a model act', *Wake Forest Law Review*, vol. 17, no. 4, pp. 535–560.

Simpson, B. 2013, 'Challenging childhood, challenging children: Children's rights and sexting', *Sexualities*, vol. 16, no. 5/6, pp. 690–709.

Slane, A. 2013, 'Sexting and the law in Canada', *Canadian Journal of Human Sexuality*, vol. 22, no. 3, pp. 117–122.

Slipper, P. 2004, *Parliamentary Debates*, House of Representatives, Commonwealth, Canberra, 4 August, 32035–32036.

Svanesson, D. 2011, '"Sexting" and the law – how Australia regulates electronic communication of non-professional sexual content', *Bond Law Review*, vol. 22, no. 2, pp. 41–57.

Tallon, K., Choi, A., Keeley, M., Elliott, J., and Maher, D. 2012, 'New voices/new laws: school-age young people in New South Wales speak out about the criminal laws that apply to their online behaviour', National Children's and Youth Law Centre and Legal Aid NSW, Sydney.

Tangen, R. 2008, 'Listening to children's voices in educational research: some theoretical and methodological problems', *European Journal of Special Needs Education*, vol. 23, no. 2, pp. 157–166.

Tankard-Reist, M. 2008, 'The pornification of girlhood', *Quadrant*, vol. 52, no. 7/8, pp. 10–16.

Taylor, I. 1999, *Crime in context: a critical criminology of market societies*, Polity, Cambridge.

Thill, C. 2015, 'Listening for policy change: how the voices of disabled people shaped Australia's National Disability Insurance', *Disability and Society*, vol. 30, no. 1, pp. 15–28.

Thompson, S. 2014, 'Sexting prosecutions: minors as a protected class from child pornography charges', *University of Michigan Journal of Law Reform Caveat*, vol. 48, no. 1–2, pp. 11–19.

United Nations Committee on the Rights of the Child 2007, *General comment no. 10: children's rights in juvenile justice*, 44th session, UN Doc. CRC/C/GC/10 (25 April).

Vanderbosch, H., Simulioniene, R., Marczak, M., Vermeulen, A., and Bonetti, L. 2013, 'The role of the media', in P. K. Smith and G. Steffgen (eds), *Cyberbullying through the new media: findings from an international network*, Psychology Press, Florence, pp. 99–118.

Victorian Law Reform Committee 2013, *Inquiry into sexting: report of the Law Reform Committee for the Inquiry into Sexting*, Parliamentary Paper no. 230, Session 2010–2013, Victorian Government Printer, Melbourne.

World Health Organization 2006, *Defining sexual health: report of a technical consultation on sexual health 28–31 January 2002*, Geneva.

Cases

DPP v. Eades (2009) NSWSC 1352
Miller v. Mitchell (2010) 09-2144 US
New York v. Ferber, (1982) 458 US 747, 759
Osborne v. Ohio (1990, 495 US 103)
R v. Schultz (2008) 450 AR 37
R v. Sharpe (2001) 1 SCR 45

7 Representations of sexting and sexual violence on legal dramas. Implications for teenagers' sexual citizenship

Emily Lockhart

Introduction

Often framed within a discourse of risk, the dominant message about teenage sexting seems to be a strategic effort to construct boundaries around who can and who cannot engage in the practice. Using a sexual citizenship framework, this chapter analyses how sexting has been used as a tool to keep certain subjects on the outskirts of full sexual citizenship. By employing a cultural studies of law approach, I will explain how popular television dramas that engage with topics involving teenagers, sexuality, technology, and the law have aided in the construction of 'deserving' and 'undeserving' sexual citizens. By deserving I mean deserving of the right to sexual agency and to protection from sexual violence. Tracing the ways in which 'the social life of law's texuality' (Coombe 2001, p. 55) takes form in popular legal representations of sexting and sexual violence among teens, this chapter will highlight examples of the porous relationship between law and popular culture (Sherwin 2008). It will examine storylines from 2009 to 2014 that centre on teenage sexuality, technology, and the law, to highlight their successes and failures in representing teenagers as sexual citizens.

Law in popular culture

A cultural studies of law focuses on meaning and materiality as these are produced across social sites, including popular culture. Rosemary Coombe (2001, p. 55) argues that 'a cultural studies of law should become more attentive to social fields of inscription' and notes that the emergence of identity-based scholarship and work on legal consciousness has allowed this to be done. It is important, according to Coombe (2001), to focus on sites where law is doing cultural work. For example, Richard Sherwin (2008, p. 106) states that cultural legal studies has branched out into the world of film, television, and other sources of popular culture in search of the constitutive elements of legal consciousness – to understand the role of popular cultural materials in shaping, disseminating, and absorbing legal meanings. Therefore, popular legal studies 'reflects a broader scholarly move to elucidate how meanings are made and conveyed in society' (Sherwin 2008, p. 109). According to Sherwin (2008, p. 97), visual mass media, especially television, has become the major source of worldly knowledge and common sense and is 'similarly changing the practice and consumption of law'. Television and film are the principal source of stories and storytelling styles in our time and they 'serve as the measure of reality as most people know it' (Sherwin 2008, p. 103). Shaping common sense, popular legal representations can help us gauge shifts in dominant discourses around teenage sexting and sexual violence.

Popular legal dramas confront viewers with questions about the relationship between youth sexuality, technology, and sexual violence, highlighting important political debates and timely cases that have captured public attention. The role of popular cultural representations of teenage sexual citizenship when considered in the context of their rights to consensual sexual self-expression (e.g. sexting) and their rights to guaranteed protection from sexual violence should they feel[1] that they did not consent to sexual acts should be investigated. Considering the social location of youth and the ways in which their lives are often shaped by digital culture, it is helpful to combine studies of law in popular culture and legal consciousness with ideas of sexual citizenship to understand how discourses about youth, sexuality, and technology have shifted since initial moral panics about teenage sexting and how these stories have been told on television.

Teenage sexual citizenship

Sexual citizenship is particularly interesting as a framework for examining, as Brenda Cossman (2007) does, the intersection between law and popular culture and what it reveals about the sexing, privatising, and self-disciplining of citizenship. Cossman (2007, p. 17) argues that 'law and popular culture are both discourses that produce social meaning and constitute subjects'. She considers the ways in which images, norms, and narratives of popular culture seep into legal discourse, and how legal discourse casts its shadow over popular culture (Cossman 2007, p. 18). Cossman pays particular attention to the ways in which citizenship borders are constructed through the creation of sexual subjects.

Sexual citizenship is a contested concept without any one agreed-upon definition and has been advanced in different ways to achieve different ends. It grew out of citizenship literature more generally as scholars were concerned with the lack of attention given to the politics of intimacy in everyday life (Weeks 1998). Sexual citizenship scholars argue that sex has long been implicated in citizenship in that broader conditions of belonging have been conditional on a set of sexual norms and practices (Weeks 1998; Cossman 2007). However, sexual citizenship emerged as a distinct paradigm for study in the late 1980s as an important notion for sociological analysis alongside feminist and queer theorists' critiques of the limitations of the liberal model of citizenship. Sexual citizenship offers a way of thinking about sexual rights as an important extension of T. H. Marshall's model of the three stages of citizenship (Richardson 2000). According to Jeffrey Weeks (1998, pp. 37–38):

> The idea of sexual or intimate citizenship is a sensitizing concept, which alerts us to new concerns, hitherto marginalized in public discourse: with the body, its possibilities, needs and pleasures; with new sexualized identities; and with the forces that inhibit their free, consensual development in a democratic polity committed to full and equal citizenship.

This concept is particularly useful as a way of understanding accelerating social change, the transformation of the social world, and new possibilities of sexual self and identity for young people. However, while there is a large body of literature exploring questions of sexual and intimate citizenship in the lives of adults, that which focuses on minors[2] is limited. This may be attributed to young people's contingent relationship to sexual citizenship, which, according to Kerry Robinson (2012, p. 258), is due to a strategic effort on the part of adults to maintain adult–child relations of power and the status quo in society.

This deliberate effort to keep teenagers from sexual citizenship is perhaps most obvious if we look at age of consent laws. In Canada, 'age of consent' or 'age of protection' is commonly understood to mean the age at which individuals can legally consent to sexual activity. In May 2001, the age of consent for sexual activity in Canada was raised from 14 to 16 years as a result of the Tracking Violent Crimes Act.[3] Scholars argue that the enactment of legislation to increase the age at which individuals can consent to sexual activity has been equated with a culture of fear about the sexual abuse of children by adults and ultimately a concern for the protection of their sexual innocence (see Sutherland 2003; Sutherland 2006; Carpenter et al. 2014). According to Belinda Carpenter et al. (2014, p. 24), 'Such an increase in the age of sexual responsibility demonstrates quite clearly that we are in the midst of a cultural paranoia about young people and sex.' Therefore, we continue to see socially constructed notions of *childhood innocence* and the *hypersexual teenager* serving as dominant narratives in the effort to keep teens on the outskirts of sexual citizenship.

The literature on age of sexual consent is also attentive to gendered forms of protection and violence, which is important when thinking about sexual citizenship. Carpenter et al. (2014, p. 25) argue that

> Although legislation is now gender neutral, traditional cultural scripts of male sexuality as active and pursuant, and female sexuality as passive and resistant, position sexual consent as a predominately feminine activity within heterosexuality, especially for young women around the age of consent and despite recent gains in 'girl power'.

According to Carpenter et al. (2014, p. 53), 'the sexual citizenship of young people is a more complex and nuanced relation than child sexual abuse narratives are currently able to articulate. In the shift to identify and protect some children from the harm of sexual abuse, all children, often up to the age of eighteen, are positioned as victims.' The sexual citizenship model recognises the importance of sexual autonomy and sexual self-efficacy of minors and encourages us to think critically about state control of childhood sexuality and the importance of sexual citizenship rights in those contexts.

Keeping this in mind, it is important not to lose sight of the legal definitions of consent that are aimed at protecting all Canadians from rape, including minors when they are incapable of giving informed and ongoing consent to sexual activity. This is outlined in the Canadian Criminal Code subsection 273.1(2). Therefore, when it comes to the rape of someone who is vomiting due to intoxication, which happened to Rehtaeh Parsons (discussed below; see Canning 2016), the legal response should be clear. However, the Parsons case is an example of what sociolegal scholars call 'law-in-the-books' versus 'law-in-action'. The case also highlights how narratives about 'risky adolescence' play a part in the inadequate formal and informal responses to sexual violence (including rape) *among* minors as well as the inappropriate policing of consensual teenage sexual expression (including sexting). Given the current political debates about the sexual citizenship rights of minors, including their right to engage in forms of sexual expression while also living without fear of sexual violence, it is important to investigate how these discourses operate.

Shifting sexual citizenship borders? Responses to and representations of teenage sexting

Legal, social, and educational responses to sexting have attracted scholarly attention since the so-called sexting epidemic captured public attention in 2008. Scholars have traced the developments of sexting legislation in the United States (Calvert 2009; Graw-Leary 2010; DeMitchell and Parker-Magagna 2011; Walters 2011; McLaughlin 2012; Kushner 2013; Hessick 2014) and Canada's increased prosecution of minors under child pornography laws (Bailey 2014; Karaian 2014). There is also a growing body of scholarship that addresses and often critiques the gendered nature of the moral panic over teenage sexting (Bailey and Hanna 2011; Hasinoff 2012; Karaian 2012; Renold and Ringrose 2011; Salter et al. 2012). Emma Renold and Jessica Ringrose (2011, p. 402) are critical of the 'sexting as risk' discourse that targets girls, insisting that the approach to sexting should be more cognisant of girls' feelings of pleasure and power in the context of 'their experiences of virtual and embodied networks colonized with real and symbolic (hetero)sexualized violence in their everyday lives'. Lara Karaian (2012) agrees, arguing that there is a need for more research and theory addressing how sexual pleasure exists alongside danger and risk, particularly for teenage girls. In other words, girls might be using sexting as a way to claim their sexual citizenship in societies that continue to deny them the same rights to sexual citizenship as heterosexual men and boys.

Moreover, scholars have challenged the tendency for the legal system to group all incidences of sexting into one category and have been exploring the different ways that teens engage in the sharing of intimate media. Keeping the sexual citizenship conversation in mind, scholars have argued that there is a significant difference between consensual sexting between consenting teens and non-consensual sharing of nude or semi-nude images for the purposes of harassment, belittlement, embarrassment, and so forth (Bailey and Hanna 2011). According to Ringrose et al. (2012), this shift in perspective highlights that abusive sexting emerges out of a larger context of ubiquitous gender- and sexuality-based victimisation. Lara Karaian and Katherine Van Meyl (2015, p. 21) argue that 'extant frameworks, which conflate consensual and non-consensual sexting and which equate both with negative risks that purportedly outweigh the value and benefits of the practice, rely on a calculus that is fundamentally flawed'. Therefore, the dominant opinion from critical scholars working on these issues is that responses to and representations of sexting should focus on those forms which are non-consensual, and not on those which are consensual expressions of sexuality (Bailey and Hanna 2011; Albury and Crawford 2012; Hasinoff 2013; Karaian and Van Meyl 2015).

Others have found that criminalising teenage sexting will have undue effects on already marginalised youth including low-income youth, youth of colour, and those who are members of the LGBTQ community. According to Amy Adele Hasinoff (2015) non-heterosexual and non-gender-confirming youths' sexual activities are already closely scrutinised. She argues:

> since any minor's relationship that violates local age-of-consent laws or that involves explicit pictures can be reported to police by disapproving family members, parents' and prosecutors' opinions of what constitutes acceptable teenage sexuality determine who is charged with these types of crimes.
>
> (Hasinoff 2015, p. 38)

Hasinoff also suggests that criminalising sexting may have serious impacts on low-income youth who are already heavily monitored by the state. She argues that 'since private counseling services are largely inaccessible to low-income families, these families tend to rely on or allow public justice systems to discipline and control their children, especially their daughters' (2015, p. 39). Upper and middle-class youth are more likely to receive reduced charges because officials feel that their parents have the resources to address their children's problems (Hasinoff 2015, p. 39). Moreover, Danielle Egan (2013, p. 81) explains that middle-class anxieties have been a longstanding part of '*Anglophone cultural fantasies, projections, and ideological formations about the eroticism, bodily comportment, and the taste of the poor and working class*' and that 'Constructing the working class, poor, colonial, and non-white immigrant as more bodily, bawdy, erotic, and wanton has a long history in the Anglophone cultural imagery' (p. 81). Against this, the white middle-class body has been represented with purity and the white middle-class child as innocent, pure, and part of the bright future of the class, race, and nation (Egan 2013). Analysing who and what gets defined as the problem is an important task in understanding how sexual citizenship borders are constructed for and between teenagers. Egan (2013, p. 103) argues that 'the entire edifice of class, gender, race, and heterosexuality assumed in the discourse on sexualization becomes fragile at best, if the girl child is a sexual subject from the start or, better yet, if all girls are conceptualized as complex sexual citizens'.

Despite the potential for an excessive impact that criminalising sexting may have on LGBTQ, low-income youth, and youth of colour, scholars have found that there is an overrepresentation of white, heterosexual, middle-class girls in media messaging and campaigns designed to educate about the dangers of the practice. According to Karaian (2012, p. 60) 'fueling the moral panic over sexting is an apparent desire to protect white, heterosexual, middle and upper class, "respectable" girls from both sexual predators and themselves'.

Finally, some scholars have argued that adult sexting is often normalised while teenage sexting is criminalised. Drawing on the work of Kath Albury and Kate Crawford (2012), Michael Salter et al. (2012, p. 303–304) argue

> the moral opprobrium that has greeted revelations of teenage sexting is further confounded by evidence that adults are much more enthusiastic sexters than minors, casting doubt on claims that the popularity of sexting among teenagers is a function of their psychological or neurological immaturity. This highlights the double standard evident in moral panics about teenage sexting that excludes young people from forms of sexual citizenship and representation exercised by adults.

In fact, Karaian and Van Meyl (2015, p. 31), highlight the ways in which adult sexting is encouraged by mainstream print media and online sources. Through a language of protection, teenage sexting is relegated to a category of risky behaviour regardless of its potentially consensual and expressive nature, while heterosexual monogamous adults are encouraged to use sexting as a tool to build healthy relationships (see Coté 2011; Roberts 2015).

Representing legal norms about teenage sexting and sexual violence on television

According to Richard Sherwin (2008, p. 109) 'Changes in dominant storytelling practices portend changes of mind and culture'. He notes:

> The study of law in popular culture embraces a multidisciplinary analysis of the manifold ways in which the interpretation of law and popular culture constitutes legal consciousness. Along the way, it uncovers sites of

resistance and creative affirmation. It also encounters new forms of dominance.

(2008, p. 109)

In other words, by taking a closer look at law in popular culture we may be able to understand who gets to assign meaning to public symbols of law and the potential legal and political effects that this might have. Through an analysis of television dramas that turned topical political and legal issues into entertainment, I am particularly interested in whether popular culture followed suit with increased feminist and activist discourses around teenage agency, consensual sexting, and the meaning of informed consent to sex. These counter hegemonic representations continue to stress the importance of the recognition and validation of teenage sexual citizenship.

The legal responses to teen sexting outlined in the scholarship have been used as storylines about the dangers of teenage sexuality and technology. For example, in 2009, shortly after several states updated their laws to account for teen sexting, *Law and Order: SVU* aired an episode entitled 'Crush' which presented a gendered narrative about the risk of sexting. The blame was entirely on a teenage girl who sent a semi-nude photo of herself to her boyfriend who, in turn, forwarded the photo without her consent. The writers remove the girl's agency completely by scripting her experience of sexting as something that she did under pressure from an abusive boyfriend as if that is the only way that a teen girl would engage in the practice. The storyline largely ignores the gender violence that led to the girl's hospitalisation and instead focuses exclusively on her role in her own demise for transgressing the age and gendered boundaries of sexual citizenship.

The normalisation of adult sexting in television episodes focused on the dangers of teenage sexting is a good example of the sexual citizenship boundaries for adults and teens around sexting explained by Karaian and Van Meyl (2015). In 'Crush', the adult detectives joke about the idea of sexting each other. This boundary-setting narrative is also presented on a 2010 episode of *Drop Dead Diva* entitled 'Bad Girls'. The main character of this legal comedy is Jane, a lawyer who overcomes low self-esteem in many of the episodes. In this particular episode she is competing for a man by sending 'spicy text messages' while, at the same time, representing a teenage girl who is the victim of slut-shaming after an ex-boyfriend non-consensually forwarded a semi-nude photo of her to others. The two storylines scripted side by side highlight the different disciplinary codes for adults and minors. While the teenage girl is slut-shamed and facing child pornography charges for consensually sharing an intimate photo with a boyfriend, Jane is encouraged to use the same technique to win over a man.

There is another issue of representation to consider in both episodes. While 'Crush' only depicts the experience of a white, middle-class, heterosexual girl, 'Bad Girls' includes the experiences of teens of colour. However, they are scripted as secondary characters who are too intimidated to come forward with their own experiences of harassment. This representation is in line with Karaian's (2012) argument that white, middle-class, heterosexual girls are more often represented as the victims of the potential harms of sexting.

In line with scholarly work that criticises the homogeneous understanding of teenage sexting and the unfair impact that the criminalisation of the practice has on girls who engage in consensual expressions of sexuality, a 2011 episode of *The Secret Life of the American Teenager* called '4–1–1' demonstrated a turn of direction in the targets of the 'sexting as risk' message. The focus, unlike in 'Crush' and 'Bad Girls' is entirely on Ethan, a hormone-driven, girl-obsessed, parentless, juvenile delinquent teenage boy who has spent most of his life in and out of foster care. Although white and heterosexual, the writers have portrayed the sexter as a horny teenage boy with a history of theft and a lack of parental guidance or a father-like role model. This episode helps put the gendered representation into perspective. While girls are represented as sexually deviant, boys are represented as deviant in other ways, which is used as justification for their sexting behaviours. According to Karaian and Van Meyl (2015, p. 31), concerns about boys who sext centre around risks posed to their futures should they be imprisoned as distributors of child pornography, while concerns about girls focus on the potential damage to their sexual reputations.

When sexual violence takes a backseat in storylines focused on the 'dangers of technology'

While the scholarly focus to date has been on the distinction between consensual and non-consensual sexting and the gendered regulation of the practice, there has been little work done on instances where visual evidence of sexual assault have been erroneously placed under the 'sexting' umbrella and used to highlight the dangers of technology for teens. This is exactly what continues to happen with the Rehtaeh Parsons case.[4]

On 4 April 2013, after months of being shamed by her peers for a much-shared photograph depicting her rape, 17-year-old Rehtaeh Parsons ended her life. Rather than a sexual assault case, however, Parsons' death has been transformed into a cautionary tale about the harms of sexting and cyberbullying and has become a backdrop case for Canadian anti-sexting and cyberbullying platforms. Soon after Parsons' death the government of Nova Scotia launched a Cyber-safety Act and a CyberSCAN Unit to investigate cyberbullying cases.

The federal government responded by introducing Bill C-13 (Protecting Canadians from Online Crime Act) which was an act to amend the Criminal Code by adding section 162.1 which addresses the non-consensual sharing of intimate images. In its transformation from a story about sexual assault to becoming the backdrop case for state cyberbullying platforms, it has become the case to be referenced in Canadian courtrooms dealing with teenagers and the production and distribution of sexually explicit photographs and has changed the way law enforcement in Nova Scotia approach cases involving the non-consensual sharing of sexual images among teens, often improperly categorised as 'sexting' cases.[5]

Moreover, while Rehtaeh's parents have been front-runners speaking out against sexual assault and gender-based violence, the state responses to the case remain largely focused on addressing the dangers of cyberbullying. This is not to say that the cyber harassment that Parsons experienced played a harmless role. It is very clear that it had seriously damaging effects on her mental health and was a contributing factor in her death. However, we should not forget that what happened to Parsons was rape and she was let down by many systems supposed to protect her. Referring to the Parsons case, Beth Lyons (2013) argues

> We should be discussing how tragedies like this are part of a broader context of oppression of women that extends beyond peer conflicts amongst youth – a context that young women aren't going to simply age out of. If we want to prevent future tragedies like Parsons', we must insist on telling her story truthfully and explicitly link it to the broader context of violence against and oppression of women that it occurred within. If we allow the narrative of this story, and the reporting of sexual violence amongst youth in general, to remain focused on bullying and sexting, we are contributing to the ongoing minimizing, dismissing, and normalizing of violence against women.

The complete failure by police to respond to an issue of sexual assault and the subsequent state efforts to remedy the issue by focusing exclusively on questions about the dangers of technology must have effects on the way young people understand their own sexual agency and legal responses to sexual violence. Parsons' story is not unique and shares similarities with other cases that occurred shortly before in 2012. These include the rape of Audrie Pott which was labelled a 'cyberbullying suicide' by the *New York Daily News* (see Stebner 2013), the case of Savannah Dietrich where she was charged for tweeting the names of her sexual abusers (see Pesta 2012), and the Steubenville high school rape case where a teenage girl was sexually assaulted, filmed, and photographed by high school football players (see D. Kushner 2013). The photographs were later shared with friends and hactivist group Anonymous leaked a video of members of the football team joking about the rape while it was taking place.

It is important to think about how meaning is infused through representations of the intersection of teenage sex and technology for the ways that they engage with questions of sexual citizenship including the right to sexual agency as well as protection from sexual abuse if individuals feel that they have been violated. While it is not enough to engage with two television examples and draw any widespread conclusions, the purpose of the following analysis of law in popular culture is to demonstrate how certain texts represent different conceptions of gender, sexuality, responsibility, violence, and technology which is helpful when thinking about the impact that popular culture may have on teenagers' and adults' legal consciousness.

The Good Wife – *'Rape: A Modern Perspective'*

The episode of *The Good Wife* entitled 'Rape: A Modern Perspective' (2013) seems to draw together themes and details from the Savannah Dietrich, Rehtaeh Parsons, Audrie Pott, and Steubenville rape cases to tell a story about the complexities of teenage sexual violence in the age of social media.

Just like the case of Dietrich, in this episode Rainey, a 17-year old girl, is being charged for violating a gag order by tweeting the name of her rapist, Todd Bratcher. Her character is scripted to exercise agency in many scenes. For example, when asked by the judge if she wrote the tweet she goes against her lawyers' Alicia and Will's advice to exercise her Fifth Amendment rights by saying 'Todd raped me, so I wrote that.' Then when the court requests that she apologise for the tweet she states, 'If I do that, what's out there is not Todd Bratcher is a rapist, what's out there is that I'm sorry for calling Todd Bratcher a rapist. I'm sorry, I'm scared to be in here [jail] but I can't live with myself apologising for saying something that is true.' It is this determination that inspires Rainey's lawyers to continue digging into the case to find a way to get justice for Rainey.

The lawyers are joined by 'Anonymous' in this fight for justice. Shortly before the episode was aired, Anonymous captured widespread media attention for their involvement in the Dietrich, Parsons, and Steubenville cases. The storyline presented in 'Rape: A Modern Perspective' most closely resembles the way that Anonymous was involved in the Steubenville case. In the episode, Alicia's son receives an Anonymous text with a video of teenage boys joking about Rainey's rape which included details about the assault.[6] The boys in the video revealed that Bratcher had penetrated Rainey's vagina with a hairbrush.

Bratcher claims that he and Rainey had consensual sex and that she does not remember the details of the night because it was spring break and she was drunk. Relying on other rape myths and attempting to discredit the victim, Bratcher claims that Rainey was unhappy about her decision to hook up with him so lied about the sex being non-consensual, after the fact. In cross-examination, Rainey's lawyer asks Bratcher 'You did not take advantage of Rainey's intoxicated state by having sex with her while she was unconscious? You did not insert a hairbrush into her vagina? And you did not make fun of these claims in your deposition?' With this line of questioning they win the right to show the video of the boys joking about the rape with the hope that the video will convince the jury that Rainey had the right to release Bratcher's name over Twitter because the claim that he raped her was true.

In the next court appearance members of Anonymous are in the courtroom and give Will and Alicia information to help them win the case – a paper written by the doctor testifying that the bruises on Rainey's body were caused by gymnastics not rape. Alicia asserts that the doctor has theories that women cannot really be raped. She argues, 'The defence's expert's attitude towards rape is directly relevant to his testimony on rape.' This scene is clearly scripted in a feminist dialogue that is critical of rape myths that often influence legal decision-making.

In the next court scene, members of Anonymous wearing Guy Fawkes masks stand up in court and chant 'Justice for Rainey, justice now'. They then release a public broadcast similar to that released in the Dietrich, Steubenville, and Parsons cases. The judge calls a mistrial, linking Anonymous to the prosecution, so Kalinda Sharma, the detective for the law firm, finds another way to get Bratcher's confession. She obtains the police video recording of Bratcher confessing to raping Rainey, where when asked if Rainey said yes to sex, Bratcher responds 'I guess not'. Will presents the video in court stating, 'Rainey is being imprisoned for speaking the truth … and that is wrong, and this video proves it.' This move ultimately wins the case and Rainey is released from jail.

Overall, this episode does show victim agency and is written, for the most part, according to the increased feminist discourse about the importance of informed and ongoing consent. However, it does not get to the discussion of consent until the last three minutes. The focus is predominately on the dangers of technology, given that it draws on cases where this danger is emphasised, including one where the victim of rape is prosecuted for identifying her rapists on social media. The legal focus is entirely on getting Rainey off the hook for speaking out and not on prosecuting a rapist.

Scandal's 'Like Father, Like Daughter' (2014)

The title of this episode of *Scandal* is evidence of the writers' attempt to script something in line with feminist discourse that suggests that women and girls have sexualities and that it is not so strange to think that they would want to explore them as white, heterosexual men have always had the freedom to do.

The scene opens with Karen Grant, the US president's teenage daughter, throwing up over the edge of a bed in her underwear at a rave that she got to after sneaking out past her security detail and hijacking her friend's father's private jet. Scared, drunk, and high on both marijuana and some form of intravenous drug, Karen calls Olivia Pope, the show's lead female character, to help her get out of the situation. The first thing Karen says to Olivia is 'Don't tell my parents.' Of course, Olivia does tell Karen's parents.

Fitzgerald Grant, the President, is at first very angry but then, after realising that his daughter is under the influence of drugs and alcohol, asks his daughter calmly if she was raped. Here the writers might be letting the viewers know that consent cannot be obtained if someone is under the influence of drugs and/or alcohol, but they do not make that very clear. Karen then shows sexual agency when she says to her father 'Dad. I cut class. I ran away from my secret service goons. I helped some girl I barely know jack her father's private jet to go to a party. I got drunk. I smoked weed. I shot up something awesome. And yet the only way that you think I could have sex with two guys is if I were raped?'

This statement demonstrates a move towards recognition of both female and teenage sexual agency and the ability and right to decide who and how many people they have sex with. In doing so, however, it glosses over the fact that Karen did not consent to being filmed. The writers are attempting to represent a fuzzy legal line here, but I am concerned that their attempts could confuse teenagers who, unlike Karen, did not want to have sex or be filmed, by implying that consent can be given by someone who is inebriated, which is not the case in many jurisdictions. Although Karen does not imply that she gave continuous consent during sex, she questions why her father would jump to the conclusion that she was raped even though there was a strong feminist discourse after multiple widely covered teenage rape cases in the US and Canada about what legally constitutes consent. Nonetheless, the writers miss an opportunity to explain this. Informed and ongoing consent therefore is not at the forefront of this episode and it should be. The sex tape is presented as one of the many consequences of teenage sex. It is presented as an assumed risk and a penalty for transgressing the boundaries of sexual citizenship.

Conclusion

While trying to show teenage agency and deal with the dangers of technology, 'Rape: A Modern Perspective' and 'Like Father, Like Daughter' make consent and the underlying issue of rape secondary considerations. Therefore, while there is concrete evidence that academics are challenging the 'sexting as risk' discourse and arguing that dominant representations of teenage sexting have negative impacts on their sexual citizenship, my analysis of television legal dramas shows that primary storylines continue to emphasise the dangers of technology and only marginally present teenagers as sexual citizens by scripting them to exercise increased agency but not emphasising the importance of their right to protection from violence within their peer groups. According to a popular legal studies understanding of the role of television as an important site where legal discourse filters through to society, it is more likely that teens and the adults in their lives (i.e. parents and teachers) will be reached by popular culture than by academic literature. With this in mind, it is important that the message that they receive does not downplay the seriousness of sexual violence, confuse the meaning of informed consent, and discourage victims from accessing support services.

Notes

1 I note that I use the term 'feel' here to recognise that when talking about alcohol and consent I want to prioritise the importance of agency and not allow legal

discourse exclusive reign to define how we can talk about sex and desire. As Andrew Archard (2007, p. 212) argues, 'a concern to defend and protect persons against their ill treatment should not be pursued at the expense of their ability to make their own choices'. This is particularly complicated in the case of minors who, historically, have been kept outside the boundaries of sexual citizenship in an effort to protect them. A sexual citizenship approach wants to ensure minors are protected from sexual violence but recognises that they are capable of making their own decisions.

2 For the purpose of this chapter, I refer to 'minors' as those under the legal age of sexual consent. This includes the legal age at which persons can consent to sending digitally transmitted sexual images. In Canada this age is 16, however, police have not prosecuted minors for consensual sexting. In other contexts, including many states in the US, minors have been prosecuted for both consensual sexting and the non-consensual sharing of intimate images via digital devices (Calvert 2009; Graw-Leary 2010; DeMitchell and Parker-Magagna 2011; Walters 2011; McLaughlin 2012; A. Kushner 2013; Hessick 2014).

3 The age of consent in Canada is 18 in contexts involving exploitation, including prostitution, pornography, or when a person in a relationship of trust, authority, or dependency commits the sexual acts. Additionally, there are close-in-age exceptions for 14–15-year-olds when the sexual partner is less than five years older and there is no relationship of trust, dependency, or authority. This exception also applies to 12- and 13-year-olds in that they can consent to sexual activity with a person who is less than two years older and not in a position of trust, dependency, or authority. Further, the age of consent for anal sex is 18 and scholars have linked this to law's role in producing heteronormativity.

4 For example, Chris Hansen, a spokeswoman for the Public Prosecution Service in Nova Scotia explained that there was no policy on 'sexting' prior to Parsons' death. According to Hansen, 'the sexting policy was the first such policy we ever had. There was nothing before that. The Parsons case identified a gap we had in our policy manual and we filled that gap.' Further, a recent case in Bridgewater Nova Scotia involving the non-consensual distribution of sexual images has been investigated and police say it was handled differently from previous cases because of the Rehtaeh Parsons case and the new Bill C-13.

5 In *R. v. C.N.T* (2015) the judge stated: 'It is important to note the date of these offences: 9 November 2014. That is over a year and a half since the tragic death of Rehtaeh Parsons. In that intervening time, this province and this country underwent a transformational shift in recognizing the vulnerability of young people – particularly females – to trauma, psychological harm, serial victimization and predation as a result of people (including – perhaps particularly including – age peers) doing precisely what C.N.T. did to his victims. Legislative action was swift. *Protecting Canadians from Online Crime Act* criminalized the non-consensual sharing of intimate photos. Nova Scotia enacted the Cyber-safety Act, permitting the issuance of protection orders to stop cyberbullying' (*R. v. C.N.T.*, 2015 NSPC 43) (CanLII).

6 Anonymous leaked a twelve-minute video (which is available to the public via YouTube) of Steubenville high school boys joking about the rape of a teenage girl.

References

Albury, K. and Crawford, K. 2012, 'Sexting, consent, and young people's ethics: beyond Megan's Story', *Continuum: Journal of Media and Cultural Studies*, vol. 26, no. 3, pp. 463–473.

Archard, A. 2007, 'Book reviews', *Journal of Applied Philosophy*, vol. 24, no. 2, pp. 209–221.

Bailey, J. 2014, *Submission to the House of Commons Standing Committee on Justice and Human Rights Regarding Bill C-13*, Ottawa, Ontario.

Bailey, J. and Hanna, M. 2011, 'The gendered dimensions of sexting: assessing the applicability of Canada's child pornography provision', *Canadian Journal of Women and the Law*, vol. 23, no. 2, pp. 405–441.

Calvert, C. 2009, 'Sex, cell phone, privacy, and the First Amendment: when children become child pornographers and the Lolita effect undermines the law', *Common Law Conspectus*, vol. 18, no. 1, pp. 1–65

Canning, G. 2016, 'My years without Rehtaeh taught me that kids need to know consent', *Huffington Post*, 6 June, viewed 23 January 2017, www.huffingtonpost.ca/glen-canning/rehtaeh-parsons-consent-dad_b_9623792.html.

Carpenter, B., O'Brien, E., Hayes, S. and Death, J. 2014, 'Harm, responsibility, age and consent', *New Criminal Law Review*, vol. 17, no. 1, pp. 23–54.

CityNews 2015, 'Rehtaeh Parsons' father on the dangers of sexting', 23 February, viewed 23 January 2017, www.citynews.ca/video/2015/02/23/rehtaeh-parsons-father-on-the-dangers-of-sexting.

Coombe, R. 2001, 'A cultural studies of law?', in T. Miller (ed.), *A companion to cultural studies*, Blackwell, Cambridge, pp. 36–62.

Cossman, B. 2007, *Sexual citizens: the legal and cultural regulation of sex and belonging*, Stanford University Press, Stanford, CA.

Coté, E. 2011, 'Relationship news: 10 ways to become a sexting pro', *Elle Canada*, 4 October, viewed 23 January 2017, www.ellecanada.com/life-and-love/article/relationship-news-10-ways-to-become-a-sexting-pro#.Vyd973QrLfY.

DeMitchell, T. and Parker-Magagna, M. 2011, 'Student victims or student criminals? The bookends of sexting in a cyber world', *Cardoza Public Law, Policy and Ethics Journal*, vol. 10, no. 1, pp. 1–41.

Egan, D. 2013, *Becoming sexual: a critical appraisal of the sexualization of girls*, Wiley, Cambridge and Malden, MA.

Graw-Leary, M. 2010, 'Sexting or self-produced child pornography? The dialogue continues – structured prosecutorial discretion within a multidisciplinary response', *Virginia Journal of Social Policy and the Law*, vol. 17, no. 3, pp. 486–566.

Hasinoff, A. A. 2012, 'Sexting as media production: rethinking social media and sexuality', *New Media and Society*, vol. 15, no. 4, pp. 449–465.

Hasinoff, A. A. 2013, 'Watching slut-shaming', 12 April, viewed 23 January 2017, https://amyhasinoff.wordpress.com/2013/04.

Hasinoff, A. A. 2015, *Sexting panic: rethinking criminalization, privacy and consent*, University of Illinois Press, Urbana-Champaign.

Hessick, C. 2014, 'The limits of child pornography', *Indiana Law Journal*, vol. 89, no. 4, pp. 1437–1484.

Karaian, L. 2012, 'Lolita speaks: "sexting", teenage girls and the law', *Crime, Media, Culture*, vol. 8, no. 1, pp. 57–73.

Karaian, L. 2013, 'Policing "sexting": responsibilization, respectability and sexual subjectivity in child protection/crime prevention responses to teenagers' digital sexual expression', *Theoretical Criminology*, vol. 18, no. 3, pp. 282–299.

Karaian, L. 2016, 'Data doubles and pure virtu(e)ality: selfies, scopophilia, and "surveillance porn"', in E. van der Meulen and R. Heynen (eds), *Expanding the gaze: gender and the politics of surveillance*, University of Toronto Press, Toronto, Buffalo, and London, pp. 35–55.

Karaian, L. and Van Meyl, K. 2015, 'Reframing risque/risky: queer temporalities, teenage sexting and freedom of expression', *Laws*, vol. 4, no. 1, pp. 18–36.

Kushner, A. 2013, 'The need for sexting law reform: appropriate punishments for teenage behaviors', *University of Pennsylvania Journal of Law and Social Change*, vol. 16, no. 3, pp. 281–302.

Kushner, D. 2013, 'Anonymous vs. Steubenville', *Rolling Stone*, 27 November, viewed 23 January 2017, www.rollingstone.com/culture/news/anonymous-vs-steubenville-20131127.

Lyons, B. 2013, 'On calling things by name: rape, exploitation and victim-blaming aren't bullying', *Shameless Magazine*, 11 April, viewed 23 January 2017, http://shamelessmag.com/blog/entry/on-calling-things-by-name-rape-exploitation-and-v.

McLaughlin, J. 2012, 'Exploring the First Amendment rights of teens in relationship to sexting and censorship', *University of Michigan Journal of Law Reform*, vol. 45, no. 2, pp. 315–350.

Marshall, T. H. 1950, *Citizenship and social class and other essays*, Cambridge University Press, Cambridge.

Pesta, A. 2012, 'Thanks for ruining my life', *Europe Newsweek*, 12 October, viewed 23 January 2017, http://europe.newsweek.com/thanks-ruining-my-life-63423?rm=eu.

Renold, E. and Ringrose, J. 2011, 'Schizoid subjectivities? Re-theorizing girls' sexual cultures in an era of "sexualization"', *Journal of Sociology*, vol. 47, no. 4, pp. 389–409.

Richardson, D. 2000, 'Constructing sexual citizenship: theorizing sexual rights', *Critical Social Policy*, vol. 20, no. 1, pp. 105–135.

Ringrose, J. 2011, 'Are you sexy, flirty, or a slut? Exploring "sexualisation" and how teen girls perform/negotiate digital sexual identity on social networking sites', in R. Gill and C. Scharff (eds), *New femininities: postfeminism, neoliberalism and subjectivity*, Palgrave, Basingstoke and New York, pp. 99–116.

Ringrose, J., Gill, R., Livingstone, S., and Harvey, L. 2012, *A qualitative study of children, young people and 'sexting'*, NSPCC, London.

Ringrose, J., Harvey, L., Gill, R., and Livingstone, S. 2013, 'Teen girls, sexual double standards and "sexting": gendered value in digital image exchange', *Feminist Theory*, vol. 14, no. 3, pp. 305–323.

Robinson, K. 2012, '"Difficult citizenship": the precarious relationships between childhood, sexuality and access to knowledge', *Sexualities*, vol. 15, no. 3/4, pp. 257–276.

Roberts, S. 2015, 'How sexting could actually save your relationship', *The Sun*, 15 October, viewed 23 January 2017, www.thesun.co.uk/sol/homepage/features/6693159/Can-sexting-save-your-relationship.html.

Salter, M., Crofts, T., and Lee, M. 2012, 'Beyond criminalisation and responsibilisation: sexting, gender and young people', *Current Issues in Criminal Justice*, vol. 24, no. 3, pp. 301–316.

Sherwin, R. 2008, 'Law in popular culture', in A. Sarat (ed.), *The Blackwell companion to law and society*, Wiley-Blackwell, Oxford, pp. 95–112.

Stebner, B. 2013, 'Audrie Pott suicide', *New York Daily News*, 18 September, viewed 23 January 2017, www.nydailynews.com/news/national/new-details-revealed-audrie-pott-cyber-bullying-suicide-article-1.1459904.

Taber, J. 2014, 'Defendants allege abuse of process in Parsons case over "sexting policy"', *Globe and Mail*, 23 April, viewed *23 January 2017*, www.theglobeandmail.com/news/national/lawyer-for-accused-in-parsons-case-takes-aim-at-ns-sexting-policy/article18122923.

Waites, M. 2005, *The age of consent: young people, sexuality, and citizenship*, Palgrave Macmillan, Basingstoke.

Walters, L. 2011, 'How to fix the sexting problem: An analysis of the legal and policy considerations for sexting legislation', *First Amendment Law Review*, vol. 9, no. 1, pp. 98–148.

Weeks, J. 1998, 'The sexual citizen', *Theory, Culture and Society*, vol. 15, no. 3–4, pp. 35–52.

Part III
Ethnographies of young people's education

8 MOOCs and widening participation in higher education

From competency to capability in the evaluation of educational technologies

Remy Yi Siang Low

Introduction

> A good educational system should have three purposes: it should provide all who want to learn with access to available resources at any time in their lives; empower all who want to share what they know to find those who want to learn it from them; and, finally, furnish all who want to present an issue to the public with the opportunity to make their challenge known.
>
> (Illich 1971 p. 44)

The *New York Times* declared 2012 to be the 'Year of the MOOC'. MOOCs is an acronym for Massive Open Online Courses. Simply defined, MOOCs are 'massive' because they are designed to enrol tens of thousands of learners; 'open' because, at least in theory, anyone with an Internet connection can enrol in the course for free without prerequisites; 'online' because the content is delivered in modules through online video lectures and interaction takes place in web discussion groups; and, finally, they are 'courses' because they have specific start and end dates, student assessments, online tests and quizzes, and proctored exams. Upon completion, some may offer a 'verified certificate' of completion. A key claim of MOOCs providers and advocates is that through this innovative format, high quality education can and should be made available to everyone (e.g. see Agarwal in Parr 2013).

By the end of 2013, the largest MOOC provider Coursera had over 4 million enrolments while its closest competitor, edX, had over one million users (Anders 2013; Conway 2013). At its peak in the 2012–2013 period, there were almost daily reports in the print and online media about some aspect of MOOCs, with the foci of discussion mostly centred on their astronomical enrolment numbers or their extremely high drop-out rates of up to 90 per cent ('The attack of the MOOCs' 2013). There are also daily commentaries on whether MOOCs represent a mere ripple in the world of higher education or a tsunami that will bring down the walls of the traditional university, and whether this will be for the better or worse. In focusing on how the effects of such new educational technologies may be measured and evaluated, however, these types of commentary often leave unexplored the more immediately empirical issue of how people actually experience and interact with such technologies (Jackson 2002).

In the midst of this media maelstrom, a key issue about MOOCs can perhaps be encapsulated in the question posed by Australian Broadcasting Corporation Radio National host Anthony Funnell on 8 April 2013: are they 'the future of education or mere marketing?'. From the perspective of those seeking to widen the participation of historically underrepresented populations in higher education, this question assumes additional gravity and urgency owing to the promise that MOOCs appear to offer in opening up higher education to those for whom it appears distant. If MOOCs are to be the future of education, then its potential to be a resource for those otherwise excluded from higher education will almost certainly be one of its key selling points. However, if MOOCs are to be more than mere marketing exercises for higher education, then the question of what real-life opportunities they offer to participants needs to be addressed.

This chapter contributes to the discussion around MOOCs particularly, and educational technologies more broadly, by centring on the profiles of five young people from the Mount Druitt region in Sydney who are at different stages of their educational and work lives, and who have been linked to MOOCs through a project for widening participation in higher education – the Mount Druitt University Hub (MDUH). I begin by sketching an overview of Mount Druitt as a region and why it has been identified by the institutional partners of the MDUH project as a site of intervention. Following this, I will offer brief profiles of the five MOOCs participants' experiences, focusing specifically on the MOOCs they undertook, their experiences of taking them, and what they hoped to achieve from their undertakings. Methodologically, I follow Michael Jackson's (2002, p. 334) existential–phenomenological approach in 'bracketing out, or setting aside, questions concerning the large-scale social impact of new technologies in order to explore the intersubjective dynamics of the human encounter with technology'. I will then challenge us to think of the forms of recognition that are appropriate for those who have undertaken MOOCs and, with reference to the experiences of participants from Mount Druitt, what implications such recognition might have on those studying and working in areas where higher education opportunities have been scarce. I do this by drawing broadly on a framework known as the 'capability approach' (CA) advanced by the economist and Nobel laureate Amartya Sen (1999) and the US legal philosopher Martha Nussbaum (2011). The CA proposes that we should measure human development not only by the quantity of wealth or skills accumulated by people, but also by the life opportunities that they are able to access with those resources. MOOCs, I argue, may present a promising platform for offering higher education options and increasing the capabilities of people who live and work in a region like Mount Druitt. However, its promise can only be actualised if the work and achievements of MOOCs participants from such regions can achieve adequate recognition from authorities like higher education institutions, government agencies, and employers, who function as the institutional gatekeepers of opportunity (Bourdieu 1988, 1994; Teese and Polesel 2003).

Context

Mount Druitt is a suburb located in the City of Blacktown 43km west of the Sydney Central Business District and encompasses smaller suburbs such as Bidwill, Blackett, Whalan, Tregear, Lethbridge Park, and Emerton. It boasts extraordinary levels of cultural diversity, with 52.2 per cent of the population born outside Australia and nearly 60 per cent of residents speaking a language other than English at home (Australian Bureau of Statistics 2011). However, Mount Druitt is more popularly known in Australia for other well-publicised reasons. As it is popularly represented in the media, Mount Druitt is a region beset by violent crime (Howden and Ralston 2011), outlaw gang activity (ABC 2011; Morri 2011; Coote et al. 2012) and is a chronically disadvantaged neighbourhood with 'toxic effects' on those who live there (SMH 2004).

The social indicators for the Mount Druitt region offer some statistical justification for the media's negativity. For example, employment statistics for Mount Druitt in 2011 shows that there was a higher proportion classed as unemployed (12.2 per cent), compared with 5.7 per cent for the Sydney Metropolitan region as a whole (ABS 2011). Youth unemployment in Mount Druitt is reported to be 21.1 per cent, about four times Sydney's average unemployment rate (ABS 2009).

An analysis of the distribution of the population by income quartile in Mount Druitt compared to the Sydney Metropolitan region overall shows that there was a lesser proportion of persons in the highest income quartile and a greater proportion in the lowest income quartile. The most significant change in Mount Druitt from 2006 to 2011 was in the lowest income quartile, which showed an increase of 1,006 persons.

With regard to educational attainment specifically, the highest level of schooling attained by the population in Mount Druitt shows that there was a higher proportion of people who had left school at an early level (Year 10 or less, 34.9 per cent) and a lower proportion of people who completed Year 12 or equivalent (50.6 per cent) in Mount Druitt compared with the Sydney Metropolitan averages of 31.2 per cent and 55 per cent (ABS 2011). There is also a relatively lower proportion of people holding university-level qualifications (15.6 per cent versus 24.1 per cent) and a higher proportion of people (50.4 per cent versus 40 per cent) with no formal qualifications (ABS 2011). A worrying sign for the area is that from 2006 to 2011, although the numbers of people with formal qualifications (i.e. bachelor or higher degree; advanced diploma or diploma; or vocational qualifications) increased – an additional 684 people had university-level qualifications, for example – the largest growth was still represented by those who had no formal qualifications, with an increase of 771 persons (ABS 2011). Based on the latest census data, the

National Centre for Social and Economic Modelling's 'Child Social Exclusion Index' has placed the south-western area of Blacktown encompassing Mount Druitt and its surrounds as an area of 'highest risk' whether measured by distance from the mean or by quintile ranking (National Centre for Social and Economic Modelling [NATSEM] 2013).

The Mount Druitt University Hub (MDUH) project was conceived as a particular response to the perceived problem of poor educational outcomes in the Mount Druitt region (see Mahar 2010). The MDUH is a product of a partnership between a public university – the Australian Catholic University – and Loyola Senior High School in Mount Druitt, a co-educational school for Years 11 and 12 and a partner school in the Australian government's 'Smarter schools national partnership for low socio-economic status school communities' program. The MDUH was formed with a view to enhancing local understanding of university course offerings and student support structures, and in so doing increase higher education participation of all students from the Mount Druitt area. In addition, the MDUH seeks to undertake research into the patterns and trends of university entry and retention in the Mount Druitt region through the maintenance of records and databases of student contacts, course selections and post-school destinations, as well as coordinating regular follow-up discussions with students from the region who are undertaking undergraduate studies.

In August 2012, I was appointed as the MDUH's project officer with a brief to coordinate its activities and determine the most effective way to deliver the project's goals. What is most peculiar about the MDUH and the position of project officer is the 'outsider-in' location of the project officer within the MDUH, which offers unique perspectives on the delivery and reception of higher education widening participation programs within schools without being formally part of either institution. The position also affords a unique perspective on what sociologists of youth social exclusion have for some time focused on: the transition between school and post-school activities like work or higher education (see Raffo and Reeves 2000; Schoon et al. 2001; Bynner and Parsons 2002). Sociologist Matthias Drilling (2010, p. 61) has helpfully used the term 'status passages' to denote such transitional times in the life of young people where they pass over the threshold of entry into new spheres of activity, times where they are also at their most vulnerable. In the context of the MDUH, it is the transition from school to work via higher education that is the primary focus. Here, research has suggested that it is not only economic capital, but also social and cultural capital – that is, those competencies and opportunities arising from being embedded in networks (e.g. successful alumni groups) or possession of certain literacies (e.g. knowledge of professional lingo) – that have an effect on the life courses of young people (Drilling 2010).

An important caveat to the above contextualisation of the MDUH project should be added at this point: while such a project does necessitate being conscious of factors that may affect the life opportunities of young people, it is equally important not to reduce their experiences to class, culture, crime, or capital of whatever sort, but to regard such categorisations as instrumentalities and not finalities (Jackson 1989, p. 1). It is especially vital in a context like Mount Druitt to avoid lapsing into 'deficit thinking' that places the responsibility of low educational attainment or employment outcomes squarely on the shoulders of young people themselves, their families, and/or their communities. According to Richard Valencia (1997, p. xi):

> The deficit thinking paradigm, as a whole, posits that students who fail in school do so because of alleged internal deficiencies (such as cognitive and/or motivational limitations) or shortcomings socially linked to the youngster – such as familial deficits and dysfunctions ... The popular 'at risk' construct, now entrenched in educational circles, views poor and working class children and their families (typically of color) as predominantly responsible for school failure.

While Valencia's definition of deficit thinking derives from his work with Mexican youth in the United States, a similar assumption can be detected in various Australian higher education initiatives and government policy discourses on 'raising aspirations' towards university participation (see 'Bridges to higher education' 2012; Department of Education and Training 2013). Low rates of participation in higher education, such a view assumes, have to do with 'subjective' factors immanent to areas such as Mount Druitt rather than with the arrangements of social institutions like schools, universities, and the economy (Smit 2012). Contrary to the notion that there is a deficit in aspiration, the young people of Mount Druitt I spoke to in my capacity at the MDUH suggest that the families and youth cultures they were involved in did not necessarily run counter to aspirations towards higher education (see Low 2013a, 2015). Rather, a more commonly cited concern lay with *accessing* higher education. And it was here that 'open' element in MOOCs seemed to hold some promise.

In 2013, I was commissioned by the steering committee of the MDUH – consisting of school executives from Loyola Senior High School, representatives from the Australian Catholic University's Widening Participation Unit, and the Institute for Advancing Community Engagement, as well as executives from the Catholic Education Diocese of Parramatta and two middle schools in the Mount Druitt region – to investigate if and how MOOCs may be used to further the project's goal of increasing engagement in higher education amongst young people in the region. The results of this study, of which the present chapter is an extended reflection, was tabled to the MDUH steering committee in the form of a report and subsequently made publicly available through the Parramatta Catholic Education Office's website (see Low 2013b).

So, what, then, might MOOCs have to do with Mount Druitt? Are not the rearguard actions of university-widening participation programmes a matter quite apart from the vanguard questions about learning technologies and the future of content delivery in higher education? In this chapter, I want to suggest that the common treatment of these two trends in higher education as separate issues elides the opportunities presented by MOOCs not only to *bring in* potential students from historically underrepresented areas into the universities, but for universities to *go to* the students in those areas in order to generate some positive social outcomes. I do not pretend to know in advance what the impact of MOOCs will be for students from regions like Mount Druitt, if any. However, the five short profiles that follow suggest that the small uptake of MOOCs in Mount Druitt has generated varied benefits in the lives of the five pseudonymous and deidentified participants profiled below. How these benefits can be secured and translated into more long-term capabilities for the individuals involved is the challenge, I argue, that lies ahead if the promise of MOOCs as expanding access to higher education and its benefits is to have any purchase.

Participant 1: Sam

Sam is a 17-year-old high school student. He is one of four children of parents who left Afghanistan after the Soviet invasion. Sam's parents have no experience of universities either in Australia or Afghanistan and of his peer group, he guesses that 'maybe five out of a hundred are at uni and out of a hundred, maybe two are even studying after school'. Yet for as long as he can remember, Sam has aimed to undertake higher education.

In 2013, Sam's father had brain surgery with severe complications, the consequences of which include regular seizures, loss of cognitive and basic motor functions and drastic mood swings. This means that he misses school to help his mother with caring duties: 'What can you do? It's family.' Sam first intended to do engineering, but did not know much about what that might entail. Via the MDUH, he enrolled in the Coursera course 'Introduction to Engineering Mechanics' taught by Wayne E. Whiteman from Georgia Institute of Technology to sample what engineering may entail. After two weeks of the course, Sam realised that he was uninterested in the content of engineering and was not disposed to the prerequisite knowledge of physics and mathematics that such a course assumed. He then attempted the course 'An Introduction to Operations Management' taught by Christian Terwiesch of University of Pennsylvania via Coursera. Sam enjoyed this course a lot more and it has enriched his understanding of his interests, strengths, and weaknesses, and not only what decisions he is going to make beyond school but also how to make them (i.e. getting information and 'test driving' various areas of study). He says of his experience:

> I didn't finish the 'Intro to Engineering Mechanics' course and I don't think I will be able to finish the 'Intro to Operations Management' one either because there's a lot happening at home at the moment, you know,

with dad being sick and stuff. But I got lots out of trying both of them and I think I know what I want to do now [in 2014]. And maybe when things settle down a bit, I wouldn't mind actually starting one and finishing it. It'll be pretty cool to get a certificate at the end to say you got through it even though there's all this shit that's happening in your life, you know what I mean?

Participant 2: Dipesh

Dipesh was born in Fiji and came to Mount Druitt as a young boy. Neither his mother nor father had been to university, although they are very supportive of his desire to pursue higher education in the fields of science and engineering. Dipesh achieved good grades at school in all his subject areas, but his study had been affected by a chronic spinal condition, which means that he suffers from constant pain and cannot remain seated for more than twenty minutes without having to get up and move around. He said: 'This [condition] really interrupts my concentration, class times and exam times because even if I am halfway into a problem, I have to get up and move around ... Sometimes I don't get up until I finish what I am doing, but then it really kills when I get back up.'

In 2013, Dipesh enrolled and completed over ten MOOCs through Coursera in fields ranging from astronomy to finance to neuroscience. He said that he 'enjoys what the top universities in the world had to offer, and for free!'. Dipesh points out some of the courses he has completed such as 'Combinatorial Game Theory', 'Exploring Quantum Physics', and 'Energy 101' as especially relevant to what he wants to study further at university in 2014:

> Completing these MOOCs gave me a unique learning experience of what I am told is similar university study. This experience has allowed me to take a more efficient approach to studies as it allowed me to develop skills relevant to school and beyond, including organisation and time management. Due to my broad academic interests in a variety of areas, I was able to get familiar with what university courses would be like so that I can expand or narrow down my preferences.

Dipesh also hoped that the completion of courses may benefit him and his friends in some way in the future. He says:

> At the end of each course, the instructor gives certificates to everyone who has successfully completed the course. This certificate allows people who want to explore other options, such as university, TAFE or work to distinguish themselves from everyone else.

I asked Dipesh if the MOOCs format of content broken down into smaller modules helped him to learn, especially given his medical condition. His response was: 'Yes, absolutely. I can watch a part, do the quiz and then take a break. Or I sometimes even stand up and walk around and watch the lecture video on my iPad.'

Participant 3: Pilli

Pilli moved with his family to Australia from Samoa in 2010 via New Zealand. His father is a computer technician, which interested Pilli in computers from a young age. He had been interested for some time in information technology networking and network security as a profession, but had no friends or relatives who worked in the field. His father gave him some encouragement, but he was still unsure what study in this field might involve, as it was not in his training.

In January 2013, Pilli attempted the 'Introduction to Computer Networks' taught by David Wetherall, Arvind Krishnamurthy and John Zahorjan from the University of Washington via Coursera. Pilli was very engaged in the course lectures and homework, but did not finish the course due to higher school certificate commitments, which he had to complete in order to matriculate.

As of the latter half of 2013, Pilli was enrolled in a diploma in IT networking (CISCO) and plans to pursue the study of network security at university level. He said of his MOOCs experience that:

> It was amazing that you just click on the button and you're enrolled. One minute I was just trying to finish my Year 12 and not sure about what I was doing, then suddenly I was doing a course from the University of Washington. Haha! I had to tell my dad and watch his face. It's really good but, the course. It was heaps interesting and I think after trying it, I was pretty sure I wanted to get into it. Now I'm on the train and people ask me what I'm doing and I say 'IT Networking' and they go 'What? Oh, ok … ' I think they expect me to be going to the gym or rugby training or something.

Pilli was not an Australian citizen (although at the time of writing, he was in the process of applying for citizenship status), which means that he cannot access government provisions like the deferral of higher education payments (via the Higher Education Loan Program) or income support (i.e. Youth Allowance) while he is undertaking his further education. This means Pilli has to find adequate employment to support the cost of his study. In this regard, he wondered if completing his MOOC may have been beneficial:

> Would've been good but, to finish it and get a certificate, put it on my resume and stuff for getting a job. It's hard trying to find a part-time job while studying and maybe if I got the certificate it would help a bit.

Participant 4: Alisha

Alisha is a young teacher from the local area who graduated in 2012 and returned to Mount Druitt in February 2013 to begin her first full-time year of teaching. She became aware of MOOCs via the emails and Facebook posts of the MDUH. Alisha expressed interest in further study in the field of education studies because: 'I genuinely enjoy studying and learning new things, so I think it will be incredibly interesting.' In late 2013, she enrolled in two MOOCs via Coursera – namely, 'Art and Inquiry: Museum Teaching Strategies for Your Classroom' and 'Archaeology: Dirty Little Secrets'. She explained that these courses:

> [B]oth appeal to me as I did a few archaeology units at USyd [the University of Sydney] and also did a lot of work on Museums and Curatorship. I thought using that in a classroom setting would be interesting! Through MOOCs I hope to be a more desirable candidate for jobs, especially as I want to extend my contract here [at a particular Mount Druitt high school] if possible!

Participant 5: Bobby

Bobby is a local resident and a young teacher in a leadership role in a Mount Druitt school. In 2013, he completed the 'Introduction to Philosophy' course taught by a group of instructors from the University of Edinburgh. At the time of our discussion, he was also halfway through 'Democratic Development' taught by Larry Diamond from Stanford University. Bobby has also enrolled in the 'Introduction to Psychology' and 'Soren Kierkegaard' courses delivered by instructors from the University of Toronto and the University of Copenhagen respectively. When I asked him what aspects of MOOCs had generated his enthusiasm for them, he immediately pointed to accessibility as an important feature:

> Studying through MOOCS allowed for flexibility, choice and a space to have a voice. The flexibility to study at your time and location, the choice to study what interests you and a voice to participate in discussion forums.

So, for Bobby, the opportunity for flexible learning and interaction with other like-minded students spurred him on to further his knowledge in various fields, despite having to then 'juggle work, young family and study'. He sees MOOCs as enabling him to connect from Mount Druitt to the world:

> I enjoy learning new things so my experiences have been positive and inspiring. Highlights include participating on a thread involving students from Africa and South America ... and I have been exposed to resources online and professors of renown in their fields.

More specifically, while Bobby does repeatedly emphasise his love of learning, he also sees his MOOCs participation as related to his professional practice. Bobby stated clearly: 'I am attempting to widen my knowledge of education by participating in courses that have a direct or indirect influence on education theory, and that can improve the ways I approach the task of education out here [in Mount Druitt].'

So what? From competencies to capabilities

So where do we go from here? What promise do MOOCs hold as a higher education resource for young people such as those profiled above? I suggest that any evaluation of MOOCs must take into account how this form of educational technology is taken up by people with particular aspirations and whether it does, in fact, enable them to achieve the goals that they desire within the existing social world that they inhabit. As Tim Ingold (1997, p. 107) argues, relations between humans and technologies are embedded in social relations, and 'can only be understood within this relational matrix, as one aspect of human sociality'. To evaluate whether MOOCs may be efficacious for such purposes for the five individuals from Mount Druitt mentioned above, I propose that the capability approach (CA) to development advanced by the Nobel laureate for economics Amartya Sen and the American legal philosopher Martha Nussbaum may offer a useful perspective.

Broadly speaking, it is an approach to human development that aims at moving beyond a focus on resources like wealth and skills towards also considering people's opportunities to achieve the things they value in life (Sen 1999, p. 18). It poses the questions: 'What are people actually able to do and be? What real opportunities are available to them?' (Nussbaum 2011, p. x). With regard to the evaluation of educational technologies, then, the CA will tend to focus on the extent to which they afford opportunities for people to be able to make decisions they value and work to remove obstacles to those freedoms – that is, its effects on their capabilities (Walker and Unterhalter 2007, p. 2). Such an approach to evaluation presents an alternative to the methodological individualism of market-driven approaches that purportedly 'merely' reflect what particular people say they want on the one hand, and broader structural approaches that focus on material inputs on the other. As Melanie Walker and Elaine Unterhalter posit, a CA to evaluation attempts to hold both structural and contextual factors alongside an appreciation for human agents' capacity to make decisions about what matters to them:

> Evaluating capabilities, rather than resources or outcomes, shifts the axis of analysis to establishing and evaluating the conditions that enable individuals to take decisions based on what they have reason to value. These conditions will vary in different contexts, but the approach sets out to be sensitive to human diversity; complex social relations; a sense of reciprocity between people; appreciation that people can reflect reasonably on

what they value for themselves and others; and a concern to equalize, not opportunities or outcomes, but rather capabilities.

(2007, p. 3)

I submit that at present, in contrast to the human-centred view of the CA, educational technologies like MOOCs tend to be framed by policymakers as a means of increasing the *competencies* of students for industry needs and economic ends (e.g. Goldsworthy and Coenen 2013; Burdon 2014). I define competency as 'the specification of knowledge and skill and the application of that knowledge and skill to the standard of performance required' as per the Australian government's *Assessment – Technical Manual* (Hager et al. 1994). In this reckoning, competencies are associated with enhancing skills and abilities for a given task or job. The standard assumption underlying the focus on increasing competencies is to treat units of education as skill investments in human capital, so that the average quantity of education in the labour force is taken to be an input into economically productive capacity (Schultz 1961). Underlying such an approach is an assumption that depicts the 'poor' student as simultaneously lacking in competencies and as the hope for economic growth – a discourse that has come to frame educational policy initiatives both in Australia and internationally (see respectively, Quiggin 1999; McCormick 2012). With regard to MOOCs, this can be seen in how the chief executive officer of the Australian government-contracted firm OpenLearning, Adam Brimo, describes its key quality: 'They allow businesses and government to upskill their staff for minimal cost' (in Redrup 2015). When applied to the case of MOOCs in Mount Druitt, then, we may surmise from a competencies perspective that it allows participants to accumulate particular knowledge and skills rather cheaply, and which then enables them to be more productive for businesses and consequently, generate economic growth for the national economy (Benhabib and Spiegel 1994).

However, in the absence of appropriate opportunities, accumulating competencies in the form of new skills and abilities will not be sufficient to enable people to actualise the lives they have reason to value. When we apply the CA to the question of MOOCs in Mount Druitt, we are led to ask: what are MOOCs participants in Mount Druitt actually able to do and be? What real opportunities are available to MOOCs participants from Mount Druitt?

It appears from a cursory look at the participants profiled above that there are certain capabilities that can be developed from undertaking MOOCs. These are summarised in Table 8.1.

For Sam, Dipesh and Pilli, for example, participation in MOOCs has increased their capabilities in making decisions about higher education, thus increasing their sense of how to navigate post-school options. As well as developing generic skills that may be useful in considering further study, the way MOOCs are delivered allowed Sam to access higher education content despite the complicated home situation he was involved in at the time. For Dipesh, the modular format of MOOCs and its online mode of delivery accessible

Table 8.1 Capabilities derived from participation in MOOCs

Participant	Capabilities
Sam	• Decision-making about higher education • Access to higher education content despite disruptions at home
Dipesh	• Decision-making about higher education • Access to higher education content despite physical disability
Pilli	• Decision-making about higher education • Access to higher education content despite non-citizen status
Alisha	• Knowledge for professional practice
Bobby	• Knowledge for professional practice • Networking and sharing of ideas across different locations

through mobile devices also appeared to enable participation in learning despite Dipesh's chronic spinal condition. Access is also a key feature in the case of Pilli, where MOOCs made the experience of higher education available for free at a time when he was not able to access government loan assistance for higher education due to the citizenship requirements that are a condition for such assistance.

In the case of Alisha and Bobby, MOOCs appear to have provided both professionals at different stages of their careers with content that may be of use to them in their practice. It is interesting to note that the MOOCs chosen by Alisha and Bobby were not necessarily ones that appeared directly linked to their teaching or leadership tasks, but both nonetheless sought applications for what they had learned in their practices. For Bobby, the process of undertaking MOOCs also offered opportunities for networking and the sharing of ideas across national boundaries, thus in part compensating for the issues of workplace isolation that may be experienced by teachers in low socio-economic status schools on the margins of large metropolitan cities (see Schlichte, Yssel and Merbler 2005).

However, there are further unanswered questions about the capabilities that participation in MOOCs actually confers. With particular reference to the accounts of the participants from Mount Druitt above: can Sam, given his participation in MOOCs as a way of broadening his understanding of university options, be recognised for what he has accomplished in light of his family circumstances? Will any of Dipesh's 10–12 completed MOOCs certificates count towards his university career? Is Pilli right to assume that a MOOC certificate will help him to get a job? And will the courses completed by Alisha and Bobby count towards their professional development as educators, especially given their passion for applying their knowledge to practice?

For, if competencies might look at the accumulation and application of skills and knowledge, *capabilities*, by contrast, signify people's freedom to achieve the actualisation of various life goals and exercise control over their own individual social and economic lives (Otto and Ziegler 2010, p. 10). In the literature on education and development, the notion of capabilities highlights the attainable (future) life alternatives by pointing to 'the scale and scope of the real, actual possibilities and positive power of young persons to choose and enjoy different worthwhile activities and to pursue different meaningful life paths he or she has reason to value' (Otto and Ziegler 2010, p. 10). In this view, the linkages between individuals and local groups and broader institutional processes – including regulatory, legal, political, and economic institutions – need to be taken into account. Inevitably, this will also involve unpacking the power relations between individuals, groups, and institutions that act as impediments to the life opportunities of young people (Frediani 2006).

How, then, do we get from competency to capability? I propose that the gap between competencies and capabilities can be bridged by *recognition*, which is the endowment with authorisations and rights to act in certain arenas, as well as access to opportunities to exchange competencies for certain goods (Sen 1999, p. 74; Drilling 2010, p. 53). Recognition thus functions at the intersection of the skills and knowledge that individuals may possess through doing MOOCs on the one hand, and the actual opportunities that are open to them for exchanging those competencies for goods (both monetary and non-monetary) that are valued by the individual on the other. Formal accreditation and recognition for knowledge and skills acquired is thus crucial for conferring legitimacy to the competencies that individuals have come to possess, articulating these into broader institutions like higher education and the labour market and giving such individuals access and agency within those fields. By combining a focus on the accumulation of knowledge and skills with attention to institutional recognition, the narrow focus on competencies is broadened to include a consideration of what capabilities they enable within the social worlds that young people inhabit.

So, what might that look like for the participants from Mount Druitt profiled above? The following may offer some provisional answers. First, for Sam, the award of 'points' and 'badges' for work completed at different stages, such as those popularised by the Khan Academy (see Taton 2011), may provide a means to testify to his initiative in exploring different courses and some recognition for what he has completed. This may also be a formal means of indicating his acquisition of broad understandings of different academic fields, some degree of academic and professional language acquisition, etc.

For Dipesh, some articulation between the courses he has already completed and his intended university career, including a consideration of his MOOCs achievements as a supplement to his university entry score or as equivalent to some undergraduate credit, may benefit both him and the university that is forthcoming with such opportunities. However, the costs of such accreditation and whether such costs may limit the opportunities available to those from lower-SES regions like Mount Druitt remain an open question.

For Pilli, the increasing visibility and acceptance of MOOCs through identity verification procedures such as that introduced by Coursera's 'Signature Track' (Coursera, n.d.) may enhance the legitimacy of any MOOCs achievements for the purposes of seeing employment. Whether employers will hire those like Pilli even with identity-verified certificates received from the completion of MOOCs instead of or alongside those with traditional university degrees remains an open question.

And, finally, for Alisha and Bobby, the recognition of learning through MOOCs as professional development from the relevant professional teacher accreditation authorities (e.g. the New South Wales Institute of Teachers) will enable schools to formally acknowledge a range of educationally relevant knowledge and skills – including leadership skills – that are possessed by educators who have completed MOOCs.

Conclusion

According to the anthropologist Michael Jackson (2002, p. 336), the ways in which we experience our relationships, whether with persons or technologies, 'depend upon the degree to which we feel in control of these relationships, as well as the degree to which these relationships are felt to augment rather than diminish our own sense of well-being'. This is to say that human relationships with others – whether people, machines, institutions, or technologies – are potentially a source of fulfilment and frustration. Accordingly, evaluations of educational technologies such as MOOCs can only be made with reference to how they are experienced in the lives of the people using them. If we take as axiomatic that human beings should have a hand in the self-determination of their own lives, as does the CA as a framework for human development, then perhaps the question of whether MOOCs are 'good' or 'bad' need to be evaluated on the basis of what capabilities they may offer to people to live lives they have reason to value.

What I have attempted to show in the five profiled MOOCs participants from Mount Druitt furnished above is how certain forms of recognition may serve to increase the capabilities of young people who live and work in contexts where opportunities for higher education have been scarce. I submit that if the promise of MOOCs for widening participation in higher education is to be realised, then we need to consider the forms of recognition that can translate the competencies attained by its participants in such contexts into capabilities for accessing the range of opportunities in work, study, and life that they have hitherto been unable to access.

References

Australian Bureau of Statistics 2009, 'Census data 2006', ABS, Canberra, viewed 23 January 2017, http://abs.gov.au/websitedbs/censushome.nsf/home/historicaldata2006.

Australian Bureau of Statistics 2011, '2011 Census QuickStats', BS, Canberra, viewed 23 January 2017, www.censusdata.abs.gov.au/census_services/getproduct/census/2011/quickstat/SSC11613.

Benhabib, J. and Spiegel, M. M. 1994, 'The role of human capital in economic development evidence from aggregate cross-country data', *Journal of Monetary Economics*, vol. 34, no. 2, pp. 143–173.

'"Bikie links" to torched industrial unit' 2011, ABC News, 19 September, viewed 10 May 2017, www.abc.net.au/news/2011-09-19/bikie-links-to-torched-industrial-unit/2905568.

Bourdieu, P. 1988, *Homo academicus*, Stanford University Press, Stanford, CA.

Bourdieu, P. 1994, 'Rethinking the state: genesis and structure of the bureaucratic field', *Sociological Theory*, vol. 12, no. 1, pp. 1–18.

'Bridges to Higher Education' 2012, viewed 23 January 2017, www.bridges.nsw.edu.au/about.

Burdon, S. 2014, 'Will Australia catch the next digital wave?' ABC Radio National, 7 October, viewed 23 January 2017, www.abc.net.au/radionational/programs/ockhamsrazor/will-australia-catch-the-next-digital-wave3f/5779808.

Bynner, J. and Parsons, S. 2002, 'Social exclusion and the transition from school to work: The case of young people not in education, employment, or training (NEET)', *Journal of Vocational Behavior*, vol. 60, no. 2, pp. 289–309.

Coote, A., Cuneo, C. and Klein, N. 2012, 'Gang bashed boy and tied him to a tree on Luxford Road Mount Druitt', *Daily Telegraph*, 8 August, viewed 23 January 2017, www.news.com.au/national/nsw-act/gang-bashed-boy-and-tied-him-to-a-tree-on-luxford-road-mount-druitt/news-story/9aa2ed0a0a6c0367170bce306f11cba9.

Coursera n.d., 'Earn a verified certificate: official recognition to advance your lifelong education', viewed 23 January 2017, www.coursera.org/signature.

Department of Education and Training 2013, *Higher education participation and partnerships program (HEPPP)*, Australian Government, Canberra, viewed 23 January 2017, http://education.gov.au/higher-education-participation-and-partnerships-programme-heppp.

Drilling, M. 2010, 'Capability deprivation and capability enlargement: rethinking the role of welfare', in H.-U. Otto and H. Ziegler (eds), *Education, welfare and the capabilities approach: European perspectives*, Barbara Budrich Publishers, Opladen and Farmington Hills, MI, pp. 51–70.

Frediani, A. A. 2006, 'Participatory methods and the capability approach', Hum Development and Capability Association, viewed 23 January 2017, http://hd-ca.org

Funnell, A. 2013, 'MOOCs: the future of education or mere marketing?', ABC Radio National, 8 April, viewed 23 January 2017, www.abc.net.au/radionational/programs/futuretense/moocs-revolution/4616500.

Goldsworthy, C. and Coenen, L. 2013, 'Is borderless learning the answer?', Business/Higher Education Round Table Commentary Paper, viewed 23 January 2017, www.bhert.com/events/2013-02-06/FoME-CommentaryPaper-Mar2013.pdf.

Hager, P., Athanasou, J., and Gonczi, A. 1994, *Assessment – technical manual*, Australian Government Publication Service, Canberra.

Howden, S. and Ralston, N. 2011, 'Residents turn fury on accused child killer', *Sydney Morning Herald*, 30 April, viewed 23 January 2017, www.smh.com.au/nsw/residents-turn-fury-on-accused-child-killer-20110429-1e0te.html

Illich, I. 1971, *Deschooling society*, Harper & Row, London.

Ingold, T. 1997, 'Eight themes in the anthropology of technology', *Social Analysis*, vol. 41, no. 1, pp. 106–138.

Jackson, M. 1989, *Paths toward a clearing radical empiricism and ethnographic inquiry*, Indiana University Press, Bloomington and Indianapolis.

Jackson, M. 2002, 'Familiar and foreign bodies: a phenomenological exploration of the human-technology interface', *Journal of the Royal Anthropological Institute*, vol. 8, no. 2, pp. 333–346.

Low, R. 2013a, 'Can the "under-represented" student speak? Discerning the subjects amongst the objects of widening participation in higher education', *Australasian Journal of University–Community Engagement*, vol. 8, no. 1, pp. 1–24.

Low, R. 2013b, 'MOOCs and widening participation in higher education: case studies from Mount Druitt', Mount Druitt University Hub, Report No. 2, Catholic Education Diocese of Parramatta, Sydney. Viewed 23 January 2017, www.loyolamtdruitt.catholic.edu.au/SiteData/213/UserFiles/PublicationLinks/moocs-in-mount-druitt-report-case-study-2013-09-03.pdf

Low, R. 2015, 'Raised parental expectations towards higher education and the double bind', *Higher Education Research and Development*, vol. 34, no. 1, pp. 205–218.

McCormick, A. 2012, 'Whose education policies in aid-receiving countries? A critical discourse analysis of quality and normative transfer through Cambodia and Laos', *Comparative Education Review*, vol. 56, no. 1, pp. 18–47.

Mahar, J. 2010, 'Painful memories of Mount Druitt's maligned class of '96', *Sydney Morning Herald*, 29 January. Viewed 23 January 2017, www.smh.com.au/national/education/painful-memories-of-mount-druitts-maligned-class-of-96-20100128-n1sd.html

Morri, M. 2011, 'Lawless Sydney thugs copy mayhem of US organised crime groups', *Daily Telegraph*, 14 February, viewed 23 January 2017, www.dailytelegraph.com.au-/lawless-sydney-thugs-copy-mayhem-of-us-organised-crime-groups/news-story/0000000ef5b5fc1d5829cfa3ed50eb4edc275

National Centre for Social and Economic Modelling [NATSEM] 2013, 'Child social exclusion index, NSW and ACT', University of Canberra, Canberra.

Nussbaum, M.C. 2011, *Creating capabilities*, Belknap Press, Cambridge, MA.

Otto, H. U. and Ziegler, H. 2010, 'Introduction – capability perspectives on education and welfare', H.-U. Otto and H. Ziegler (eds), *Education, welfare and the capabilities approach: European perspectives*, Barbara Budrich Publishers, Opladen andFarmington Hills, MI, pp. 9–14.

Quiggin, J. 1999, 'Human capital theory and education policy in Australia', *Australian Economic Review*, vol. 32, no. 2, pp. 130–144.

Raffo, C. and Reeves, M. 2000, 'Youth transitions and social exclusion: developments in social capital theory', *Journal of Youth Studies*, vol. 3, no. 2, pp. 147–166.

Redrup, Y. 2015, 'OpenLearning secures federal government MOOC contract', *Australian Financial Review*, 4 June, viewed 23 January 2017, www.afr.com/technology/openlearning-secures-federal-government-mooc-contract-20150604-ghged2.

Schlichte, J., Yssel, N., and Merbler, J. 2005, 'Pathways to burnout: case studies in teacher isolation and alienation', *Preventing School Failure*, vol. 50, no. 1, pp. 35–40.

Schoon, I., McCulloch, A., Joshi, H. E., Wiggins, R. D., and Bynner, J. 2001, 'Transitions from school to work in a changing social context', *Young*, vol. 9, no. 1, pp. 4–22.

Schultz, T. W. 1961, 'Investment in human capital', *American Economic Review*, vol. 51, no. 1, pp. 1–17.

Sen, A. 1999, *Development as freedom*, Anchor Books, New York.

SMH 2004, 'Pick your neighbours with care: it may determine your chances', *Sydney Morning Herald*, 9 March, viewed 23 January 2017, www.smh.com.au/articles/2004/03/08/1078594301538.html.

Smit, R. 2012, 'Towards a clearer understanding of student disadvantage in higher education: problematising deficit thinking', *Higher Education Research and Development*, vol. 31, no. 3, pp. 369–380.

Taton, J. A. 2011, 'It's school organized like a giant videogame: participation structures embedded within the mathematics content and curriculum of the Khan Academy', *Working Papers in Educational Linguistics*, vol. 26, no. 2, pp. 7–42.

Teese, R. and Polesel, J. 2003, *Undemocratic schooling: equity and quality in mass secondary education in Australia*, Melbourne University Publishing, Carlton.

Valencia, R. R. 1997, *The evolution of deficit thinking: educational thought and practice*, Falmer, London.

Walker, M. and Unterhalter, E. 2007, 'The capability approach: its potential for work in education', in M. Walker and E. Unterhalter (eds), *Amartya Sen's capability approach and social justice in education*, Palgrave Macmillan, Basingstoke, pp. 1–18.

9 Technologies of orientation
Pathways, futures

Anna Hickey-Moody and Valerie Harwood

I: Would you consider going to one [a university]?
P: In the future.
I: Yes?
P: After I pass school and all that stuff.
(Christa, young woman, Beachpoint)

I: What are unis for, how would you explain what a university is for? Why do we have them?
P: It helps you get a job and do what you want to in the future.
(Maree, young woman, Barford)

P: Well, maybe this is my second chance to be able to go to uni and actually get a proper future rather than be stuck in retail for the rest of my life.
(group interview with two young women, aged 17–18, Flindersvale)

Introduction

These three quotes are from participants in the Imagining University Education (IUE) project, a study that sought to understand how university was imagined by young people from disadvantaged communities who have 'precarious' (Butler 2004) relationships to education. Participants in our study have either been permanently excluded from school or have left and returned to school. We draw on Judith Butler's (2004) use of the term 'precarious' to describe the relationships these students have to education, rather than terminology such as 'drop out' or 'non-attender' which negatively construct the young subjects in question. We have chosen these quotes as they highlight how these young people see university as a way of making the future better. But, as we go on to explain, there are few methods, or as Michel Foucault might characterise them, 'technologies of thought' (Foucault 1991) available to young people with such precarious relationships to education. This is problematic, since particular ways of thought are crucial for bridging existing divides between early school leavers and university attendees. Aspiration for educational futures, let alone university attendance, is precious, and most rare. Arguably such aspiration is very important as it is so rare and can lead to class transition. If it can be sustained, aspiration for university attendance is a key ingredient for success in higher education.

The three quotes with which we begin the chapter construct the relationship between the present and the future differently. For Christa, at school in a low socio-economic area we call 'Beachpoint', the future is something that can only be dealt with seriously after the present pains inflicted by schooling have been managed. For Maree in Barford, the future is an ongoing imperative. Perhaps most promisingly, for the young person in Flindersvale, university is a chance to 'get a proper future', and this chance is being negotiated right now. The promise that the future could be actualised at university is embedded in the present. Different temporal orientations (and different kinds of time), as well as different relationships to career, were discussed by the young people in our study, and we present and analyse these discussions in this chapter. In spite of the largely difficult circumstances and often troubled lives of our research participants, as we show, a group of twelve remained aspirational about their professional and educational futures.

The research we discuss in this chapter is drawn from a large Australian study funded by the Australian Research Council (DP160371009), involving over 250 young people living in disadvantaged communities who also had precarious relationships to education. We sought to understand their context using Jonathan Wolff and Avner de-Shalit's (2007) plural conceptualisation of disadvantage, examining how this context impacted on the ways they imagined university and university education. Fieldwork was conducted using a youth-focused approach (Harwood et al. 2013) in youth centres in disadvantaged communities in five Australian states. Research sites have been deidentified to protect confidentiality, with pseudonyms used for both places and young people's names.[1] The young people were aged 11–25 years old, with most aged 14–17. A small number of participants stated to us that they were Aboriginal or Torres Strait Islander.

We thematically analysed our extensive data set for discussions of 'feelings and places', 'feelings and futures', 'unique futures', the words 'dream' and 'imagine'. These themes captured descriptions of emotions and feelings related to the future, and emphasised explanations of present actions in terms of the future. Relationships between place and future were captured in young people's descriptions about where they want to be in the future, or of being 'stuck' in place where they are (Knopp 2004; Hickey-Moody and Kenway 2014). Our themes also pointed to how young participants at times described their future plans as different from those of their families and peers. Considered together, these five themes referenced data from 46 transcripts of interviews (from 88 transcripts in the complete dataset) with 151 unique participants (57 per cent of total participants).[2]

Two sub-themes focused on life orientations and vocational pathways were also chosen in response to the data. These emphasised the pleasures of lifestyle, object attainment, and vocational aspiration. Despite the geographic distances between our participants, all the conversations highlighted by these analytics could be clustered under one of these sub-themes. These similarities of approach when thinking about futures are striking, and while we do not have the space here to closely examine the stories of all 151 participants, we have chosen quotes that we feel are representative of the broader concerns and methods of approaching the future that our participants expressed.

The ways these young people's plans for the future were organised can be mapped across their orientations towards careers and education, their relationships to objects, and what they see as desirable lifestyles. We were acutely aware that these participants had very different levels of knowledge about available pathways towards achieving their goals. Their lack of knowledge about educational pathways, along with comments about their educational 'present', suggested the support they had for achieving their educational goals was minimal. We think through the values expressed by young people's aspirations, and make some suggestions for how youth-focused spaces or schools might better support such young people by building accessible and responsive pathways to higher education. Philosophies of time can help us understand how young people live in their present and imagine their future. We draw on contemporary work on time (Coleman 2008), outlining how it provides new insights into the critical role feelings play in the production or disavowal of careers and educational futures.

Less than half our participants said they wanted to pursue educational or professional futures, and their dreams were not necessarily aligned with social class (Lehmann 2009). They wanted to be vets, youth workers, criminologists, lawyers, midwifes, nurses, plumbers, dancers, ambulance drivers, paramedics, psychologists, veterinary nurses, filmmakers, musicians or music producers, artists, illustrators, special education teachers, landscapers, soldiers (or wanted to 'join the army'), journalists, childcare workers, doctors, boat captains, IT workers, a game developer, a hairdresser, a mechanical engineer, and structural engineer, work in tourism and marketing, justice administration, be a cleaner, legal secretary, policeman, psychologist, landscaper, or to travel. This is neither a list of middle- or upper-class aspirations nor a list of clearly working-class or 'disadvantaged' aspirations. Some of these aspirations were very clearly gendered; for example, only young women wanted to be hairdressers and models. Most popular potential careers were veterinary science, youth work, IT or game development, and military service.

The ways young people came to have a career goal also varied: some wanted a particular career because it matched their identity or personality, others as a means of getting things they wanted. Many were still not sure what they wanted, as this young woman from Jonestown evidences:

basically what I want to do ... I'm an action person so I just ... if I want to go to uni, I will go to uni but it's not a choice up ahead. I just want to finish school first.

(group interview with three young people, aged 15–18, Jonestown)

Young people also had very different kinds of knowledge about what university was, why one might want to attend one, and how to go about doing so. Too often university seemed like a purely imaginary option:

I: Okay. What does a university do?
P1: It helps you get better jobs ...
P2: I think ... isn't it when you finish TAFE and you want to get a better degree or something you go into university.
P1: Get more educated.
I: Yes, more educated, it helps you get a better job and stuff.
P2: Yes, and get your dream job pretty much.

(group interview with two young people, aged 15–17, Flindersvale)

The simple equation of getting a 'dream' job with going to university shows us how far removed some participants were from the reality of life after university education, and how special, and unattainable, university seemed. While Australian political rhetoric of recent decades has featured aspirational references to being 'the clever country', in which 40 per cent of young people will attend university, for the young participants in our study university certainly isn't something everyone aspires to, and is something even fewer people actually do. Our data shows that university attendance is a dream for the particularly aspirational, and, in these instances, these aspirational young people often needed to acquire technologies of subjectivity (Foucault 1991)[3], or key preparatory skills, to remove themselves from existing entanglements with places and people.

While some young people were oriented towards university, others actively turned away from it. Some feared they would be rejected by institutions and cultures of higher education, just as they felt they had been rejected by schools (Willis 1977). Others saw it as a place for *other people* and as a way *other people* actualised their futures. This was a defensive strategy through which young people avoided possible rejection, and shows how different they felt from those who did go to university.

Young people's orientations towards ideas about their future are necessarily about more than university (Driscoll 2014). Conversations about participants' futures were marked by concerns about lifestyles and objects, and a desire to move out of current circumstance. Odette, a 13-year-old from Silvercrest, held her father's words close to her heart:

my dad told me about two things – one thing 'Always travel around the country and do your favourite things first before you get married'. The other thing he also told me is 'Always stand up for yourself no matter if you're getting bashed or ... stand up for yourself and if anyone tries to bully you or if you know that something's not right, just stand up for yourself'.

Together they imagined that her 'future' involves travel, marriage, and the possible need to negotiate conflict. Odette's sense of her father's advice about the future is one of our most positive, complex, and grounded future stories. It emphasises care for the self – cultivating self-pride and personal pleasure – as well as orienting herself towards other cultures, and informally acquiring other knowledges through travel.

Thinking through the concept of orientation is useful, as young people are oriented towards particular relationships with themselves, their cultures, other cultures, and institutions through their learning experiences. Orientations towards futures are both expressions of young people's learning biographies and movements of self that have been learned across time. Changing an orientation or a pattern is a complex act of remaking the movements, directions, and practices through which we make selves. There were some shared orientations towards future pathways that stood out in our data and prompt our discussions here. Other recent discussion in scholarship on orientation has drawn on Sara Ahmed's (2006) relevant work. Ahmed's project is theoretically and methodologically very different from our work here, but she usefully reminds us that 'The work of repetition is not neutral work; *it orients the body in some ways rather than others*' (Ahmed 2006, p. 57). The participants in our study had often repeatedly lived through being told they were not good enough, they could not learn, and they had no educational future. In this respect, like scraping away the disbelief that had accumulated across the years, the young people who aspired to educational futures often did so in spite of difficult experiences of schooling, and had to reorient their relationships to education in order to hold on to their dreams.

Orientations

'The temporality of orientation reminds us that orientations are effects of what we tend toward, where "toward" marks a space and time that is almost, but not quite, available in the present' (Ahmed 2006, p. 20). Orientations are the ways we make futures. Even when we are not thinking about orientations we have them; they are the method through which we make our future. Young people's explanations of their orientations can be organised primarily in relation to a perceived difference between becoming a certain kind of *person* versus getting a certain kind of *job*. Seeing a job or a career as a chance to *practise* being a certain kind of person is a vocational approach to career pathways shared by a number of the participants who had future career goals. Alternatively, as we have suggested, some young people see a job as a means to survive, to eventually acquire objects, or in select cases, to meet consumption and lifestyle goals. For young people oriented towards objects, the future means surviving. Homes give shelter, and provide safety. Clothes provide protection; objects are a necessary means of survival.

As we have noted, our young participants were often looking for a way out of the place in which they are entangled:

P1: I know where I want to live. I know where I want to live ...
P2: ... get the Baby Bonus[4] and go ...
P1: ... I want to have this dream house like a Jersey Shore house and two garages and a garage for the girls and a garage for boys and split up the house for the boys and girls ...
P3: It's not going to happen so shut up.
P1: ... shut up, in the city and when you open the curtains, there's the beach.
(group interview with five young people, aged 13, Eagles Nest)

It seems that the possibility of being in another place, of having new horizons, opening the curtains and 'there's the beach' was an orientation that sustained this participant, however prohibitive real estate prices might be to a city beach view.

I: Would you consider going to uni?
P: Mm hmm. Yes, of course. From a young age I've always been told 'If you want to have a great life and you want fast cars and jumbo jets and all that you've got to go to university' ...
(group interview with nine young people, aged 15–24, Morrowsman)

The other comments surrounding this orientation to 'jumbo jets' and 'fast cars' are discussed later in this chapter and display a resilient approach to learning and an investment in education that extends beyond attaining objects. But those who were unsure what happened at university, or why it might matter, focused their attention on things they knew about:

P: In engineering, the difference between going straight to university and doing an apprenticeship first is that you earn enough to buy your own house before you get to university rather than once you hit the same level you've earned that much more money that you could have bought your own house and you'll be at the same level if you went to through the apprenticeship system as if you went through the university system.
I: Yes, it's about having the choice I think.
P: Also like I'm in automotive [practical mechanical studies] and the plan is to get an apprenticeship at the end of this year – about a four-year apprenticeship – where I can set my future up right now with the house and well I can build my own fast car ...
(group interview with nine young people, aged 15–24, Morrowsman)

In order to cultivate appetites for thinking differently in relation to educational contexts, one starting point might be showing young people the ways they already actively participate in what we describe as 'ecologies of learning'. Young people's everyday cultures constitute complex sets of knowledges and learning practices, and as such they are already capable learners. Further, the objects and lifestyles coveted by our participants who did not value university – fast cars, jumbo jets, and 'other places' – are often signifiers of mobility. While we clearly need to cultivate an appetite for engaging with formal educational contexts, perhaps focusing on university as offering a means to build a different life will appeal to those who quite rightly see money as the most immediate form of escape available to them.

Vocational orientations

As we foreshadowed in the introduction to this chapter, a striking aspect of the statements made by young people about their future, and the role that university might play in actualising this future, was a sense that university can help them find a job where they can do something that suits their character. The following discussions illustrate some of these vocational approaches to careers:

I: Why would you consider going to uni?
P: Well I want to go to university because, oh well I'd like to study psychology because that's what I'm interested in and I'd just like to, to keep on sort of broadening my knowledge ... so that I'm able to think better so I can understand problems.
    (group interview with five young people, aged 14, Toban Peninsular)

This passage is notable, as while the participant is oriented towards psychology because it is what they are 'interested' in, they also demonstrate a kind of orientation towards institutional knowledge that is quite rare for our data set. Other participants needed a little more encouragement. Many of the young people in our futures discussions had a career plan because it aligned with the kind of person they thought they were or should become. Here are some further examples:

I: Would you ever consider going to uni?
P: Maybe.
I: Maybe? What would persuade you to go? What would need to happen for you to go to uni? Something that you like? That you'd like to look into?
P: I'd like to be a mechanical engineer... Yes, I want to be a mechanical engineer. I wanted to do that since I was little. I don't know, it just interests me. My dad and my brother's always fixing cars because we have a lot of old cars over at my place and I'm always there helping them, slowly getting

used to it. We were driving around down the back one day, somebody broke down and I actually fixed the car. I don't know how, but I did.

(Kim, 15-year-old, Redwell)

This young person already belongs to an ecology of learning which comprises sets of practices that show 'how things work, why they work', and cultivates 'an ability to be able to fix something you like'. The skill of being able to fix something is a reward offered by involvement in these cultures, and studying engineering at university feels like a natural extension of these skills. Family members have shown Kim that practical mechanical engineering is possible, but more than this, experience has taught Kim they are good at fixing cars: 'and I actually fixed the car. I don't know how, but I did.' Fixing machines is something Kim is 'getting used to' and it makes Kim feel close to family. So, there are sets of practical knowledges and relationships that might make the start of a pathway towards a future in engineering, even if university entry is not figured yet in terms of prerequisite subjects and pathways. In the following interview excerpt, another vocationally oriented participant imagines their career as a way of extending what they are most interested in and becoming more like who they feel they are:

P1: I want to be a forensic pathologist.
I1: Wow, that would be so interesting.
P2: What's that?
P1: It's like you find out how people died and when and stuff.
P2: Like CSI?
I2: Yes, like *CSI*
P2: I love that show – and *Bones*.
P1: Yes, *Bones*.
I1: That would be very interesting. You wouldn't get creeped out?
P1: I love scary stuff.
P2: That'd be so cool.

(Joslyn and Shelly, aged 12, Jonestown)

The capacity to imagine a career as a space for stuff you 'love' shows the importance of the imagination in furnishing young people's desires to develop a professional subjectivity that excites them. For others, the imagination was less important than feeling like they wanted a career that capitalised on their existing skills. The young woman below thinks she has the natural desire to help people, and can cope with argumentative people, both of which will help her to be a good lawyer:

P1: I want to go into uni and do my degree in law. I've always had a fascination in it. I've always ...
P2: I used to [want to] be a lawyer and then my sister got into a lot of trouble, I'm like 'I don't want to be your lawyer' and she's like 'Why?' 'Because I

don't want to save your arse.' I don't know why – from there I actually lost my interest.

P1: No but you of all people you know what I'm like; you've seen what I was like when I helped you ...

P2: I am so argumentative.

P1: ... you saw what I was like when I helped you with everything with Ned.

P2: I am so argumentative ...

P1: I've always been like that. I've always been one to help people. I've never been one to turn around and say 'No' to people. I've always just had that urge to, you know, go out and help people.

(Eileen and Bethany, aged 17 and 18, Flindersvale)

Again, here we see the student's awareness of the existing ecologies of learning to which they belong furnish their belief in university. The sets of skills and practices that are referenced above – enjoying argument, a concern with justice, and being engaged with other people's needs – are clearly existing cycles in her life, made up of sets of practices of which she feels proud.

A significant portion of the participants who had plans for the future which involved university wanted to make video games – it was in the top few career goals for participants. As a vocational goal expressed by young people, being a game designer again illustrates the desire to extend belonging to a culture in which they have found enjoyment, and build an environment where they feel at home. Boys in a number of focus groups were clearly confident with their gaming and IT skills. There were positive and ongoing relationships between boys, screens, and machines constructed on a regular basis. Our focus groups proved a ripe place for growing student knowledge. Such an environment, which we call an ecology of learning, is referred to by Jane Bennett as the conjunctions and actancy that occur around 'Thing-Power', the capacity to be able to

> adjust ... relations of movement and rest in relation to other bodies ... Each human, as one mode, is always in the process of entering into a set of relationships with other modes ... Nature according to Spinoza is a place wherein bodies strive to enhance their power of acting by forming alliances with other bodies in their vicinity ... we may learn to alter the quality of our encounters but not our encountering nature.
>
> (2004, p. 353)

These young men want to change the quality and depth of their encounters with technology, with games and programming systems. They are keenly aware of their encountering nature; they are embedded in relational activities with machines and possess rich sets of knowledges about these machines, which institutional learning environments need to build upon.

Technologies for making futures

Thinking through Baruch Spinoza, we see that the process of actualising a future is actually a very practical matter of growing an ecology, and building particular kinds of associational pathways. The young people in our study who dared to dream about going to university were trying to make new associational pathways. However, the practice of making steps towards achieving these goals, having the intuitive knowledge of what was required in order for them to come to fruition, was not evidenced in their learning biographies. In order to achieve at university, students need adults like teachers, family, or youth workers to see and reinforce their existing participation in educational environments. Young people need to be shown they already participate positively in educational experiences to be able to *imagine participating* in ways that expand upon their existing interests. Such an act of imagination often contradicts dominant narratives that students have internalised about their aptitude for learning. Yet, even when students were resilient enough to think about educational futures, we were acutely aware that none of our interviews or focus groups discussed topics like subject prerequisite pathways or tertiary entry scores with any level of understanding. Work in the sociology of education (Kenway and Fahey 2014) shows us that students in elite schools have knowledge about pathways to tertiary education built into their schooling.

Earlier we introduced a young person who wants to work in criminology because they like 'scary stuff' and they want to find out 'how people died and when and stuff'. This discussion went on to feature one of the young people in the group suggesting they might be 'a scientist or a lawyer or something'. Again, the relevance of tertiary entry scores and subject prerequisites to realising such dreams are largely lacking from such aspirational comments. One of the boys who wanted to be a computer programmer knew he had to get better at maths in order to realise his goal and Kim was practising fixing cars, so there were some pathway knowledges being developed. However, from what we could tell, these knowledges were not being taught in school. In order to think about the role that feelings and the imagination play in making further education a realistic possibility for those with precarious relationships to schooling, we refer back to our earlier discussion of Spinoza's conceptualisation of the imagination as initially, and primarily, embodied. Young people need to not only be taught about subject selection processes, but to intuitively know about the ways in which learning institutional knowledges happens: the kinds of knowledge that institutions want us to put together and the ends that can be achieved through making different kinds of knowledge combinations.

If feelings provide raw material that is then processed, traversed, and negotiated through reason, young people need more than an orientation towards or away from school, or university. They need to develop an understanding of, and confidence in, the capacity to learn in day-to-day life. They need familiarity with skills sets and knowledge bases, and aptitudes for performing particular kinds of tasks and undertaking certain practices and kinds of learning.

If the imagination is our sensory experience of the world, an experience that is a kind of collective awareness, then engaging with institutionalised knowledges, or knowledges that matter within institutionalised learning spaces, exposes young people to communities of knowledge production that are much wider than their embodied communities, and also represent knowledge generated in different historical and geographical places.

Pathways: knowing other people who have successes

There were a number of students who showed us that their understanding of educational pathways was created through knowing someone who had achieved some level of educational success, although, again, due to the nature of the cohort with which we were working, these cases were rare. One of the students in regional New South Wales wanted to follow in the footsteps of their grandmother, who had been a special education teacher:

I: Where did you do your work experience then?
P: It was a hairdresser's that was at ... where's that ... ? Valentine.
I: What, was it just boring?
P: It was just like I got that bored that I got down and scrubbed the floors and windows and stuff like that – it was that boring, I just thought 'Am I going to want to do this for the rest of my life if I do it' and then I also wanted to go to university and be a special ed teacher ...
I: Oh yes? That would be good.
P: ... because my grandma – that's how I get my looks and everything from her (heaps close to her) – she did that for seventeen years. Everywhere ...
(group interview with two young women, aged 15, Gemsvale)

This young woman wants a career that engages her intellect and emotions, which her work experience of scrubbing floors and windows did not give her. She did not enjoy the mainly physical nature of her work experience and turned her goals towards a more intellectually engaging career, and one which also allowed her to follow in the footsteps of her grandmother: a special education teacher.

As we noted in our discussion of the themed data set analysed for this chapter, some of the young men wanted to work in game development: 'Usually at home I'm the one talking about university. I want to go and learn how to make games' (group interview with three young men, aged 11, Gilchrist North). James's sister suggested he would be well suited to a career in games:

I: James, do you know when you first started thinking uni might be a place to go? It's a hard question isn't it? Or do you know where the idea came from – if people aren't talking about it so much – it would be really interesting to know where you got the idea from.

P: I got it from my sister because I was at the computer one night playing this game called 'Habbo' – my sister used to play it and I used to get free stuff from my friend's dad because he used to play it all the time; he was so rich on it. But he sold his account for I think it was $15,000 ... because he didn't want to play it any more. She told me because I liked it ... because do you know how you can make your own 'Habbo' things? I've always wanted to do that because my sister and her friend used to do it – I've always wanted to do that.

I2: So what did your sister actually say about university?

P: She didn't say anything about that but she told me IT would be pretty good for me so I figured that it was probably at university because that's where all the technology stuff is.

(group interview with seven young people, aged 15, Gilchrist North)

James's sister saw his aptitude for excelling in online spaces and his skills with computers and has built on the existing confidence he has in the sets of practices he uses here to help him believe he can go to university: 'the past "lives" through how memory endures in the present' (Coleman 2008, p. 97).

Adequate ideas of educational pathways

A functional educational pathway needs to be both grounded in existing ecologies of learning and sufficiently aligned to university knowledge systems to be practically realisable. The concept of an 'adequate idea' is explored by Spinoza, and it is more than an imagining: it is an engagement between imagination, reason, and intuition. An 'adequate idea' (Spinoza 2001, Def II.3) is a knowledge that reconciles practical, intuitive, and academic knowledges.

Adequate ideas are composites of different kinds of knowledges and they include the special memories we discussed above that young people hold on to, memories that tell them they can succeed and which have an 'indefinite continuance of existing' (Spinoza 2001, Def II.3). The memories stay in the present as long as they keep presenting themselves in the young people's subjectivity. But adequate ideas are more than imagination and memory. They also involve reason and intuition.

For Spinoza, what we take to be ideas of external objects (what universities look like from the outside) are largely ideas of bodily states and do not supply us with adequate knowledge of external bodies. 'Inadequate ideas' of external objects grow as opinion or imagination. What makes imagination inferior (Spinoza 2001, Prop II.41), although a necessary basis for all thought, is that imagination is knowledge of effects, *without knowledge of their cause*. Many of the young people we spoke to who knew about university had ideas based on inaccurate imaginings of what university might be like. Such young participants would have benefited greatly from knowledge about how universities work, what they teach, and why school subject pathways matter in terms of relationships in thought and transferrable skill sets.

We have whole ecologies of learning that are deprived of adequate ideas of university education. Young people whose knowledge ecologies are not enriched with links between their practical competencies and the knowledge pathways needed to get to university will be far less likely to participate in higher education. We need to move young people who have precarious relationships to education out of these confused imaginings of university and into what Spinoza calls reason, which involves engaging with institutionalised or abstract knowledge. Reason grasps the 'necessary relations between things' (Spinoza 2001, Prop II.44), such as knowledge systems assembling together to form not only extended competencies but also meeting higher education prerequisite subject pathways. Once reason can traverse the imagination we can come to know intuitively. By building on existing ecologies of learning with knowledge of university pathways and the kinds of knowledge needed to achieve these pathways we can help young people connect their everyday skills to their educational goals, and develop intuitive knowledges about higher education.

The following student needed more encouragement to keep his educational hope alive:

P: I probably would, I did when I was a little kid because I wanted to become a structural engineer, that's what I wanted to do, I wanted to do buildings and that kind of stuff but yeah, it dropped off since Grade 7, yeah I'd go to one if I needed to, I wouldn't, no I wouldn't just go there to learn something that I didn't really need to because it costs money.

(Jye, 14-year-old male, Woodhall)

The idea of being a structural engineer is not being developed in the existing ecology of learning to which this young person belongs, and their dream 'dropped off since Grade 7'. The imagination of a career couldn't be reconciled with the reason needed to achieve the career, or the intuition required to navigate the knowledges and contexts that lead to engineering. A focus group in Towers Estate tells a similar story:

I: It's sort of like about how you might imagine your future and how you might imagine your future education or your future employment and whether education plays a role in that.
P: Yes. Well, for me, I'm really, really, really interested in music. Currently relearning guitar because I used to learn it when I was younger. I stopped after I broke my finger. Like it's kind of hard to imagine what career I could get out of going to university for music, you know, what career I can get that I would actually want to have because a lot of those courses kind of lead towards different things, more like working in the music industry isn't ... you

know, doing technical stuff or orchestral stuff like a bit more prestigious sort of things that I don't really want to do because I don't really ...
                      (group interview with three young people, Towers Estate)

These young people are grappling to connect their imaginative knowledges, comprising what they know through doing and what they dream of doing, with formal educational pathways. If further support around the kind of career they 'could get out of going to university for music' was offered, they may well think differently about what tertiary education had to offer.

P1: Yes. I look at how much effort I've ... even though it's not that great, I look at the effort that I've taken to ...
P2: Put back into school.
P1: ... fix what my mistakes and ... like when I left school and started being a chef, my life did go downhill a lot and when I see people's lives going downhill and how hard it was for me to come out of it ...
P2: You try and help them.
P1: ... it is really disappointing to see the number of people that are making the same mistakes is growing. As hard as it is, it's still something that I wish that a lot more people could do; pick yourself back up and actually go 'My future's more important than the fun I'm having'.
             (Bethany and Eileen, 17- and 18-year-old females, Flindersvale)

As this passage suggests, many young participants worried about their future, and a huge amount of effort is required to build institutionalised educational pathways for those in disadvantaged situations. We need to support this 'huge amount of effort' with 'reason' about university and subject pathways, taught through an engagement with existing ecologies of learning. The following quotation evidences an intuitive approach to an educational pathway, in which a young person has combined imagination with reason, or abstract knowledge of subject areas, to develop a vocational goal that shows an enduring engagement with the power of visual cultures as a mode of expression for young people.

P1: Well as I said, I left just before Year 11 started, the day Year 11 started again, I went in to my mum and signed out, started being a chef and, it did, because of the stress levels and things like that, I got myself into some really bad things; started being a chronic smoker, was partying all the time just to try to relax a bit and it wasn't very easy but, as I said, some of my friends decided 'Let's go back to school' and that was when I was like 'You know what, I need to fix my life'. Then I started remembering how I'd always wanted to be a youth worker which is ironic because, you know, bad youth experiences ...
P2: Ex-partner.
P1: Yes and my ex-partner and his friends now work with the youth – it's just seeing what they've done makes you want to go ...

P2: And what they've achieved.

P1: ... maybe I could help do that and I want to actually go and do a degree in community and youth services. I also want to do ... it will be a double degree so it's going to be a lot of work. One is only for two years, the other is three.

P2: You're going to have fun.

P1: Yes. My other one is a bachelor of arts and basically I'll work as a youth worker Monday through Friday, spend my weekends at an arts school and I eventually want to be able to draw cartoons for kid's books and things like that.

(Bethany and Eileen, 17- and 18-year-old females, Flindersvale)

Widening participation programmes can, our data suggests, strengthen the amount of intuitive knowledge young people have about higher education, but these programmes need to emphasise practical knowledge pathways and recognise the existing ecologies of learning to which young people belong.

Conclusion: pleasures of making the future self

We hope to have shown that, often against staggering odds (Stehlik 2006), young people maintain a belief in their capacity to learn and the role that learning plays in educational pathways. We make three recommendations arising from our data. First, when young people demonstrate object attachment as a way of both escaping and bettering their life, this can be the result of desire for survival, mobility, higher income, and long-term health which are also associated with university education. This connection could be made more explicit. Second, the concept of ecologies of learning can be used as a way of extending student-centred learning practices. Thinking through the knowledges, things, people, and objects that make up the daily life cycles of young people can be a way of empowering students to learn about their 'encountering nature' (Bennett 2004, p. 353) and to extend and improve their learning encounters. Third, and most crucially, part of enriching young people's ecologies of learning needs to focus on building new associational pathways in thought that act as pathways to higher education. These pathways might begin within an existing ecology of learning, but will need to extend existing knowledges with a practical focus on university entrance requirements. We make these recommendations in the knowledge that university is not the answer for all young people, and that, in the present historical conditions, their participation will necessarily involve the accrual of significant debts.

However, thinking forward, for those that decide to go to university and are able to succeed in being admitted, we also need to plan for retention at university. Just getting in isn't enough. New associational pathways of thought would not only mean thoughts that act as pathways *to* higher education but also creating pathways *through* higher education. Showing how young people already have skills to succeed, and identifying existing useful associational pathways will help this happen in effective ways.

Notes

1 See Harwood et al. (2016) for detailed description of the places in this study as well as further information on methodology.
2 Samantha McMahon from the University of Wollongong generated this numerical detail of the data set that we analyse in this chapter.
3 Foucault describes technologies of subjectivity as the way we make ourselves, the beliefs and practices through which we become 'who we are'.
4 The 'Baby Bonus' can no longer be claimed. It began in 2002 and was abolished in 2014. The Baby Bonus was an Australian government payment of $5,000 per eligible child made in thirteen fortnightly instalments intended to help families with the costs of a newborn baby or adopted child (under the age of 16). It was payable to families who have not received Paid Parental Leave and whose estimated combined adjusted taxable income (ATI) is $75,000 or less.

References

Ahmed, S. 2006, *Queer phenomenology: orientations, objects, others*, Duke University Press, Durham, NC.
Australian Bureau of Statistics 2011, 'Census of population and housing: socio-economic indexes for areas (SEIFA)', ABS, Canberra, viewed 3 February 2017, www.abs.gov.au/AUSSTATS/abs@.nsf/DetailsPage/2033.0.55.0012011?OpenDocument.
Australian Bureau of Statistics 2013, 'Socio-economic indexes for areas', ABS, Canberra, viewed 3 February 2017, www.abs.gov.au/websitedbs/censushome.nsf/home/seifa.
Bennett, J. 2004, 'The force of things: steps toward an ecology of matter', *Political Theory*, vol. 32, no. 3, pp. 347–372.
Butler, J. 2004, *Precarious life: the powers of mourning and violence*, Verso, London.
Coleman, R. 2008, '"Things that stay": feminist theory, duration and the future', *Time and Society*, vol. 17, no. 1, pp. 85–102.
Department for Education and Children's Services 2010, 'ICAN: innovative community action networks', DECS, Government of South Australia, viewed 3 February 2017, www.decd.sa.gov.au/supporting-students/flexible-learning-options-flo.
Driscoll, C. 2014, *The Australian country girl: history, image, experience*, Ashgate, Farnham and Burlington, VT.
Foucault, M. 1991, *The history of sexuality: volume one*, Penguin, London.
Foucault, M. 1997, 'On the genealogy of ethics: an overview of work in progress', in P. Rabinow (ed.), *Ethics: subjectivity and truth (The essential works of Michel Foucault, 1954–1984, vol 1)*, New Press, New York, pp. 253–280.
Harwood, V., Hickey-Moody, A., McMahon, S., and O'Shea, S. 2016, *The politics of widening participation and university access for young people: making educational futures*, Routledge, Oxon.
Harwood, V., O'Shea, S., Uptin, J., Humphry, N., and Kervin, L. 2014, 'Precarious education and the university: navigating the silenced borders of participation', *International Journal of School Disaffection*, vol. 10, no. 2, pp. 23–44.

Harwood, V. and Rasmussen, M.L. 2013, 'Practicing critique, attending to truth: the pedagogy of discriminatory speech', *Educational Philosophy and Theory*, vol. 45, no. 8, pp. 874–884.

Hickey-Moody, A. and Kenway, J. 2014, 'Spatio-temporal and spatio-sensual assemblages of masculinity', in P. Hopkins and A. Gorman-Murray (eds), *Masculinity and place (gender, space and society)*, Ashgate, Abingdon., pp. 43–56.

HM Treasury and Department for Education and Skills 2007, *Policy review of children and young people: a discussion paper*, HMSO, Norwich.

Kenway, J. and Fahey, J. 2014, 'Staying ahead of the game: the globalising practices of elite schools', *Globalization, Societies and Education*, vol. 12, no. 2, pp. 177–195.

Knopp, L. 2004, 'Ontologies of place, placelessness, and movement: queer quests for identity and their impacts on contemporary geographic thought', *Gender, Place and Culture: A Journal of Feminist Geography*, vol. 11, no. 1, pp. 121–134.

Lehmann, W. 2009, 'Becoming middle class: how working-class university students draw and transgress moral class boundaries', *Sociology*, vol. 43, no. 4, pp. 631–647.

Spinoza, B. 2001, *Ethics*, Wadsworth, Herts.

Stehlik, T. P. 2006, *Levels of engagement: report of findings of the school retention action plan action research project*, University of South Australia, Adelaide.

Vinson, T. 2007, *Dropping off the edge: the distribution of disadvantage in Australia*, Jesuit Social Services/Catholic Social Services, Richmond, Vic.

Watkins, M. 2011, *Discipline and learn: bodies, pedagogy and writing*, Sense Publishers, Rotterdam.

Willis, P. 1977, *Learning to labour*, Saxon House, Aldershot. Wolff, J. and de-Shalit, A. 2007, *Disadvantage*, Oxford University Press, Oxford.

10 The use of mobile and new media technologies in a health intervention about HPV and HPV vaccination in schools

Cristyn Davies, S. Rachel Skinner, Harrison L. Odgers, George P. Khut and Angie Morrow

Introduction

The uses of mobile apps (application software) in health interventions to affect health behaviour change and/or disease management has become increasingly popular with the rise of mobile technologies (Guse et al. 2012; Lupton 2014; 2015). Mobile apps are self-contained programs or pieces of software generally downloaded by a user to a mobile device to fulfil a specified purpose. They are available through application distribution platforms such as Apple's App Store, Google Play, Window's Phone Store, and Blackberry app World to a target mobile device, or sometimes a laptop or desktop, either free or for a fee. Young people's ubiquitous use of technology and new media provides opportunities to educate them about a variety of health issues, including human papillomavirus (HPV), HPV vaccination, and also management of needle-related fear and anxiety. Young people's use of mobile and new media technologies are frequently constructed through discourses of risk, especially in relation to their interactions with sexual content (Davies and Robinson 2010; Albury, et al. 2013; Byron et al. 2013; Robinson, 2013; Albury and Byron 2015), too much screen time and lack of physical activity (Olds et al. 2006; Hardy et al. 2010; Guse et al. 2012). However, in this discussion we focus on the innovative capacity of mobile and new media technologies to educate, engage, and make accessible accurate health information and relaxation/distraction techniques to assist young people to become informed, agentic citizens.

First, we provide some brief background on children and adolescents' use of mobile and new media technologies, specifically mobile phone and app use. Second, we outline constructions of adolescence; and, third, we provide some background about children and adolescents' access to sex education. Understandings of adolescence and young people's access to sex education more broadly impact the development and implementation of educational resources about HPV and HPV vaccination in a school setting. We also provide some background about HPV and HPV vaccination and the limited knowledge adolescents have about these areas, which motivated the development and trial of our educational and relaxation/distraction resources. We provide brief details of the larger study HPV.edu, which is a cluster randomised controlled trial (RCT) evaluation of education, decisional support, and logistical strategies in school-based HPV vaccination of adolescents (Skinner et al. 2015).[1] Then we discuss the design and use of two apps trialled as part of this study (Skinner et al. 2015). We designed an app called 'HPV.edu' to teach Australian students eligible for the vaccine about HPV and HPV vaccination. This app also contains a distraction/relaxation component that can be used by young people leading up to, and on, vaccination day. For this app, we will also discuss student feedback. The second app is 'BrightHearts' – a biofeedback controlled interactive art app that combines relaxation training with multimedia distraction for the management of anxiety related to procedural pain. For this app, we will discuss some preliminary feedback based on qualitative research observations from its use during vaccination day as part of the HPV.edu trial.

Background

Children and adolescents' use of mobile and new media technologies

In Australia, the Australian Bureau of Statistics (2008–2009) Children's Participation in Cultural and Leisure Activities Survey collected data on children's (aged up to 14 years) mobile phone ownership and usage for the first time. At this time, an estimated 841,000 children, almost one-third (31 per cent) of all children, owned a mobile phone (ABS 2011). Mobile phone ownership increased with age; three-quarters (76 per cent) of 12–14-year-olds owned a mobile phone, compared with 2 per cent of 5–8-year-olds (ABS 2011). According to this survey, children primarily used mobile phones to contact family (60 per cent) rather than friends (36 per cent), and 4 four per cent of children had used their phone to access the Internet (ABS 2011).[2]

More recent Australian data (December 2013) indicates that 89 per cent of adolescents aged 14–17 years of age have a mobile phone and 69 per cent of mobile phone users have a smart phone (ACMA 2014). Of adolescents in this age group, 56 per cent used their mobile phone to go online and 72 per cent go online more than once per day (ACMA 2014).[3] According to ACMA, a key factor making social media, user-generated content, and professional online video desirable for adolescents is the convenience of mobile apps that facilitate easy access to viewing, streaming, and contributing to content. Of adolescents with a smartphone aged 14–17, 65 per cent downloaded an app during 2013 (ACMA 2014).

Given young people's engagement with technology, and specifically mobile technologies, our HPV.edu study advisory board composed of representatives from the fields of education, health, and medicine, recommended developing an app about HPV and HPV vaccination that could be easily downloaded by students onto their mobile devices.

Constructions of adolescents

In contemporary sociological and cultural theory, childhood, adolescence and adulthood are understood as socially constructed terms that are defined in relation to one another (Davies and Robinson 2010; Robinson 2013; Robinson and Davies 2014). Social constructionism refers to the complex ways society produces knowledge and understandings through diverse social practices that give meaning to and define objects, subjectivities and relationships (Davies and Robinson 2010). Adolescence has frequently been characterised in public discourse as a liminal space, or borderland, between childhood and adulthood (Robinson and Davies 2008; 2015). In 1986, the World Health Organization (WHO) suggested that the term 'young people' be used to refer to individuals between 10–24 years of age, which derived from the overlapping categories of 'adolescence' (10–19 years) and 'youth' (15–24 years) (WHO 1986; Bennett and Robards 2013). The concept of adolescence is a modern term that emerged at the beginning of the twentieth century (Hall 1916; Bessant et al. 1988; Bennett and Robards 2013). Like childhood, adolescence is culturally located and temporally specific. What it means to be an adolescent has changed historically, differs among cultural contexts, and is experienced differently in relation to social class, gender, ethnicity, sexuality, and so on. Understandings of adolescence are influenced by social, political, economic, and cultural contexts.

Current concepts of adolescence are frequently marked by the onset of puberty and influenced by biopsychosocial changes that lead into what is constituted as adulthood. Adolescence is most frequently divided into three sub-phases: early adolescence (10–14 years), middle adolescence (15–17 years), and late adolescence (18–20 years) (Leffert and Petersen 1996; Bennett and Robards 2013). Adolescent development encompasses increasing independence, autonomy from the family, greater peer affiliation and importance, sexual awareness, identity formation and physiological and cognitive maturation (Igra and Irwin 1996). While much research on adolescents focuses on the risks and challenges that may be encountered during the second decade of life, a positive, strengths-based youth development framework expands the traditional focus primarily on reducing risk to creating opportunities for adolescents to experience and learn (McNealy and Blanchard 2009; Saltmarsh and Davies 2010). This is not to deny that many adolescents do, indeed, live in situations where risks associated with violence, abuse, neglect, poverty, discrimination, and social exclusion are part of everyday lifeworlds, nor is it to minimise the effects of such situations on young people's lives and futures (Saltmarsh and Davies 2010). However, reframing development as a positive process is critical to support, socialise, challenge, and educate young people, which requires supportive relationships, accurate information, and skills-building opportunities. A strengths-based youth development framework includes: competence (the perception that one has the abilities and skills), confidence (the internal sense of self-efficacy and self-worth), connection (positive bonds with people and institutions), character (ethics, integrity, understanding standards of behaviour), and caring (sympathy and empathy for others) (McNealy and Blanchard 2009). Media literacy and sexual health and relationships literacy are imperative skills for adolescents to negotiate decision-making that impacts their current and future health and well-being.

Children and adolescents' access to sex education

Children's and adolescents' access to sexual health and relationships education is critical for building awareness and understandings of sexual ethics early in life (Robinson 2013). It is also crucial for fostering resilience in children and young people, and for developing their health and well-being, not just in the early and adolescent years but throughout one's life. However, cultural values associated with childhood and adolescence in many industrialised Western countries, such as 'childhood innocence', have hindered children's and young people's access to sexual health and relationships education (Robinson 2008; 2013; Robinson and Davies 2008; Davies and Robinson 2010). Childhood innocence is a sociocultural, legal, and political construction, fostered and maintained through everyday practices and interactions with children (Robinson 2013). Childhood innocence has been mobilised by some adults to justify or rationalise strictly regulating children's and adolescents' access to 'difficult knowledge', such as sexuality (Davies and Robinson 2010; Davies and Robinson 2013; Robinson 2013). Perspectives of adolescents as hypersexual, resistant to authority, and engaging in risky behaviours, can influence the regulation of adolescents' access to sexual health and relationships knowledge (Davies and Robinson 2010), including sexually transmitted infections. The myth that if you provide young people with too much sexual information it will encourage them to engage in those behaviours has hindered their access to appropriate sexual health and relationships education for adolescents (Robinson and Davies 2008; Fonner et al. 2014; Haberland and Rogow 2015). On the contrary, in their systematic review Fonner et al. (2014) found that school-based sex education is an effective intervention for generating 'HIV-related knowledge and decreasing sexual risk behaviors among participants, including delaying sexual debut, increasing condom use, and decreasing numbers of sexual partners'.[4] Nicole Haberland and Deborah Rogow (2015) point out that the 1994 International Conference on Population and Development's (ICPD) Programme of Action (United Nations Population Fund), explicitly calls on governments to provide sexuality education to promote the well-being of adolescents and 'clarifies that such education should take place both in schools and at the community level, be age appropriate, begin as early as possible, and foster mature decision making' (S15). Cultural values and beliefs around childhood and adolescence that limit young people's access to accurate, accessible information about sexual health and relationships education and HPV and HPV vaccination, prevent young people from effectively participating in decisions about their own health.

HPV and HPV vaccination

HPV infection, if persistent, can cause cancer of the cervix, vulva, vagina, penis, anus, and throat. The worldwide prevalence of infection with HPV in women without cervical pathology is 11–12 per cent with higher rates in sub-Saharan Africa (24 per cent), Eastern Europe (21 per cent), and Latin America (16 per cent) (Forman et al. 2012). The two most prevalent cancer-causing genotypes are HPV16 (3.2 per cent) and HPV18 (1.4 per cent).[5] Of the estimated 12.7 million cancers occurring in 2008, 610,000 (population attributable fraction = 4.8 per cent) could be attributed to HPV infection (Forman et al. 2012). According to incidence data from the Australian Institute of Health and Welfare (AIHW), which is estimated at a rate per 100,000 people, in Australia in 2015 cervical cancer affected 885 people, while 395 were affected with anal cancer (AIHW 2016).[6] According to AIHW, the total number of head and neck cancers diagnosed in Australia in 2009 was 3,896, accounting for 3.4 per cent of all cancers diagnosed (114,137) (AIHW 2014).[7] HPV has been recognised as contributing to some cancers of the head and neck, particularly cancers affecting the oral cavity and oropharynx (the area at the back of the throat) (AIHW 2014). In Australia in 2009, 82 people were affected with penile cancer, which is rare (AIHW 2012).[8] The National HPV Vaccination Program in Australia commenced school delivery in April 2007 for girls and February 2013 for boys, using the quadrivalent HPV [4vHPV] vaccine.[9] This vaccine protects against two major HPV genotypes: 16 and 18, which are responsible for 70–80 per cent of cervical cancers (de Sanjosé et al. 2013) and also genotypes 6 and 11, which cause most types of genital warts (Garland et al. 2007).

In Australia, adolescents aged 11–14 years (Years 7 or 8 in secondary school depending on jurisdiction) are vaccinated as part of the School-based Immunisation Program (SPIB), which is subsidised by the Commonwealth government. The HPV vaccine is offered alongside other vaccines in the national school vaccination programme (e.g. diphtheria, tetanus, and pertussis (DTaP) booster and varicella vaccines). The Australian National HPV Vaccination Program Register reports that for girls aged 14–15 years (as of mid 2012), 82 per cent received HPV dose 1, 78 per cent received HPV dose 2, and 71 per cent received HPV dose 3 (2013) (Register 2015). For a comprehensive reduction in HPV disease burden at a population level, vaccination uptake needs to be consistently high (Tabrizi et al. 2012; Drolet et al. 2015; Skinner et al. 2015). HPV vaccines are now recommended as part of vaccination programmes for adolescent girls in many countries (Markowitz et al. 2012), and more recently some countries have extended this recommendation to boys. Implementation of HPV vaccination programmes varies considerably by country, as do vaccination coverage levels (Drolet et al. 2015; Wigle et al. 2016). Generally, school-based programmes have higher coverage than non-school-based programmes (H. S. Marshall et al. 2013).

Limited knowledge and understanding about HPV and HPV vaccination

Many adolescents have limited or no understanding of the vaccines they receive, including the HPV vaccine, or the diseases they are intended to prevent (C. Cooper Robbins et al. 2010; Davies and Burns 2014; Burns and Davies 2015; Skinner et al. 2015). Research in Australian schools (C. Cooper Robbins et al. 2010; 2011; Burns and Davies 2015) indicates that adolescents' understanding, self-efficacy, and involvement in decision-making about the HPV vaccine are low, while vaccination-related fear and anxiety is high (S. Cooper Robbins et al. 2010; Bernard et al. 2011). Australian girls offered the vaccine as part of the school programme had limited or no understanding about HPV, HPV vaccination, their future risk of cervical cancer, and other sexually transmitted infections (C. Cooper Robbins et al. 2010; Burns and Davies 2015; Cooper et al. 2015). In addition, poor understanding about HPV and the HPV vaccine was also linked to heightened anxiety on vaccination day (S. Cooper Robbins et al. 2010). Limited knowledge about the HPV vaccine may contribute to poor acceptance, initiation, and completion of the vaccine series (Fu et al. 2014). Knowledge of HPV and vaccination has been found to be even lower in Australian boys than girls (Agius 2010).

Despite media awareness (Davies and Burns 2014; Burns and Davies 2015), adolescents still experience some uncertainty about where they can and should obtain reliable information about the vaccine (C. Cooper Robbins et al. 2010; Kessels et al. 2012). In Australia, CSL Biotherapies (now known as Sequirus),[10] the pharmaceutical company responsible for the production and distribution of the quadrivalent vaccine in Australia, engaged Edelman, a public relations firm, to develop a media campaign called 'I-did' to raise awareness of the HPV Program. However, this campaign primarily targeted women aged 18–26, given that the vaccine was also subsidised by the commonwealth government for this age group between 1 July 2007 to 30 June 2009. The campaign consisted of a television and online advertisement about the vaccine and a succession of posters that were displayed on public billboards and in doctors' offices (Burns and Davies 2015). Information for adolescents was made available through the 'Post-it' campaign (both print and online) run by the Australian Commonwealth. This campaign was conducted in conjunction with the consent forms provided to students by the Commonwealth. When boys were included in the SBIP, media awareness campaigns were available online through the Cancer Council (www.hpvvaccine.org.au) and the Commonwealth Government's Department of Health Immunise Australia Program (www.immunise.health.gov.au/internet/immunise/publishing.nsf/Content/immunise-hpv). However, since the SBIP was instated in 2007, no formal in-school education has been required for students eligible for the vaccine.

Informed young people are in a better position to make decisions about their health and well-being (Davies and Burns 2014; Burns and Davies 2015). Young people are unlikely to learn about HPV and HPV vaccination without structured and effective education (Cooper et al. 2015). Expecting parents/

guardians to educate young people is also unlikely to be effective as their own knowledge about HPV and HPV vaccination can also be very limited (H. Marshall et al. 2007; H. S. Marshall et al. 2013). As with sex education more broadly (Davies and Robinson 2010; Robinson and Davies 2014), parents/guardians also experience barriers such as embarrassment about discussing the sexually transmitted nature of the virus with their child.

Methods

HPV.edu is a multi-centre cluster randomised controlled trial (RCT) of a complex intervention in 40 secondary schools with 6,965 Year 8 students funded by the National Health and Medical Research Council. In the discipline of medicine, RCTs are considered the most rigorous way of determining whether a cause–effect relation exists between treatment and outcome and for assessing the cost-effectiveness of a treatment (Sibbald and Roland 1998). Generally, the unit of control in an RCT is an individual subject (patient). In a cluster RCT, groups of subjects (such as schools) are randomised to receive an intervention or act as a control (usual practice) rather than individual subjects (such as students). Our study took place in Western Australia (WA) and South Australia (SA) with schools stratified by government, Catholic, and independent sectors and geographical location, and randomly allocated to intervention or control. The study had 21 intervention (3,806 students) and 19 (3,159 students) control schools. Intervention schools received a complex intervention,[11] which included an adolescent intervention (education and distraction), a decisional support tool for parents and adolescents, and logistical strategies (consent form returns strategies, in-school mop-up vaccination and vaccination-day guidelines).[12]

The study included a quantitative evaluation (validated student survey) and a qualitative component (17 focus groups with 111 students, 22 interviews with parents, 11 interviews with school personnel, 10 immunisation team interviews, 20 school observation logs of vaccination day processes). We also developed fidelity logs for teachers undertaking the education intervention with students, for immunisation nurses on vaccination day, and for school personnel supervising vaccination day.[13] Our mixed-methods evaluation design was implemented to explore in-depth possible mechanisms for any observed effect of the intervention on knowledge of HPV and HPV vaccination, as well as change in a range of psychosocial outcomes, such as fear and anxiety relating to HPV vaccination and HPV vaccination uptake.

Elements of the intervention package used technology as a means to achieve our study aims. We designed an app to engage students in learning about HPV and HPV vaccination and to teach them relaxation techniques through the use of distraction to be used on vaccination day. The app was available to students via iPads on vaccination day and was also available for students to download across platforms onto their own mobile devices.

Below we describe the components of the HPV.edu app available for use by students leading up to and on vaccination day. We also analyse the user experience from the perspective of students in study intervention schools. Additionally, we outline the development of BrightHearts – a heart-rate-controlled interactive artwork and biofeedback-assisted relaxation training app. Using observational data, we analyse the implementation of BrightHearts with students on vaccination day across three schools involved in the HPV.edu study.

HPV.edu app: using mobile technologies to improve adolescent knowledge about HPV and HPV vaccination

We found that technology affected change in two key areas; first, by providing knowledge in a user-friendly and engaging format for young people, increasing their understanding of HPV and HPV vaccination; and, second, through providing a distraction for students on vaccination day. The app allowed students to privately access the seven animated film chapters about HPV and HPV vaccination, a text relevant to the content of the film chapters, and an e-magazine about HPV and HPV vaccination. These components were also available outside the app format: teachers and school nurses were provided with a DVD of the film chapters to screen during class time, to be followed by a discussion with students as well as other educational activities available in a teacher supplement; and the magazine was also available in hard copy format for students to read outside of class time.

This way, young people could rewatch the film chapters privately to reinforce learning, and students who were absent could also access the film content and the magazine content by downloading the app, which was made available for all students across Apple and Android platforms. The film chapter content included the following chapters: What is HPV?; What is HPV vaccination?; Males and HPV; HPV Decision-Making; Vaccination on the day: Vaccination in the future; Recap; and Credits. Simple animation is used as the format to convey concepts, balancing the need to engage young people's attention and personalising the information, but also to ensure it was an acceptable format to convey sensitive concepts for schools across all sectors (government, Catholic, independent). The magazine entitled: *Human-Papi What?* focuses on HPV and HPV vaccination reinforcing student learning in a familiar magazine format. Students were provided with targeted information about HPV and HPV vaccination through the genre of an advice column, true stories, quizzes, health recipes, and calming exercises (Cooper et al. 2015). Each of the educational components was developed with input from focus groups and individual interviews with young people, in an iterative way (Cooper et al. 2015). Feedback on the educational components was also received from experts in the field, and the HPV.edu advisory board.

In the HPV.edu study, students primarily described the film chapters about HPV and HPV vaccination positively. They particularly liked being able to 'visualise' the content, such as the way the vaccine works in the body, rather than 'just reading off a piece of paper'. Students appreciated the simple animations, commenting on the 'nice and simple graphics', and they enjoyed the 'colourful' and 'bright' animations. The use of animation, rather than real images of nude people, was described as 'not as gross' by one student, suggesting that animated representation may reduce the embarrassment commonly experienced by young people when discussing sexually transmitted infections, and sex education more broadly. Adolescents really liked that the animations were designed and 'presented more for kids instead of adults', which assisted in engaging students in a positive learning experience. Students made fewer references to the magazine, but commented that they enjoyed the smoothie recipes and advice to eat breakfast on the day of vaccination, so as to feel less faint.

School personnel (teachers and school nurses) also responded positively to the film chapters, almost universally recognising this resource as the most beneficial aspect of the educational intervention, due to its ability to engage students and 'facilitate discussion'. School personnel found the film chapters a valuable teaching resource commenting on the 'simple but informative' and 'easy to understand' animated format that 'worked well with that [adolescent] age group' and 'grabbed their [students'] attention'. School personnel saw the utility of an audiovisual resource, commenting that the target age groups 'are very visual learners'. School personnel also observed that the use of animation led to 'less tittering' about naked bodies, and in doing so 'kept it very factual for the students'.

Development of BrightHearts

As part of the HPV.edu study, we undertook a feasibility study of BrightHearts in three secondary schools in SA. BrightHearts is a heart-rate-controlled biofeedback mediated artwork that was developed at the Children's Hospital at Westmead for the purpose of teaching children biofeedback-mediated relaxation techniques. BrightHearts uses an iPad to display a colourful geometric artwork, which responds to changes in heart rate transmitted by a wireless pulse oximeter. There is also an auditory component that responds to decreases in heart rate by producing musical sounds. Biofeedback is a process that enables the self-regulation of normally involuntary body processes (Frank et al. 2010).

The subject receives external validation in response to lowering their heart rate by employing calming techniques (breathing, visualisation). The initial prototype was developed from an interactive digital artwork, 'Cardiomorphologies', designed by one of the investigators (Muller et al. 2006). The initial prototype consisted of a PC-based digital artwork, which responded to changes in heart rate conveyed via a wireless serial port connection.

BrightHearts differs from existing commercially available biofeedback applications for mobile and desktop computers in that it has been designed to be highly accessible and user-friendly for children by focusing the user's attention on gradual changes in the quality of a 'mandala'-like circular interface. Other kinds of animation used to distract young people in clinical settings are most frequently object- and/or character-driven visuals used in regular computer games, and biofeedback displays consisting of simple time–series graphs and bar charts (Henriques et al. 2011) or animations of pleasant nature scenes or graphics (Culbert et al. 1996) or fantasy-world scenarios such as used in the biofeedback relaxation training game 'Journey to the Wild Divine' (Amon and Campbell 2008).

In contrast, BrightHearts was designed to enable the user's eye to rest on a single, central point of focus, encouraging a more relaxed quality of visual engagement and interaction. Like many other interactive artworks that explore the aesthetics of body-focused interaction (Penny 1996; Stern 2013), BrightHearts draws the user's attention to an exploration of kinaesthetic relationships between body movement and changes in the artwork's appearance. Users can contract successive layers of circular imagery from beyond the edge of the screen, inwards towards the centre of the screen using gentle, sustained exhalations, in combination with imagining pleasant relaxing sensations and situations. The more relaxed users can allow themselves to be and the slower their average heart rate, the more layers they can draw inwards towards the centre of the screen.

The BrightHearts app was developed through an interactive design process (Morrow and Khut 2014). Qualitative data was collected through focus groups of paediatric health professionals (N=24) and individual child interviews (N=42) in a hospital setting. Observations and qualitative data collected in this study were used to develop subsequent prototypes, which eventuated in an iPad app. Heart rate and heart rate variability biofeedback provides visual and/or auditory feedback in response to changes in heart rate (Frank et al. 2010; Glick and Greco 2010) elicited through a combination of paced breathing and relaxation. Studies in adults have reported benefits for heart rate variability biofeedback in the management of headaches (Christie 2009), abdominal pain (Scharff 1997), burns (Achterberg et al. 1988), chronic neck pain (Hallman et al. 2011), constipation (Heymen et al. 2011), and behaviour (Linkenhoker 1983). Paediatric studies have reported benefits from the application of biofeedback techniques in the management of pain associated with sickle cell disease (Myrvik et al. 2012), bladder and bowel dysfunction (Lee et al. 2012), headaches (Sieberg et al. 2012), respiratory conditions, and psychological disorders (McBurnett et al. 2011). The efficacy of biofeedback-mediated approaches to procedural pain management has not been evaluated in children and adolescents.

Distraction: using technology to assist in the management of adolescent related anxiety on vaccination day

Anxiety and distraction

Anxiety is an emotional state based upon the anticipation of an impending threat, defined or undefined in nature, that causes apprehension, self-doubt in one's ability to cope, and expanded interpretations over the seriousness of the perceived threat (Stein et al. 2010). Anxiety can become detrimental to an individual's normal functioning if it interferes with daily tasks or important activities, for example, receiving a vaccination. Anxiety is a commonly reported emotion in studies of paediatric and adolescent vaccination, and appears to be primarily anticipatory in nature (S. Cooper Robbins et al. 2010; Bernard et al. 2011). Anticipatory anxiety is associated with higher levels of reported pain from stimuli (Tsao et al. 2004; Kain et al. 2006). Distraction is a frequently used technique in healthcare during procedures or processes that may cause pain or anxiety.

Distraction is used to shift a person's focus from a potentially painful and/or anxiety-provoking clinical procedure, towards something engaging and attractive thus hindering their capacity to concentrate on potentially painful stimuli in an effort to reduce pain, distress, and anxiety (Lambert, 1999; Kleiber and McCarthy 2006; Koller and Goldman 2012). Effective distraction can shift attention away from anxiety-provoking stimuli, thereby reducing the capacity of a person to focus on the stimuli, and by extension cause a reduction of their anxiety and pain. A systematic review of distraction techniques for children and adolescents undergoing painful or anxiety-provoking procedures revealed that a wide range of distraction methods have been researched, from immersive virtual reality to passive listening to music (Koller and Goldman 2012). Studies analysing needle-related procedures found that use of interactive technology, such as videos games, was significantly associated with clinically meaningful decreases in pain and distress in children, compared to non-interactive measures (Dahlquist, Busby et al. 2002; Dahlquist, Pendley et al. 2002). This evidence suggests that use of interactive technology, such as games and apps, provides stimulus that is able to distract adolescents from their anticipatory anxiety. Below, we outline the components of HPV.edu and BrightHearts that we used to distract young people on vaccination day.

HPV.edu app: distraction

The HPV.edu app contained a painting component, whereby young people could design and create their own colourful artworks on an iPad that was provided while waiting in line to be vaccinated, or on their own mobile devices. The painting component required young people to engage in an active form of distraction promoting adolescent engagement in an interactive activity involving fine motor and visual skills. Our app also contained an audio component through which young people could listen to calming music for relaxation and meditation purposes on vaccination day. The auditory component is a passive form of distraction, whereby young people are invited to participate in previously learned relaxation exercises that were included in the teacher education component of the intervention. The relaxation/guided imagery activity introduced an active form of distraction that could be combined with the passive auditory component of our app on vaccination day.

In our study, students described the positive benefits of using the intervention iPad and app primarily as a means of distracting themselves prior to vaccination, with benefits coming from decreased anxiety towards the upcoming vaccination. One student awaiting vaccination commented:

> Um, so yeah, the kids that were sitting in the chairs with nothing to do you could just see on their faces that they were actually anxious but the students that had used the iPads and were distracted um ... they were smiling and chatting.

Other participants in the immunisation process also noted the benefits of distracting students in the vaccination environment, with one school personnel member noting that 'any distraction I think is helpful. Anything that is going to take their mind off what they are waiting for is good.' Our observations of the school vaccination environment revealed that students who were not distracted by the use of technology, either via the intervention app or their own device, were more likely to try to interact with other students and cause disruption. Our results supported previous studies that identified that student fear and anxiety towards vaccination was largely anticipatory in nature, and influenced by factors within the physical environment (S. Cooper Robbins et al. 2010; Bernard et al. 2011). We identified factors that could positively impact on the vaccination setting including, but not limited to, guidelines for nurses and teachers about the set-up of the vaccination room to minimise student anxiety, promote student privacy, and assist with the efficiency of vaccination processes and distraction strategies to directly assist the management of adolescent anxiety (Skinner et al. 2015). Strategically distracting students by targeted use of mobile technologies not only positively impacts on student experience of vaccination day, but also contributes to the overall calmness and efficiency of the vaccination day setting in the school environment.

Our research suggests that multimedia, technology-based education is preferred by students, that young people are receptive to being distracted by technology within the vaccination environment, and that education plays an important role in allowing students to approach vaccination with more self-efficacy. One student describes using the HPV.edu app on an iPad on vaccination day:

> I thought it was a pretty good idea just like because everyone was really nervous on the day so like if you just had something to take your mind

off it for a little bit – or to give you more information about what you are actually getting.

As our research demonstrates, adolescents are receptive to education via interactive technology such as iPads and apps, and thus further efforts targeting health behaviours employing these mediums are likely to have success.

BrightHearts: biofeedback distraction

As part of our HPV.edu intervention, we undertook a feasibility study of the BrightHearts app with students at three co-educational secondary schools (government, Catholic, independent) in Adelaide (SA). Two research staff made available five BrightHearts (iPad and sensors) for students awaiting vaccination. In each school selected students used BrightHearts while seated and waiting for their vaccinations to ensure safety of the equipment and to better focus on the use of the app. Students were given the option of using BrightHearts during vaccination, and returning it afterwards, or just using it prior to vaccination. We found that there was variability in the school vaccination environments and students appeared better able to focus on using the app when the environment was well coordinated and managed. For example, in one school, students using BrightHearts were moved to three different locations while waiting for vaccination, whereas in another school, research staff and students stayed in one location, which improved the student experience of BrightHearts. Remaining in one location without interruptions provided a setting in which students could focus on the app, and therefore have more control over slowing their breathing to enable a sense of calm before their vaccination.

Approximately 50 students (about 150 students in total) in each of the three schools piloted BrightHearts. Most students said that they liked using the app, and that it made their vaccination experience better. Some students said that they did not feel the vaccination while using the BrightHearts app, and others said that it helped their experience, even in a small way during vaccination. Few extremely anxious students did not notice much of a difference, however this appeared to occur mostly where the school environment was less well coordinated. We found that some immunisation nurses said that they felt BrightHearts helped the students who used the app while they were being vaccinated. One nurse commented that she had to change her usual position to assist a student to raise his/her uniform sleeve because students were using their hands to hold the iPad (sensors had lanyards for students to wear around their neck). In the school setting with less well-coordinated processes, the immunisation nurses commented that they thought the device made very little or no difference to students' anxiety. Factors contributing to effective coordination of school-based immunisation settings include commitment from school personnel, planning appropriate time and space for vaccinations, clear communication with and between agencies involved, and flexibility depending on school setting (S. Cooper Robbins et al. 2010).[14] In addition to education of teachers and students about HPV and HPV vaccination, our intervention included logistical strategies to improve vaccination in the school setting: guidelines for nurses and teachers about the set-up of the vaccination room to minimise anxiety and strategies to directly assist the management of adolescent anxiety; mail-out of consent forms (instead of being delivered to parents through adolescents); incentives (non-material class prizes) for classroom consent form return, regardless of whether parental consent is granted or not; and mop-ups offered for students who were absent on a previous vaccination day (Skinner et al. 2015). BrightHearts is currently being trialled in a school-based immunisation setting in WA with students, in a clinical setting in Victoria with young women getting venepuncture, and in a paediatric hospital setting with children undergoing either peripheral blood collection, intramuscular injections of botulinum toxin (Botox), or cannula insertions (emergency department).

Conclusion

Our research demonstrates that mobile and new media technologies can be used innovatively to engage, educate, and make accessible accurate health information and relaxation/distraction techniques for adolescents as part of a public health programme in a school setting. While young people's use of mobile and new media technologies is most often constructed through discourses of risk, we have developed and provided examples of two apps: HPV. edu and BrightHearts that showcase the positive potential of mobile and new media use to educate, distract, and assist young people to relax in a school-based vaccination setting. While adolescents and young people are frequently constructed through discourses that foreground associations with deviance, instability, emotionality, and irresponsibility, our use of mobile and new media technologies in a school setting offered opportunities for students to be informed about their health and well-being, participate in decision-making, and to develop skills to manage anxiety and promote relaxation through the mechanism of biofeedback. Adolescents have the right to be well informed about HPV and HPV vaccination with accurate and accessible information, so that they have an understanding of HPV-related diseases, transmission of the virus, and also how the vaccine works and what protection it offers. Our research establishes that adolescents are receptive to being distracted by mobile, new media technologies within the school-based vaccination environment and that multimedia, interactive education is a preferred mode of engagement. Significantly, education plays a critical role in allowing students to approach vaccination as informed citizens with more self-efficacy.

Acknowledgements

The National Health and Medical Research Council funded this study under grant application 1026765. GSK Australia provided an investigator-initiated educational grant for the development of HPV educational materials, which were used in this study. Trial registration: Australian and New Zealand Clinical Trials Registry, ACTRN12614000404628, 14.04.2014. We would like to thank our Advisory Board for their cooperation with this study and their invaluable advice and feedback. We would like to acknowledge Seqirus (BioCSL) for providing an investigator-initiated research grant to assist in collection of data from boys. Thank you to our research participants: the students, teachers, school nurses, parents/guardians, and immunisation team members for their invaluable input. We also wish to acknowledge Gemma Abraham, an outstanding summer scholar, for her contribution to coding the qualitative data in NVivo, enabled by the Sydney Medical School Summer Scholars Program, University of Sydney, Australia. Special thanks to members of our evaluation team on the ground in WA and SA, who worked to implement and help evaluate the intervention in two states of Australia: Helen Marshall, Tanya Stoney, Joanne Collins, Jane Jones, Heidi Hutton, and Adriana Parrella.

Notes

1. See the 'Methods' section for an explanation of a cluster RCT.
2. 'Tasmania had the highest proportion of children who owned a mobile phone (41 per cent), while in the Northern Territory, 27 per cent of children had mobile phones. All other states and territories had similar rates of mobile phone ownership, at around 30 per cent. Mobile phone ownership was also similar across Remoteness Areas. In this study, Remoteness Area (RA) is a geographical structure which intends to classify areas sharing common characteristics of remoteness into broad geographical regions (Remoteness Areas). A higher proportion of children from one-parent families than couple families owned a mobile phone (38 per cent and 29 per cent respectively)' (ABS 2011).
3. 'Given advances in mobile technology, it is unsurprising that the number of teenagers using the internet via mobile phones has more than tripled in the four years since December 2009 to reach 639,000 users during December 2013' (ACMA 2014).
4. This article is available online and does not have a page reference, see: http://journals.plos.org/plosone/article?id=10.1371/journal.pone.0089692, viewed 1 July 2016.
5. Prevalence increases in women with cervical pathology in proportion to the severity of the lesion reaching around 90 per cent in women with grade three cervical intraepithelial neoplasia and invasive cancer (Forman et al. 2012).
6. Estimates for 2012–2016 (based on 2002–2011 incidence data) are presented.
7. Head and neck cancer incidence refers to the *number of new cases* of head and neck cancers diagnosed during a specific period, usually one year. It does not refer to the *number of people* newly diagnosed (because one person can be diagnosed with more than one head or neck cancer in a year), although the two numbers are likely to be similar.
8. The 2009 incidence data include estimates for NSW and the ACT.
9. See the Pharmaceutical Benefits Advisory Committee (PBAC) decision to include the HPV quadrivalent vaccine in the National Immunisation Program: www.pbs.gov.au/info/industry/listing/elements/pbac-meetings/psd/2006-11/pbac-psd-gardsil nov06, viewed 15 July 2016. The rationale was as follows: 'The submission sought funding for Gardasil on the National Immunisation Program (NIP) for the prevention of human papillomavirus (HPV) infection in an ongoing group of 12 year

old girls and for a catch-up program for all girls and women 13–26 years ... The PBAC recommended to the Minister that a school-based program (for 12 to 18 year-old girls) be implemented under the National Immunisation Program on the basis of a high, but acceptable cost-effectiveness ratio resulting from a price reduction.' In addition: 'the PBAC subsequently recommended funding of the 18–26 year cohort on the NIP, as a catchup program for a period of 2 years based on a price reduction additional to that proposed for the second catch up group. As a consequence of this price reduction, the incremental cost per life year gained was now of a similar magnitude as that for the primary cohort (12 and 13 year olds).' See also the PBAC decision extending the quadrivalent HPV vaccine to Australian boys: www.pbs.gov.au/info/industry/listing/elements/pbac-meetings/psd/2011-11/pbac-psd-quadrivalent-nov11, viewed 15 July 2016. The rationale to extend the vaccine for boys after two former rejections was: 'The PBAC recommended extension of the National Immunisation Program listing of quadrivalent human papillomavirus (HPV) (types 6, 11, 16, 18) recombinant vaccine, solution for injection 0.5 mL, to include ongoing administration to males approximately twelve to thirteen years of age in a school-based program and for two catch-up cohorts for all males in the two year groups above the ongoing cohort, delivered over two years for Year 9 males, on the basis of acceptable cost effectiveness compared with female-only vaccination, which forms the basis of the revised economic evaluation in the re-submission.'

10 'Seqirus, formerly bioCSL, manufactures and in-licenses, markets and distributes vaccines with particular focus on vaccines for the prevention and treatment of serious disease ... In July 2015, bioCSL and the influenza vaccines of Novartis joined forces to create Seqirus, now the second largest influenza vaccine company in the world' (www.seqirus.com.au/about, viewed 1 August 2016).

11 According to Mark Pettigrew (2011, p. 397), the Medical Research Council guidance suggests 'complexity resides (among other things) in the number of interacting components; the number and difficulty of behaviours required by those delivering or receiving the intervention; the number of groups of organizational levels targeted by the intervention; the number and variability of outcomes; and the degree of flexibility or tailoring of the intervention permitted'. For further detail see Pettigrew (2011).

12 In-school mop-up vaccinations refer to the immunisation team visiting the school at another time/date to vaccinate students who were absent on vaccination day. In-school mop-ups assist to increase vaccination coverage and are more convenient for parents/guardians who may not be able to take their child to another clinic or GP for a vaccination dose.

13 Each educator (teacher and/or school nurse) was invited to complete a log documenting lesson type, student year group, number of students in attendance at the HPV.edu lesson, sex of students, lesson time spent educating student about HPV and HPV vaccination, education resources used, number of students that received the magazine, number of students that undertook the student questionnaire, kinds of questions asked by students about HPV and HPV vaccination, educator confidence with responding to student questions, educator comments and suggestions regarding the education resources.

14 In addition to education of teachers and students about HPV and HPV vaccination, our intervention included logistical strategies to improve vaccination in the school setting: guidelines for nurses and teachers about the set-up of the vaccination room to minimise anxiety and strategies to directly assist the management of adolescent anxiety; mail-out of consent forms (instead of being delivered to parents through adolescents); incentives (non-material class prizes) for classroom consent form return, regardless of whether parental consent is granted or not; and mop-ups offered for students who were absent on a previous vaccination day (Skinner et al. 2015).

References

ABS 2011, 'Australian social trends', Australian Bureau of Statistics, Canberra, viewed 24 January 2017, www.abs.gov.au/AUSSTATS/abs@.nsf/Lookup/4102.0Main+Features60Jun+2011.

Achterberg, L., Kenner, C., and Lawlis, G. F. 1988, 'Severe burn injury: a comparison of relaxation, imagery and biofeedback for pain management', *Journal of Mental Imagery*, vol. 12, no. 1, pp. 71–87.

ACMA 2014, 'Aussie teens online', Australian Communications and Media Authority, viewed 24 January 2017, www.acma.gov.au/theACMA/engage-blogs/engage-blogs/Research-snapshots/Aussie-teens-online.

Agius, P.A. 2010, 'Human papillomavirus and cervical cancer: Gardasil vaccination status and knowledge amongst a nationally representative sample of Australian secondary school students', *Vaccine*, vol. 28, no. 27, pp. 4416–4422.

AIHW 2012, *Cancer in Australia: an overview*, cat. no. CAN 88, Australian Institute of Health and Welfare, Canberra.

AIHW 2014, *Head and neck cancers in Australia*, cat. no. CAN 80, Australian Institute of Health and Welfare, Canberra. Retrieved from: www.aihw.gov.au/WorkArea/DownloadAsset.aspx?id=60129547289

AIHW 2016, 'Incidence and mortality of anal cancer', Australian Institute of Health and Welfare, Canberra, viewed 24 January 2017, www.aihw.gov.au/cancer/cancer-in-australia-overview-2014/appendixb/- t3

Albury, K. and Byron, P. 2015, *Rethinking media and sexuality education: research report*, University of New South Wales, Sydney.

Albury, K., Crawford, K., Byron, P., and Matthews, B. 2013, *Young people and sexting Australia: ethics, representation and the law*, University of New South Wales, Sydney.

Amon, K.L. and Campbell, A. 2008, 'Can children with AD/HD learn relaxation and breathing techniques through biofeedback video games?', *Australian Journal of Educational and Developmental Psychology*, vol. 8, pp. 72–84.

Bennett, D. L. and Robards, F. 2013, 'What is adolescence and who are adolescents?', in M. Kang, S. R. Skinner, L. A. Sanci, and S. M. Sawyer (eds), *Youth health and adolescent medicine*, IP Communications, Melbourne, pp. 3–19.

Bernard, D., Cooper Robbins, S., McCaffery, K., Scott, C., and Skinner, S. 2011, 'The domino effect: adolescent girls' response to human papillomavirus vaccination', *Medical Journal of Australia*, vol. 194, no. 6, pp. 297–300.

Bessant, J., Sercombe, H., and Watts, R. 1988, *Youth studies: an Australian perspective*, Addison Wesley Longman, South Melbourne.

Burns, K. and Davies, C. 2015, 'Constructions of young women's health and wellbeing in neoliberal times: a case study of the HPV Vaccination Program in Australia', in K. Wright and J. McLeod (eds), *Rethinking youth wellbeing: critical perspectives*, Springer, New York, pp. 71–90.

Byron, P., Albury, K. and Clifton, E. 2013, '"It would be weird to have that on Facebook": young people's use of social media and the risk of sharing sexual health information', *Reproductive Health Matters*, vol. 21, no. 41, pp. 35–44.

Christie, N. H. 2009, 'Integrating biofeedback into a pediatric neuroscience department', *Biofeedback*, vol. 37, no. 4, pp. 126–128.

Cooper Robbins, C., Bernard, D., McCaffery, K., Brotherton, J. M., and Skinner, S. R. 2011, '"I just signed": Factors influencing decision-making for school-based HPV vaccination of adolescent girls', *Health Psychology*, vol. 29, no. 6, pp. 618–625.

Cooper Robbins, C., Bernard, D., McCaffery, K., Garland, S. M., and Skinner, S.R. 2010, '"Is cancer contagious?": Australian adolescent girls and their parents: making the most of limited information about HPV and HPV vaccination', *Vaccine*, vol. 28, no. 19, pp. 3398–3408.

Cooper Robbins, S., Bernard, D., McCaffery, K., and Skinner, S.R. 2010, '"It's a logistical nightmare!" Recommendations for optimising human papillomavirus school-based vaccination experiences', *Sexual Health*, vol. 7, no. 3, pp. 271–278.

Cooper, S. C., Davies, C., Mahendran, K., Blades, J., Stoney, T., Marshall, H., and Skinner, S. R. 2015, 'Development of an HPV vaccination intervention for Australian adolescents', *Health Education Journal, Online First*, vol. 75, no. 5, pp. 1–15.

Culbert, T., Kajander, R., and Reaney, J. 1996, 'Biofeedback with children and adolescents: clinical observations and patient perspectives', *Journal of Developmental and Behavioral Pediatrics*, vol. 17, no. 5, pp. 342–350.

Dahlquist, L. M., Busby, S. M., Slifer, K. J., Tucker, C. L., Eischen, M. A., Hilley, L., and Sulc, W. 2002, 'Distraction for children of different ages who undergo repeated needle sticks', *Journal of Pediatric Oncology Nursing*, vol. 19, no. 1, pp. 22–34.

Dahlquist, L. M., Pendley, J. S., Landtrip, D. S., Jones, C. L., and Steuber, C. P. 2002, 'Distraction intervention for preschoolers undergoing intramuscular injections and subcutaneous port access', *Health Psychology*, vol. 21, no. 1, pp. 91–94.

Davies, C. and Burns, K. 2014, 'Mediating healthy citizenship in the HPV vaccination campaigns', *Feminist Media Studies*, vol. 14, no. 5, pp. 711–726.

Davies, C. and Robinson, K. 2010, 'Hatching babies and stork deliveries: risk and regulation in the construction of children's sexual knowledge', *Contemporary Issues in Early Childhood*, vol. 11, no. 3, pp. 249–263.

Davies, C. and Robinson, K. H. 2013, 'Reconceptualising family: negotiating sexuality in a governmental climate of neoliberalism', *Contemporary Issues in Early Childhood*, vol. 14, no. 1, pp. 39–53.

de Sanjosé, S., Alemany, L., Ordi, J., Tous, S., Alejo, M., Bigby, S. M., and Bosch, F. X. 2013, 'Worldwide human papillomavirus genotype attribution in over 2000 cases of intraepithelial and invasive lesions of the vulva', *European Journal of Cancer*, vol. 49, no. 16, pp. 3450–3461.

Drolet, M., Bénard, É., Boily, M. C., Ali, H., Baandrup, L., Bauer, H., and Brisson, M. 2015, 'Population-level impact and herd effects following human papillomavirus vaccination programmes: a systematic review and meta-analysis', *Lancet Infectious Diseases*, vol. 15, no. 5, pp. 565–580.

Fonner, V. A., Armstrong, K. S., Kennedy, C. E., O'Reilly, K. R., and Sweat, M. D. 2014, 'School based sex education and HIV prevention in low- and middle-income countries: a systematic review and meta-analysis', *PLoS One*, vol. 9, no. 3, viewed 24 January 2017, http://journals.plos.org/plosone/article?id=10.1371/journal.pone.0089692.

Forman, D., de Martel, C., Lacey, C. J., Soerjomataram, I., Lortet-Tieulent, J., Bruni, L., and Franceschi, S. 2012, 'Global burden of human papillomavirus and related diseases', *Vaccine*, vol. 30, no. 5, pp. 12–23.

Frank, D. L., Khorshid, L., Kiffer, J. F., Moravec, C. S., and McKee, M. G. 2010, 'Biofeedback in medicine: who, when, why and how?', *Mental Health in Family Medicine*, vol. 7, no. 2, pp. 85–89.

Fu, L.Y., Bonhomme, L.-A., Cooper, S., Joseph, J. G., and Zimet, G. D. 2014, 'Educational interventions to increase HPV vaccination acceptance: a systematic review', *Vaccine*, vol. 32, no. 17, pp. 1901–1920.

Garland, S. M., Hernandez-Avila, M., Wheeler, C. M., Perez, G., Harper, D. M., Leodolter, S., and Koutsky, L. A. 2007, 'Quadrivalent vaccine against human papillomavirus to prevent anogenital diseases', *New England Journal of Medicine*, vol. 356, no. 19, pp. 1928–1943.

Glick, R. M. and Greco, C. M. 2010, 'Biofeedback and primary care', *Primary Care*, vol. 37, no. 1, pp. 91–103.

Guse, K., Levine, D., Martins, S., Lira, A., Gaardeb, G., Westmorland, W., and Gilliam, M. 2012, 'Interventions using new digital media to improve adolescent sexual health: a systematic review', *Journal of Adolescent Health*, vol. 51, no. 6, pp. 535–543.

Haberland, N. and Rogow, D. 2015, 'Sexuality education: emerging trends in evidence and practice', *Journal of Adolescent Health*, vol. 56, no. 1 pp. S15–S21.

Hall, G. S. 1916, *Adolescence: its psychology and its relations to physiology, anthropology, sociology, sex, crime, religion and education* (vol. 1 of 2 vols), Appleton, New York and London.

Hallman, D. M., Olsson, E. M. G., von Scheele, B., Melin, L., and Lyskov, E. 2011, 'Effects of heart rate variability biofeedback in subjects with stress-related chronic neck pain: a pilot study', *Applied Psychophysiological Biofeedback*, vol. 36, no. 2, pp. 71–80.

Hardy, L., Denney-Wilson, E., Thrift, A. P., Okely, A. D., and Baur, L. A. 2010, 'Screen time and metabolic risk factors among adolescents', *Archives of Pediatrics and Adolescent Medicine Journal*, vol. 164, no. 7, pp. 643–649.

Henriques, G., Keffer, S., Abrahamson, C., and Horst, S.J. 2011, 'Exploring the effectiveness of a computer-based heart rate variability biofeedback program in reducing anxiety in college students', *Applied Psychophysiology and Biofeedback*, vol. 36, no. 2, pp. 101–112.

Heymen, S., Jones, K. R., Scarlett, Y., and Whitehead, W. E. 2011, 'Biofeedback treatment of constipation: a critical review', *Diseases of the Colon and Rectum*, vol. 46, no. 9, pp. 1208–1217.

Igra, V. and Irwin, C. E. J. 1996, 'Theories of adolescent risk-taking behavior', in R. DiClementine, W. Hansen, and L. E. Ponton (eds), *Handbook of adolescent health risk behavior*, Springer, New York, pp. 35–51.

Kain, Z. N., Mayes, L. C., Caldwell-Andrews, A. A., Karas, D. E., and McClain, B. C. 2006, 'Preoperative anxiety, postoperative pain, and behavioral recovery in young children undergoing surgery', *Pediatrics*, vol. 118, no. 2, pp. 651–658.

Kessels, S. J. M., Marshall, H. S., Watson, M., Braunack-Mayer, A., Reuzel, R., and Toohera, R. L. 2012, 'Factors associated with HPV vaccine uptake in teenage girls: a systematic review', *Vaccine*, vol. 30, no. 24, pp. 3546–3556.

Kleiber, C. and McCarthy, A. M. 2006, 'Evaluating instruments for a study on children's responses to a painful procedure when parents are distraction coaches', *Journal of Pediatric Nursing: Nursing Care of Children and Families*, vol. 21, no. 2, pp. 99–107.

Koller, D. and Goldman, R. D. 2012, 'Distraction techniques for children undergoing procedures: a critical review of pediatric research', *Journal of Pediatric Nursing*, vol. 27, no. 6, pp. 652–681.

Lambert, S. A. 1999, 'Distraction, imagery, and hypnosis: techniques for management of children's pain', *Journal of Child and Family Nursing*, vol. 2, no. 1, pp. 5–16.

Lee, H. S. L., Patterson, B. J., and Varma, D. R. A. 2012, 'A randomised controlled trial of anorectal biofeedback for constipation', *International Journal of Colorectal Disease*, vol. 27, no. 4, pp. 459–466.

Leffert, N. and Petersen, A. C. 1996, 'Healthy adolescent development: risks and opportunities', in P. M. Kato and T. Mann (eds), *Handbook of diversity issues in health psychology*, Plenum, New York, pp. 117–140.

Linkenhoker, D. 1983, 'Tools of behavioural medicine: applications of biofeedback treatment for children and adolescents', *Journal of Development and Behavioral Pediatrics*, vol. 4, no. 1, p. 1620.

Lupton, D. 2014, 'Critical perspectives on digital health technologies', *Sociology Compass*, vol. 8, no. 12, pp. 1344–1359.

Lupton, D. 2015, 'Health promotion in the digital era: a critical commentary', *Health Promotion International*, vol. 30, no. 1, pp. 174–183.

McBurnett, K., Arnold, L. E., and Hurt, E. 2011, 'Biofeedback and neurofeedback treatment for ADHD', *Psychiatric Annals*, vol. 41, no. 1, pp. 73–79.

McNealy, C. and Blanchard, J. 2009, *The teen years explained: a guide to healthy development*, John Hopkins University, Baltimore, MD.

Mangis, C. 2004, 'Science of the mind: the goal of journey to wild divine is to teach you how to control your body's alertness and relaxation levels', *PC Magazine*, 20 April, no. 23, p. 158.

Marshall, H., Ryan, P., Roberton, D., and Baghurst, P. 2007, 'A cross sectional survey to assess community attitudes to introduction of human papillomavirus vaccine', *Australian and New Zealand Journal of Public Health*, vol. 31, no. 3, pp. 235–242.

Marshall, H. S., Collins, J., Sullivanc, T., Tooher, R., O'Keefe, M., Skinner, S. R., and Braunack-Mayerc, A. 2013, 'Parental and societal support for adolescent immunization through school based immunization programs', *Vaccine*, vol. 31, no. 30, pp. 3059–3064.

Morrow, A. M. and Khut, G. P. 2014, 'BrightHearts: development of a biofeedback controlled interactive artwork for the management of procedural pain and anxiety', *Developmental Medicine and Child Neurology*, vol. 56, no. S2, p. 14.

Muller, L., Turner, G., Khut, G., and Edmonds, E. 2006, 'Creating affective visualisations for a physiologically interactive artwork', 10th International Conference Information Visualisation, 5–7 July, London.

Myrvik, M. P., Campbell, A. D., and Butcher, J. L. 2012, 'Single-session biofeedback-assisted relaxation training in children with sickle cell disease', *Journal of Pediatric Hematology*, vol. 34, no. 5, pp. 340–343.

Olds, T., Ridley, K., and Dollman, J. 2006, 'Screenieboppers and extreme screenies: the place of screen time in the time budgets of 10–13 year-old Australian children', *Public Health Behaviour and Education*, vol. 30, no. 2, pp. 137–142.

Penny, S. 1996, 'From A to D and back again: the emerging aesthetics of interactive art', *Leonardo Electronic Almanac*, vol. 4, no. 4, pp. 4–7.

Pettigrew, M. 2011, 'When are complex interventions "complex"? When are simple interventions "simple"?', *European Journal of Public Health*, vol. 21, no. 4, pp. 397–399.

Register, NHVP 2015, 'Coverage data', National HPV Vaccination Program Register, viewed 24 January 2017, www.hpvregister.org.au/research/coverage-data.

Robinson, K. H. 2008, 'In the name of "childhood innocence": a discursive exploration of the moral panic associated with childhood and sexuality', *Cultural Studies Review*, vol. 14, no. 2, pp. 113–129.

Robinson, K. H. 2013, *Innocence, knowledge and the construction of childhood: the contradictory nature of sexuality and censorship in children's contemporary lives*, Routledge, London.

Robinson, K. H. and Davies, C. 2008, 'Docile bodies and heteronormative moral subjects: constructing the child and sexual knowledge in schooling', *Sexuality and Culture*, vol. 12, no. 4, pp. 221–239.

Robinson, K. H. and Davies, C. 2014, 'Doing sexuality research with children: ethics, theory, methods and practice', *Global Studies of Childhood*, vol. 4, no. 4, pp. 250–263.

Robinson, K. H. and Davies, C. 2015, 'Children's gendered and sexual cultures: desiring and regulating recognition through life markers of marriage, love and relationships', in E. Renold, J. Ringrose, and D. Egan (eds), *Children, sexuality and the 'sexualisation' of culture*, Palgrave, London, pp. 174–190.

Saltmarsh, S. and Davies, C. 2010, 'Risky childhoods in uncertain times', *Contemporary Issues in Early Childhood*, vol. 11, no. 3, pp. 230–233.

Scharff, L. 1997, 'Recurrent abdominal pain in children: a review of psychological factors and treatment', *Clinical Psychology Review*, vol. 17, no. 2, pp. 145–166.

Sibbald, B. and Roland, M. 1998, 'Understanding controlled trials: why are randomised controlled trials important?', *British Medical Journal*, vol. 316, p. 201.

Sieberg, C. B., Huguet, A., von Baeyer, C. L., and Seshia, S. 2012, 'Psychological interventions for headache in children and adolescents', *Canadian Journal of Neurological Sciences*, vol. 39, no. 1, pp. 26–34.

Skinner, S. R., Davies, C., Cooper, S., Stoney, T., Marshall, H., Zimet, G., and McGeechan, K. 2015, 'HPV.edu study protocol: a cluster randomised controlled evaluation of education, decisional support and logistical strategies in school-based Human Papillomavirus (HPV) Vaccination of adolescents', *BMC Public Health*, vol. 15, no. 1, pp. 896.

Stein, D. J., Hollander, E., and Rothbaum, B. O. 2010, *Textbook of anxiety disorders*, 2nd edn, American Psychiatric Publishing, Washington, DC.

Stern, N. 2013, *Interactive art and embodiment: the implicit body as performance*, Gylphi, Canterbury.

Tabrizi, S., Brotherton, J. M., Kaldor, J. M., Skinner, S. R., Cummings, E., Liu, B., Bateson, D., McNamee, K., Garefalakis, M., and Garland, S. M. 2012, 'Fall in human papillomavirus prevalence following a national vaccination program', *Journal of Infectious Diseases*, vol. 206, no. 11, pp. 1645–1651.

Tsao, J. C., Myers, C. D., Craske, M. G., Bursch, B., Kim, S. C., and Zeltzer, L. K. 2004, 'Role of anticipatory anxiety and anxiety sensitivity in children's and adolescents' laboratory pain responses', *Journal of Pediatric Psychology*, vol. 29, no. 5, pp. 379–388.

WHO 1986, *Young people's health – a challenge for society: report of a WHO study group on young people and 'health for all by the year 2000'*, World Health Organization, Geneva.

Wigle, J., Fontenot, H. B., and Zimet, G. D. 2016, 'Global delivery of human papillomavirus vaccines', *Pediatric Clinics of North America*, vol. 63, no. 1, pp. 81–95.

Index

adolescence 36, 41, 71, 88–90, 126; anxiety 185–188; as identity 16; coming-of-age stories 18–19; common sense understanding 38; history of 4–6, 177–178; limitations and classification 13–14, 68, 73–75, 78–80; media use 176–177; minoritised adolescence 30–31, 65; sexuality 78, 80, 111, 113, 117, 178–183
art 59, 78, 160, 172, 176, 183–185; arthouse 76; artistic merit 52, 76; programmes 12, 16
Australian Classification Branch (ACB/AFCB) 73, 76, 79–80

Bennett, Tony 1, 7, 16, 33, 36
bodies 11, 20, 36, 90–91, 127, 166–169, 183; embodied networks 126; embodiment 20, 91, 167–168; industry bodies 48, 55, 57; regulatory bodies 66, 73
Bourdieu, Pierre 6, 11, 31, 143
BrightHearts 176, 182–185, 187–188
British Board of Film Classification (BBFC) 66–73, 76, 80
Butler, Judith 20, 158

capability approach 142, 150, 153
citizenship 31, 36, 38, 52, 60–61, 73, 76, 90–91, 175; citizen training 12–14, 16, 31; civility of 4; corporate citizenship 56; informed citizenship 188; mature citizen 78–79; sexual citizenship 109, 124–129, 134; status of 47, 148, 152; surveillance of 30; youth citizenship 31, 40–42, 65–66, 91, 117
Clark, Larry and Harmony Korine 78–81
cliché 8, 18, 21, 31–32, 37–39
common sense 4, 8, 13, 29–42, 87, 124

consent 13, 15, 33, 36, 50, 90–91, 94, 117, 125–126, 132–134; age of sexual consent 2, 10, 40–41, 91, 125; in ethical research 94–95, 97; involving digital images 103–105, 108–109, 114–117, 124, 127–131; involving vaccinations 180–181, 188
consumption 3, 7, 20, 40–41, 54, 56, 59–61, 66, 71–73, 75–76, 80, 124, 163; consumer advice, warnings and guidelines 60, 75–76, 78; consumer culture 3, 5; consumer identity 3, 16; consumption by minors 13, 19, 29–30, 32, 41, 81; drug consumption 8; media consumption 13, 22, 29–30, 41, 51

Dean, Mitchell 50, 52, 55, 60–61
discourse 4, 7–8, 11, 15, 18, 22, 30–31, 35–38, 40–42, 46–47, 80, 88, 90, 92, 105, 117, 128–129, 133–134, 145, 151; common-sense 29; dominant or hegemonic 7, 30, 34, 42, 104–105, 124; legal 104, 110, 124, 134; on sexual freedom 2; on youth 8, 21, 35, 104; popular or public 8, 17, 33, 87, 103, 106, 113, 124–125, 177; risk 123, 126, 134, 175, 188

education 1–2, 7–9, 11–14, 16–22, 38, 40–41, 46, 51–52, 75–76, 80, 118, 141–154, 158–164, 166, 168–171, 176–177, 186–189; about sexting 105, 115, 126, 128; education system 6; higher or tertiary education 12, 20–22, 141–142, 144–148, 150–154. 159–161, 167, 170–172; pathways 160, 16, 165, 167–172; sexual education 5, 10, 15, 18, 91–92, 115–116, 177–183; teaching 5, 13, 40, 152, 176

Erikson, Erik 5–6
ethics 13, 15, 17; 21, 30, 52–54, 61, 115, 118, 178; research 10; research committees 87–98

film 11, 37, 52, 54–57, 66–81, 123–124, 182–183; teen 7, 68
Foucault, Michel 10–11, 13–15, 30, 41, 48, 50, 55, 61, 73, 158, 161

gender 2, 3,7, 10, 12–13, 20, 47, 160, 177; diversity 15; double standards 112, 114; norms 92; pressure 111–112; victimisation 125–13
generation 3, 5–6, 8–9, 77, 111
Grossberg, Lawrence 2, 4, 6, 17

Hall, Stuart 6, 33–36, 39
Hall, G. Stanley 4–5
harm 22, 36, 46–47, 49, 60–61, 94–95, 97, 104; protection of minors from 29–31, 33–34, 36–42, 77, 93, 126; relating to child pornography 106–107; relating to sexting 104–106, 109, 114–115, 117, 130
Hasinoff, Amy Adele 105, 115, 126–127
health 12, 14–15, 22, 46, 95, 172, 175–182, 184–185, 187–188; mental 107, 131; sexual 17, 90, 92, 115, 178–179; vaccine 175–177, 179–183, 185–188
Heidegger, Martin 11, 18
human papillomavirus (HPV) 175–177, 179–183, 185–189

innocence 5, 17–20, 87–88, 94, 97, 128, 178; loss of 17, 40; sexual 10, 125

Karaian, Lara 117, 126–130

law 16, 22, 29, 32–33, 36, 40–42, 47–49, 51–53, 65, 74–75, 88–89, 91, 95, 97, 103, 112; child pornography laws 104–110, 115–117; cultural studies of 124–127; in popular culture 128–129, 131–134; soft law 55–58, 60–61
Luhrmann, Baz 2, 37

Massive Open Online Courses (MOOC) 21–22, 141–142, 145–154
maturity 2, 4, 6, 8, 13, 30, 39–41, 70, 128, 177–178; opposition between immaturity and 17–21; classifications 65–68, 70–73, 75–81

media 12, 29 39–40, 91, 96, 103–106, 109, 113–114, 117, 124, 127–128, 141–143, 178, 180; consumption by minors or children 13, 29–30, 32, 41; consumption by young people 22; content regulation 46–48, 50–52, 54–60; convergence 30; new 9, 103, 175, 188; studies 1; social 104, 110, 113, 132–133, 176; violence in 71
media classification 31, 37, 47–48, 51–55–60, 72–81; as producing minority and adulthood 65–66, 68, 80–81; systems 11, 19, 22, 31
minority 7, 30–31, 33, 35–36, 52, 77, 81; concepts of 2, 8; distinction from majority 12–13, 31, 35, 41, 66, 73; governance of 65–66, 80; limited capacities 11, 42; minoritised adolescence (see adolescence); protection of 32, 36–37, 42, 49, 66, 69, 77, 79; sexual lives of 2, 78, 116–117, 125–129; surveillance of 30, 36
Morris, Meaghan 1, 37
Motion Picture Association of America (MPAA) 67–68, 71, 77

Nussbaum, Martha 142, 150

pornography 17, 47, 54, 67, 75; child 38, 91, 103–111, 113, 115–118, 126, 129–130
pre-harm parenting 40

qualitative research 87, 91–98, 176, 181, 184, 189

race 7, 47, 128
responsibility 4, 12, 20, 38, 40, 48, 55–56, 58–60, 79, 93, 132, 145; parental 14, 29–30; sexual 125
Rousseau, Jean-Jacques 12–13, 19, 32, 40

Sen, Amartya 47, 142, 150, 153
school 12–16, 20–21, 92, 95–96, 131, 143–149, 151–152, 154, 160–162, 167, 169, 178; leaving or avoidance 40–41, 114, 143, 158–159; vaccinations in 175–176, 179–183, 186–188
sexting 10, 12, 15, 17, 20, 22, 92, 95, 103–106, 108–118, 123–124, 126–131, 134
sex offenders 29–31, 36, 39, 41, 105, 109
Skelton, Tracey 7, 92, 94, 96
Spielberg, Steven 68–71

Spinoza, Baruch 166–167, 169
surveys 76, 91–92, 103, 110–112, 114, 176, 181

teachers 13, 71, 92, 106, 134, 149, 152, 154, 160, 167–169, 181–183, 186, 188–189
teenager 3–4, 31, 125
transitions 4, 6, 8, 144

university 141, 145, 158–159, 163; qualifications 143, 153–154, 161

Weber, Max 51, 60–61
Williams, Raymond 1, 5, 17, 33, 35

youth culture 1–3, 7, 9, 16, 40, 145
youth studies 1, 6, 14–16, 20–22, 38, 89–90